PACKET SWITCHED NETWORKS - Theory and Practice

Richard Barnett and Sally Maynard-Smith

SIGMA PRESS
Wilmslow, United Kingdom

HALSTED PRESS
a division of JOHN WILEY & SONS, Inc.
605 Third Avenue, New York, NY 10158
New York • Chichester • Brisbane • Toronto • Singapore

First published in 1988 by
Sigma Press 1 South Oak Lane, Wilmslow, SK9 6AR, England.

British Library Cataloguing in Publication Data

> Packet-switched networks: theory and
> practice.
> 1. Computer networks 2. Data transmission
> systems 3. packet switching (Data
> transmission)
> I. Title II. Maynard-Smith, Sally
> 004.6'6 TK5105.5

Library of Congress Cataloguing in Publication (applied for)

ISBN (Sigma Press): 1-85058-095-2

ISBN (Halsted Press): 0-470-21392-2

Distributed by
John Wiley & Sons Ltd., Baffins Lane, Chichester, West Sussex, England.

Halsted Press, a division of John Wiley & Sons Inc, 605 Third Avenue, New York, NY 10158, USA

Printed by Interprint Ltd, Malta

Cover design by Professional Graphics, Warrington, UK

Acknowledgments: the following are trademarks or registered trademarks:
DEC - Digital Equipment Corporation; DECNET - Digital Equipment Corporation; Ethernet - Xerox Corporation; IBM - International Business Machines Corp; INTEL - Intel Corporation; IPSS - British Telecommunications plc; KiloStream - British Telecommunications plc; MegaStream - British Telecommunications plc; NETBIOS - International Business Machines Corp; Packet SwitchStream - British Telecommunications plc; PC AT - International Business Machines Corp; PDP-11 - Digital Equipment Corporation; Prestel - British Telecommunications plc; VAX - Digital Equipment Corporation; WANG - Wang Laboratories Inc; Z80 - Zilog Corporation.

The authors apologise for any inadvertent failure to acknowledge trademarks.

CONTENTS

Part 4: Future Developments   239

Network Basics

'Packet Switched Networks: Theory and Practice' has been split into four parts: Part 1 consists of a basic overview to networking; Part 2 covers protocols used in packet switched networks; Part 3 is more practical and deals with private packet switched networks; Part 4 takes a look at future developments.

This book is not intended to be an implementor's guide, but an introduction to packet switched networks. In all cases where the reader requires more information the relevant standard documents are suggested as further reading. Where views are given, they are those of the authors and not necessarily held by everyone else.

Network Basics

Part 1 starts with a guide to networking in general aimed mainly at beginners. It goes on to cover the basic concepts of packet switched networks. Finally, it covers the components of a packet switched network.

Packet Switched Network Protocols

Part 2 goes into much more detail. It covers the protocols used in packet switched networks, looks at International Standards, UK standards and X.25 (a packet switched network protocol) in detail, and higher level protocols and security.

Private Packet Switched Networks

Part 3 looks at private packet switched networks in practice, giving useful information for those installing them. It covers such things as what to look for when purchasing packet switching equipment.

Future Developments

Part 4 looks at some possible future developments, those likely to be around in the near future and others more hypothetical in nature. This part is fairly subjective - the future, of course, is unknown (to some extent anyway)!

1

A Beginner's Guide To Networking

1.1 Introduction

In this section we describe, very briefly, the major types of networks, to give some general purpose background to networking before concentrating on packet switched networks.

A large amount of networking jargon will be introduced in this section. It is not essential to be able to remember the meanings of all of the acronyms as there is a glossary at the end of the book. However, when dealing with networking, the jargon will surface and it is useful to have an idea of what the different terms mean.

1.2 Why Are Networks Required?

Imagine that networks do not exist - a situation that was almost true not too many years ago. Figure 1.1 shows the situation, a personal computer sitting on a desk. The personal computer is able to run a lot of software and do some very clever things, but the user is limited purely to the capabilities of the personal computer.

Suppose the user needs access to some information or software on another machine? If the machines are roughly compatible, then physically transferring floppy disks can provide a solution to the information transfer problem. What if the machines do not have compatible disks?

Most computers worthy of the name have a serial interface. This is sometimes referred to as an 'asynchronous interface' or an RS-232 port. Whatever the name, if 'terminal emulation' software is run on the personal computer, the serial port can be connected to a serial port of another computer. The personal computer can then act as though it is a terminal and operate the other computer. Many terminal emulation packages allow files to be transferred across the serial interface. A good example of a terminal emulation/file transfer package is the program called Kermit, which is available for most computers and ideal for transferring information between different types of computers.

What are the problems with this sort of set-up? Firstly, the computers must be close together, as the RS-232 electrical signalling cannot be driven over very long distances. Secondly, the transfer is limited by the maximum speed at which the serial interface

2

can transfer data. This is often only 9600 bits per second. Since there are usually ten bits to a byte of data, this means that the link will be limited to 960 bytes per second. At this rate, a one megabyte file would take a minimum of around 20 minutes.

Figure 1.1 Life without a network

The first problem can be solved with devices called line drivers and modems. These allow much longer links between the computers. Most modems are designed to be connected to the Public Switched Telephone Network (PSTN) (i.e., the telephone system). Modems can not only automatically dial out but also answer incoming calls. The use of modems and the PSTN means that distance is not a problem. The two communicating computers can be on opposite sides of the world, as long as one can phone the other.

Modems tend to be limited in the rate that they transfer data due to the very low capacity of telephone lines. Modems that work at up to 2400 bits per second are available at reasonable prices but if higher speeds are required, the price goes up quite rapidly. At 2400 bits per second, a one megabyte file would take a minimum of around one hour and 20 minutes.

So we have seen that it is possible for two computers to communicate at moderately low speeds over any distance, provided that they are near a phone line. Suppose that a large office complex has several hundred, possibly different, personal computers that often have to transfer data between themselves and possibly to computers located at a remote site. How can this be done?

Clearly, it is rather impractical to have directly wired connections between each pair of computers and rather wasteful to have to use the telephone system to allow the computers to communicate - not to mention the low transfer rates.

The solution is to use a network. All of the computers that need to communicate with each other are connected into the network. A link to the remote site is also connected to the network while another network at the remote site connects all of the computers there to the remote link.

Sounds good, doesn't it? If only life were that simple. There are a wide range of different network types and technologies, some good at some things, but bad at others. No network so far invented solves everyone's communication requirements.

Network technologies are often grouped into two different classes - LANs and WANs.

1.3 LANs and WANs

These are two acronyms are always being bandied about in the computing press but what are they and in which ways are they different?

LAN stands for Local Area Network. The 'Local' bit means that the network technologies in this group tend to be limited in the distance over which they can be used. A typical maximum distance between two computers connected to a LAN might be one kilometre. LANs tend to be used to interconnect computers within one building or else a set of buildings, physically very close to each other.

LANs can often support very high data transfer rates, frequently at several million bits per second. This allows users of computers connected to the LAN to share disks between the computers and allow very rapid transfer of information between them.

On the negative side, LANs are often very susceptible to hardware and software failures. Very few have decent network management facilities. (Network management facilities give information about how the network is performing, if there are any faults, etc. More about this later.)

WAN stands for Wide Area Network. The idea is that WANs take over where LANs leave off. WANs often cover extremely large distances, although they are being used more and more in LAN territory - over small distances. Packet switched networks fall into the WAN category as do some of the more esoteric networks such as packet radio networks.

The so-called 'national networks' are all packet switched networks. British Telecom's Packet SwitchStream service uses the X.25 packet switched network protocol.

Connection to Packet SwitchStream (more commonly known as PSS) is available nationwide. It interconnects with WANs in other countries, permitting PSS-connected computers to communicate with computers in most parts of the world. Another of the national networks in the UK is JANET (the Joint Academic NETwork) which allows free access for academic use to computers at any university site and soon the Polytechnics.

The main claim to fame of WANs is the interconnectivity they provide, as they can connect computers over large distances. They can also be quite resilient to hardware and software failures, and hence very reliable. Network management facilities can be very good and have to be where network availability is very important.

The main drawback of WAN technologies has been the data transfer rates available. A typical connection to a WAN may operate at 9600 bits per second, the same rate as the serial interface on the average personal computer! Certainly, this is no competition for LAN technologies.

The situation is changing as WAN technology improves. Another important improvement is the high speed communication links now available. These operate over WAN type distances and can support rates up over two million bits per second if required.

Having given some background to networking we will give more detail on some of the different network types in more detail.

1.4 Ethernet

Ethernet is probably the most successful of all of the LAN technologies. In terms of topology, it is a 'bus network'. Figure 1.2 shows the general idea. All the devices are connected to the main cable, the Ethernet cable, via transceivers. Separate Ethernet cables can be joined together using repeaters or bridges. The cable itself is a special coaxial cable, as are the connectors and the transceivers.

Data can be transferred via an Ethernet network at ten million bits per second, a quite impressive speed. Since the two computers in communication can be up to a kilometre or so apart, Ethernet can be extremely effective for communications between computers in the same building or group of buildings.

How do the computers on the network decide which is able to use the cable? Because Ethernet is an example of a 'baseband' network, only one computer can use the network at any one time. So how do they do it?

In fact, the process is a good example of ordered chaos. When a computer wants to transmit some data on the Ethernet, it first 'listens' to what is happening on the cable to see if anyone else is using it. If so, it must wait. If not, it will start transmitting the data while still listening to the cable. This is done to check that the data being transmitted is not being corrupted, the most probable reason for which is another computer on the network transmitting data at the same time. This is known as a 'collision'. If a collision occurs, then both computers must give up and try again later. They wait a random time interval before trying to send the data again. This process is known as CSMA/CD (Carrier Sense Multiple Access/Collision Detection).

What are the practical aspects of Ethernet? There are some physical details that need care. The Ethernet cable must be installed correctly, with all the paraphernalia that goes with it (taps, transceivers, terminators, etc.). Once installed, it should be fairly reliable, as there is comparatively little to go wrong. If something does go wrong, fault finding can be a little tricky, as it may not be obvious which of the various computers connected to the cable is causing the problem.

Monitoring of network performance is a fairly simple affair, as all devices connected to the cable see all of the data being transferred. The other side of this coin is that Ethernet is inherently prone to 'eavesdropping'. (Anybody can look at the data and extract things like passwords and sensitive information unless the data is encrypted at a higher level.)

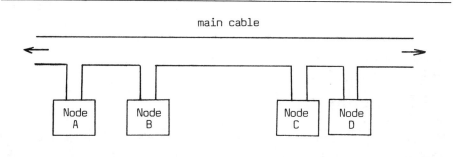

Figure 1.2 Bus network

Ethernet is good, unless a lot of computers are trying to use it at once (in other words, as long as the loading is not too high). When loading does increase, the total data throughput tends to decrease, because of the number of collisions that occur.

1.5 Broadband Networks

Networks like Ethernet are known as 'baseband' networks. All of the capacity of the cable is taken up in one fell swoop by a single node transmitting data. 'Broadband' networks are different in that they use the technique of 'frequency division multiplexing' to provide a number of simultaneous channels on the same physical cable. A typical cable may have a useful bandwidth in excess of 300MHz which, in theory at least, can support a large number of slower channels.

The concept is very much like the radio FM waveband. This is divided into a number of frequency channels that may or may not contain a signal (Capital Radio, for example). The main difference is that all of the signals are contained within the cable rather than broadcast into the atmosphere.

The main commercial example of a broad band network is the WANG network. Figure 1.3 shows the general idea. As far as a node on the network is concerned, there are two separate cables: one for received data; the other for transmitted data. It is, in fact, one cable looped at one end of the network.

In order to transmit or receive data on the broadband network, the network nodes must use a radio frequency (RF) modem to convert the data into a suitable form for the cable. One important issue is the allocation of frequency channels to nodes. If the node is to be able to utilise several different channels, then its modem must be 'frequency agile'. This means that the frequency at which the modem operates can be programmed. A central controller can then allocate one of several channels to a node, which programs its modem to operate at that frequency.

Due to the rather impressive facilities required of the broadband network interfaces, they tend to be very expensive. Also, they require that the special cable be installed correctly. So far, broadband networks have found only limited application, mainly due to the high cost involved. In terms of function, ISDN (see section 1.12) promises to offer very high bandwidth channels with guaranteed throughput and so broadband networks may never be used extensively.

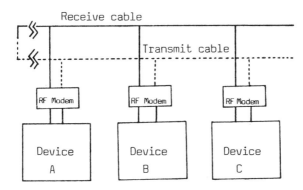

Figure 1.3 Broadband network

1.6 Token Passing

Token passing refers to the method in which nodes on a network gain access to the shared network cable. Usually this is in the form of a ring. Nodes are attached at various points around the ring. Frames of data circulate around the ring, and are inserted and removed by the network nodes.

In a token passing ring, there is usually only one 'token' circulating. Without the token, no node can insert frames of data onto the ring.

To illustrate the operation of a token passing ring we will use the example of the token passing ring network IBM has chosen for its PC LAN network. In this case, the 24 bit token circulates around the ring when no data is being transmitted. When a node wishes to transmit data to another node, it 'captures' the token and marks it as busy. That node can then transmit a data frame onto the ring.

The frame of data carries with it an address which specifies the node that is the destination of the frame. When the destination node copies the data from the frame, it sets bits in the frame to indicate to the sender that it has correctly received the data that was in it. When the sender receives the modified frame again, it removes it from the ring and releases the token back onto the ring so that other nodes may transmit data.

starting delimiter 1 byte	access control 1 byte	ending delimiter 1 byte

Token Format

starting delimiter 1 byte	access control 1 byte	frame control 1 byte	destination address 6 bytes	source address 6 bytes	information field	frame check sequence 4 bytes	ending delimiter 1 byte	frame status 1 byte

Frame Format

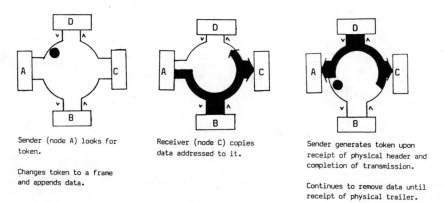

Sender (node A) looks for token.

Changes token to a frame and appends data.

Receiver (node C) copies data addressed to it.

Sender generates token upon receipt of physical header and completion of transmission.

Continues to remove data until receipt of physical trailer.

Figure 1.4 Token passing network

Figure 1.4 shows the structure of the token and data frames and gives an example of the operation of the token passing network. The IBM token passing ring operates at four million bits per second which gives good performance on small to medium size LAN rings.

1.7 Cambridge Ring

The Cambridge Ring is, as its name suggests, an example of a ring network technology. Figure 1.5 shows the concept. In common with Ethernet, a single cable is used to connect together all of the computers, except that in this case the cable forms a complete loop. Computers are connected to nodes on the cable. There can be up to 254 nodes on the ring, each with a unique eight bit address. There must also be a 'monitor station' responsible for starting up the ring and monitoring its operation.

Data is transferred, usually at ten million bits per second, in 'mini-packets' which can contain two or more bytes of user data.

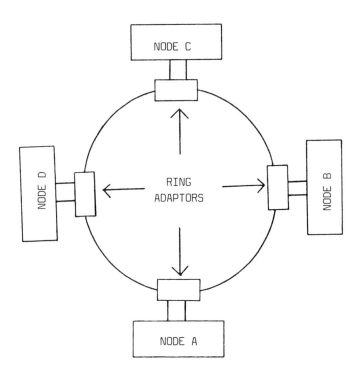

Figure 1.5 Cambridge Ring

In normal operation, a small number of empty 'slots' circulate the ring continuously. These slots are formed by the monitor station when the ring is started up. In each of the slots are various fields, including an empty/full bit that determines whether the slot contains a mini-packet.

When a node wishes to send data to another node, it must wait for an empty slot to arrive on the ring. The node can then fill the slot with a mini-packet and mark the slot as full. The mini-packet contains, in addition to the data, the sender's address and the intended recipient of the data.

If the recipient is able to accept the data when the mini-packet comes past it, it modifies the mini-packet appropriately. When the sender sees the mini-packet again, it removes it from the ring by setting the slot to empty and checks the mini-packet to see if the sender got the data.

One of the most important qualities of the Cambridge Ring is that it guarantees, no matter how busy the ring is, a certain data throughput between two nodes that is totally predictable, an important requirement for some applications.

In practice, the small amount of data transferred in each mini-packet tends to limit the usefulness of the Cambridge Ring. From the point of view of reliability, rings tend to be quite vulnerable to a node failure and this is true of the Cambridge Ring.

The Cambridge Ring's main problem is that it never really got out of the academic community where it was developed and is not an accepted International Standard protocol.

1.8 Circuit Switched Networks

Some of the very earliest, and possibly most successful, networks were circuit switched. What do we mean by circuit switching? In a typical circuit switch, a large number of RS-232 interfaces from computers, modems, terminals, etc., are connected into a single, central circuit switch. As the circuit switch is at the centre of the system, this type of network is also a 'star network'. The circuit switch can connect any of its RS-232 ports together as though there was a real cable between the two. Typically, a terminal requests that a connection is set up through the circuit switch to a host computer's serial port. The circuit switch then simulates a direct, hard wired, connection between the terminal and the host computer. The circuit switch introduces no delay and is practically invisible to the user.

The circuit switch simulates the connection by sampling the data on the inputs to the circuit switch and reproducing the sampled signals on the appropriate outputs from the circuit switch. This technique allows very large, very fast circuit switches to be built relatively cheaply.

The main limitation of circuit switches, the transparency of the connection, is also their advantage. The bit rates of all of the connected devices has to be the same unless the connected devices are capable of sensing the bit rates of incoming data. Methods for flow control also have to be the same at both ends and so on. Circuit switches are excellent flexible replacements for hard wired connections, but do not really provide the facilities offered by networks.

A variation on the circuit switch is the character switch. In character switches, whole characters are received within the switch before being sent on the appropriate output line. This allows the character switch to be cleverer than the circuit switch (the bit rates of the connected devices do not need to be the same with character switches), but this is often at the expense of throughput capability.

1.9 Packet Radio Networks

This is the first of the WAN type technologies, although a rather special one. The first of this type was the ALOHA system developed at the University of Hawaii and which went into operation in 1970. ALOHA was basically a way to allows users on the various Hawaiian Islands to access a central computer. Packets were transmitted at 9600 bits per second, using a radio frequency of about 400MHz.

In terms of operation, ALOHA is a bit like Ethernet minus the cable. If transmitted data packets collide, the transmitting stations wait a random period before re-transmitting the packets.

1.10 ARPANET

ARPANET stands for the Advanced Research Projects Agency Network and was one of the first major packet switched networks. It started in the USA in the late 1960s and has now grown to cover a large number of countries in the world, including the United Kingdom. ARPANET uses Interface Message Processors (IMPs) to route data messages across the network from sender to receiver. The IMPs are mainly connected to each other by 56k bit per second communications links.

One of the most significant features of ARPANET was that it implemented the concept of 'dynamic routing'. Essentially, the network learnt which was the quickest routes on which to send a packet towards its destination without external intervention. In this way, the network could automatically share loads between links and survive link failures without interruption to data flowing across the network. This was achieved by having the IMPs exchange their knowledge of the configuration of the network. In this way, knowledge of network configuration changes gradually becomes known throughout the network.

1.11 X.25 Packet Switched Networks

Almost all of the packet switched networks in operation today employ the X.25 protocol to define the operation of the network. Since the discussion of X.25 and packet switched networks form the main theme for this book, we will not say too much about it here.

1.12 Integrated Services Digital Network

The Integrated Services Digital Network, usually known as ISDN, will be increasingly important in years to come. The basic concept of ISDN is that it integrates voice (i.e., telephony) and data (packet switching, for example) into one unified network. The precise nature of the connection between users of the ISDN may vary but basically the ISDN provides circuit switched connections. The most important characteristic of this is the guaranteed throughput that circuit switching provides. ISDN will very likely become widely available to business users in the future as it supports the type of communications services that modern businesses need.

The ISDN supports three different types of communications channels. Any particular ISDN connection may support a number of different information channels simultaneously 'multiplexed' into a single physical set of wires.

The 'B channel' is a 64k bits per second channel. This can be used to carry digitised voice information or data information.

The 'D channel' may either be a 16k bits per second or a 64k bits per second information channel. It is mainly intended to provide control information for the operation of the other channels. In addition to controlling the circuit switching functions the D channel may be used to carry packet switched data.

The 'H channel' can be either a 384k bits per second, a 1536k bits per second or a 1920k bits per second channel. The H channel is intended for use where very high data throughputs are required - video services, facsimile and imaging in general.

The main type of ISDN access is the basic access or '2B + D'. There is also the primary rate access of '30B + D' in 2.048M bits per second networks or '23B + D' in 1.544M bits per second networks. As you may have guessed, these last two bit rates were not chosen at random. 2.048M bits per second is a standard high speed bit rate in Europe while 1.544M bits per second is standard in the USA (also known as the T1 rate).

The ISDN basic interface has been designed so that existing telephone wiring will be able to support the new digital services. Figure 1.6 shows the defined interfaces between the user and the ISDN.

Network Termination 1 (NT1) is the basic communications level and provides the line driving and termination, timing, etc.

Network Termination 2 (NT2) distributes access from the customer's equipment to the ISDN.

Terminal Equipment (TE) is the customer's equipment and can be things like terminals, digital telephones, etc. There are two type of TE. TE1 are devices which have ISDN user-network interfaces. TE2 are devices which do not have ISDN user-network interfaces (i.e., almost all current digital equipment).

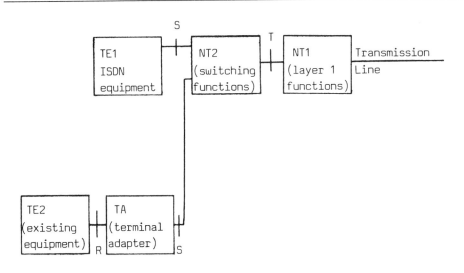

Figure 1.6 ISDN interfaces

1.13 Summary

Networks are required to give the user access to more computing facilities than is possible from equipment on the user's desk. Networks enable information to be transferred from machine to machine both locally and at a distance.

There are two types of network technologies, LANs (Local Area Networks) and WANs (Wide Area Networks). LANs are used to connect computers locally (typically up to one kilometre apart). WANs are used over longer distances (for example, across the country).

Packet switched networks come into the WAN category. British Telecom's PSS service and JANET, the Joint Academic NETwork are examples of packet switched WANs.

Examples of different networks types are:-

Ethernet - a bus network where all the devices are connected to the main cable via transceivers.

Broadband Networks - use the technique of frequency division multiplexing to provide a number of simultaneous channels on the same physical cable.

Token Passing - Network nodes access a shared cable which is usually in the form of a ring. A token (a special packet) circulates around the ring. A network node can insert frames of data onto the ring, but only when it has the token. Without the token, no node can insert frames of data onto the ring.

Cambridge Ring - works with a number of slots circulating around the ring. When a node wants to send data to another node it waits until an empty slot arrives. The node can then fill it with a mini-packet.

Circuit Switched Networks - (also called Star Networks) A large number of RS-232 interfaces are connected into a central circuit switch. The switch can connect any of its RS-232 ports together as though there was a real cable between the two.

Packet Radio Networks - Packets are transmitted using a radio frequency. If transmitted data packets collide, the transmitting stations wait a random period of time before re-transmitting the packets.

Arpanet - one of the first major packet switched networks. It started in the USA in the late 1960s.

X.25 Packet Switched Networks - X.25 is an international standard protocol which defines the operation of the network. Almost all packet switched networks in operation today use the X.25 protocol.

Integrated Services Digital Network - (ISDN) integrates voice and data onto one unified network.

Packet Switched Network Basics

2.1 Introduction

In this section of the book, we are going to describe the basic theories underlying packet switched networks. As the ISO seven layer model is to be used as a framework for this description, the first thing done is to describe the model. Then follows a description of the theory of packet switched network protocols. Finally, a practical example is used to show how the theory is used in practice.

2.2 The ISO OSI Seven Layer Model

The task of implementing communications systems to cope with the problems encountered in the real world is very large indeed. The task is too large to be dealt with as a single task. In order to make things manageable, the task has to be broken down into a number of sub-tasks. Each of these can be thought of as a self-contained task.

One such subdivision is the ISO 'seven layer model'. This is particularly important as it forms the basis of the 'Open Systems Interconnection' network protocols, usually known as the OSI protocols. ISO stands for the International Organisation for Standardisation, a standards organisation heavily involved with the standardisation of network protocols.

Figure 2.1 shows the seven layer model in a diagrammatic form. The lowest levels deal with the job of transferring information in an orderly way across communications networks. The highest levels provide a very abstract view of the network to the ultimate user of the network, the 'application'.

There are a large number of different network technologies currently in use. Each has its own particular characteristics making it suitable for a specific set of applications. Sooner or later, it becomes necessary for devices on networks with different technologies to communicate without having to worry about the underlying network.

OSI specifies a set of protocols that can be used to implement a network. At some levels, especially the lower levels, there are several alternative protocols that may be employed. This allows networks to use different sets of protocols depending on the type of network in use while still allowing 'interworking' with other OSI networks.

We will now go on to briefly describe the seven layers in the ISO OSI model (they are covered in more detail in Chapter Four).

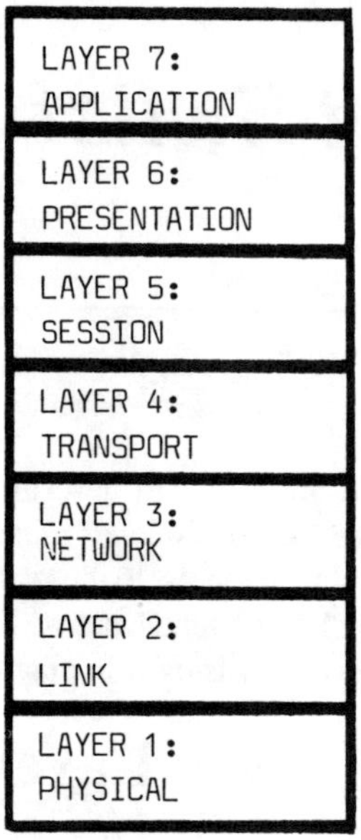

```
LAYER 7:
APPLICATION

LAYER 6:
PRESENTATION

LAYER 5:
SESSION

LAYER 4:
TRANSPORT

LAYER 3:
NETWORK

LAYER 2:
LINK

LAYER 1:
PHYSICAL
```

Figure 2.1 ISO OSI seven layer model

2.2.1 Layer 1 - The Physical Layer

The physical layer deals with the most fundamental aspects of network connection (connector types, connector pin-outs, electrical signalling and signalling conventions). The standards for the physical layer specify how to design drivers and receivers for the interface, what type of cable to use to wire devices together and precisely how the interface operates.

The most important physical layer standards relevant to packet switched networks are 'X.21' and 'X.21bis'. The latter is known variously as 'V.24' and 'V.28'.

Standards with names starting with 'V.' belong to the V series of CCITT recommendations (their name for standards). Standards with names starting with 'X.' belong to the X series of CCITT recommendations. CCITT stands for the International Telephone and Telegraph Consultative Committee which, along with ISO, form the two most important standards bodies for network protocols.

2.2.2 Layer 2 - The Link Layer

The link layer is responsible for transporting information from the higher level protocols across the physical layer interface between two devices connected together.

The link layer provides mechanisms for detecting errors in the information transferred. This may be in the form of 'corrupted data' possibly due to electrical noise coupling into the link wiring. The link layer has to include mechanisms to detect such errors and correct them in a way that is transparent to the higher level protocols.

Another facility provided by the link layer is 'flow control'. A device connected to one end of the link may not be able to process information at the same rate as the device transmitting the information. The link layer has to include a flow control mechanism that stops the information being transmitted when required, so that the receiver has enough time to process the information.The OSI link layer protocol for packet switched networks is known as 'X.25 level 2'.

2.2.3 Layer 3 - The Network Layer

The network layer is the first of the protocols that is 'end-to-end'. Layers 1 and 2 deal with two devices connected together directly. Layer 3 on the other hand deals with 'end-point devices' connected to each other across a network that may incorporate many device-device links. End-point devices actually use the network, rather than being part of the network.

The network layer is used to establish connections between end-point devices across a network, or interconnected networks. The network layer must include an 'address' concept, so that devices can identify each other. The network layer controls the transfer of information from the higher level protocols across the connection. This includes a flow control mechanism to match the transmitted and received information processing rates individually for each connection. It also includes a mechanism for detecting that information is received in the correct sequence and that the underlying link and physical layers have not failed in some way.

The OSI network layer protocol for packet switched networks is 'X.25 level 3'. Together with X.25 level 2 as the link layer and X.21bis or X.21 as the physical layer, this forms the complete X.25 protocol.

2.2.4 Layer 4 - The Transport Layer

The transport layer provides a standard interface between the higher level protocols and the underlying lower levels of the network. The transport layer is needed because different network and link layers may have different characteristics. These need to be hidden from the higher levels if interworking between different types of network is to be possible.

2.2.5 Layer 5 - The Session Layer

The session layer is really the lowest layer that deals with an abstract view of the underlying network. It basically uses the transport service to provide the mechanism for transferring information and so does not have to worry about the messy details of the network and link layers. The session layer provides support for the information transfer between applications. This includes a mechanism for restarting information transfer at the correct point after a failure that cannot be transparently corrected at the lower levels.

2.2.6 Layer 6 - The Presentation Layer

The presentation layer deals with the way in which the information being transferred is represented. The presentation layer incorporates a 'transfer syntax' to define rules for how the information is to be represented in such a way that any OSI application can understand the information. The actual structure of the information is defined in a standard known as 'ASN.1'. This stands for Abstract Syntax Notation One.

2.2.7 Layer 7 - The Application Layer

This layer provides the ultimate in high level support for the application using the network. The application layer includes facilities like file transfer, job transfer and message handling. Support is also included for interactive use of the network in the form of 'Virtual Terminal' (VT) support.

2.3 Packet Switched Network Concepts

Figure 2.2 shows the classic packet switched network diagram. The packet switches inside the 'cloud shape' are those that form part of the network itself. The things outside are the end-point devices that make use of the facilities provided by the network.

The 'packet switches' are route 'packets' of information between the various network links connected to the packet switch. The end-point devices may be host computer systems providing a service accessible from the network or devices providing special types of interface to the network. Examples of the latter are gateways between the packet switched network and another type of network, and devices that allow terminals to be connected to the packet switched network.

2.3.1 The Physical Layer

Using the ISO OSI seven layer model to describe the concepts used in packet switched networks, layer 1 deals with the physical connection between devices in the network. Within the cloud, these connections are between the packet switches that go to form the network. Outside of the cloud, the connection is between an end-point device and one of the packet switches in the network. Because each link is distinct from any other link, a single packet switched network may make use of many different types of communications links. Each link type can be chosen on the basis of the distance over which the link has to run, the 'capacity' of the link (the rate at which information can be transferred over the link), the maximum permissible error rate, etc.

The information at the physical layer consists of three types of signals. These are the data, control and clock signals. The data signals are those used to transfer the higher level information between the two devices. There are two data signals: one for data in one direction and another for data in the other direction.

The control signals are used to control the operation of the link and whether or not the link is in a usable state. The number of control signals varies depending on the particular type of interface used.

The clock signals are used in conjunction with the data signals to reconstruct transmitted information at the receiver.

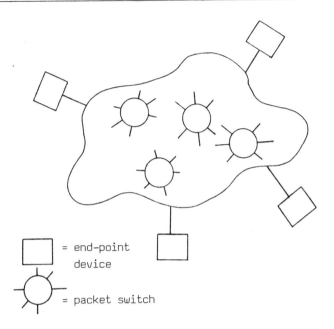

Figure 2.2 Cloud model of network

Where the link is to be run over a fairly short distance (less than about one kilometre) and on private property, ordinary telephone cable or twisted pairs are by far the most common types of wiring used to connect devices together. Depending on the electrical signalling used, it may be possible to directly connect devices together using such wire. In other cases, line drivers or modems may be required to carry the signals over large distances. As these are transparent to the network, we will not worry too much about line drivers and modems here.

Twisted pairs can be used quite effectively up to about one million bits per second over short to medium distances. Above that, it may be necessary to resort to fibre optic links to ensure that the error rate on the link is not so high that the link layer is unable to cope with the errors reliably. Fibre optic cables are particularly effective in electrically noisy environments, as they are completely insensitive to electrical noise.

Where the link between devices has to run over very large distances, it is necessary to make use of the communications link services provided by companies like British Telecom and Mercury. In the case of British Telecom, KiloStream and MegaStream are point-point links suitable for connecting together parts of a packet switched network over large distances. KiloStream can support bit rates up to 64 thousand bits per second while MegaStream can support bit rates of 2.048 million bits per second.

2.3.2 The Link Layer

Having dealt with the physical layer, we can now move on to the link layer. The link layer is responsible for moving information between devices in such a way that the information transferred is error free and correctly ordered.

There are many different ways in which the objectives of the link layer in packet switched networks can be achieved and many of these are currently in use in real networks. We will choose X.25 level 2 as it is the most important packet switched network link layer in current use.

Link layer information is transferred between the two devices at the ends of a communications link in the form of 'frames'. Figure 2.3 shows a basic X.25 level 2 frame. The 'flag' is a specific bit pattern transmitted on the link when there are no frames to transmit. The 'address' field is used to identify to which direction of transfer the frame belongs. The 'control' field is used to specify what the frame contains and other useful control information. If the frame contains higher level protocol information, then this follows the control field. The last thing in the frame is the 'fcs' field. This contains a 'checksum' and is used by the receiver to determine whether or not the frame has been received correctly. Finally, there is another flag which indicates that the end of the frame has been reached. This frame format is from a protocol called 'HDLC'. This stands for High level Data Link Control. Elements of HDLC are used in the X.25 level 2 protocol.

FLAG	ADDRESS	CONTROL	HIGHER LEVEL INFORMATION	FCS	FLAG

Figure 2.3 X.25 level 2 frame

There are two fundamentally different types of frames that are used. The first type are just used to initialise the link when the link comes into use and to correctly close down the link when it is going out of service. These are known as 'unnumbered' frames in X.25 level 2. The second type are those used to transfer and control the transfer of higher level protocol information. These are known as the 'information' and 'supervisory' frames in X.25 level 2.

Much of the complexity of link level protocols is concerned with the transfer of higher level information. The link start up and close down procedures, although very important, are relatively straightforward. With this in mind, we will concentrate on the procedures for the transfer of higher level protocol information and not worry too much about how the link was brought into use.

X.25 level 2 uses a concept known as 'positive acknowledgement' in order to provide error correction and flow control. In simple terms, this means that the receiver must acknowledge that a frame has been correctly received. An alternative to this is 'negative acknowledgement'. In this case, the receiver only responds to a received frame if it is not received correctly. Most link layers use positive acknowledgement however.

The simplest form of the positive acknowledge system is the 'window 1' system. Figure 2.4 shows this in operation. The transmitter transmits a frame and waits for the acknowledgement from the receiver. As far as the receiver is concerned, the frame is either received correctly (i.e., checksum is correct), or else incorrectly (checksum is incorrect, implying that the frame has been corrupted). In the former case, the receiver sends back an acknowledgement frame telling the transmitter that the frame has been correctly received. In the latter, the receiver discards the incorrect frame and waits.

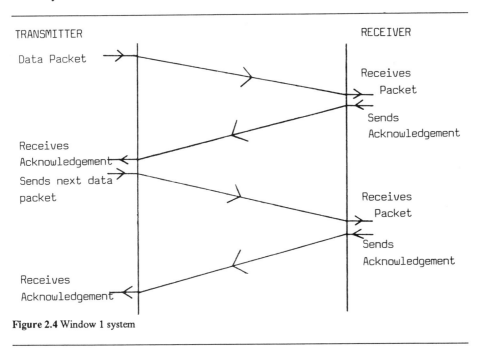

Figure 2.4 Window 1 system

Having transmitted a frame, the transmitter waits for the reply from the receiver. If the reply arrives and is received correctly, the transmitter can assume that the frame has been correctly transferred and goes on to transmit the next frame. If no reply is received within a certain time period, i.e., the acknowledgement timer has expired, it must assume that the receiver has not correctly received the frame. The transmitter then again sends the frame and again awaits a response. Usually, there is a limit to the number of times that the transmitter will retry a frame. Once the frame has been tried again the appropriate number of times without success, the transmitter assumes that the link has failed in some way.

This sounds all very nice and easy. If only life was this simple! What can go wrong with the process described above? It is important to remember that any frame, at any time, may be corrupted or lost. Equally, false frames may appear due to particularly clever electrical noise, although this is unusual and can normally be detected by the receiver.

Suppose that the reply received by the transmitter is not correctly received (the checksum is in error). If a frame is not correctly received, it cannot be processed. The transmitter must not guess that it was an acknowledgement, it just cannot know. The transmitter now does not know whether or not the receiver correctly received the frame. It cannot just send the frame again in case the receiver has already correctly received it (this would result in the contents of the frame being duplicated at the receiver).

In order to solve this problem, something must be added to the frame so that the transmitter and receiver can uniquely identify it. This it does with the use of a 'sequence number'. The transmitter and receiver both initialise the sequence number to be used to zero. The first frame carries this sequence number (in the case of X.25 level 2 it is in the control field). When the receiver acknowledges the frame, the acknowledgement carries the sequence number of the frame to which it refers. The receiver then increments its sequence number. This is, in effect, the next expected frame sequence number. When the transmitter receives this acknowledgement correctly, it increments its sequence number and the whole process can repeat.

How does this solve the problem of the corrupted reply from the receiver? The transmitter ignores the corrupted frame as before and waits for the acknowledgement timer to expire. It can then send the original frame again. Assuming that the receiver had correctly received the first attempt to transmit this frame, it will be expecting to receive a frame containing the next sequence number. The receiver can then correctly deduce that the transmitter did not receive the acknowledgement correctly. The receiver discards the received frame and sends the acknowledgement again.

One refinement needs to be added to this process to enable it to be used in practice. If the sequence number was incremented every time a frame is correctly transferred, the sequence number could grow to be very large and take up a lot of space in the frame. A method is required to ensure that the sequence number does not grow to be too large. How many distinct sequence numbers are required for the window 1 system? Take the case where the link has just started up so that the sequence number is 0. The first frame is transmitted and received correctly, but the acknowledgement from the receiver to the transmitter is lost. The receiver's sequence number is 1. The re-transmitted frame from the transmitter carries sequence number 0. This is sufficient to determine what has happened. Therefore it can be seen that just two values for the sequence number, 0 and 1, are required to ensure that all frames are transferred without loss or duplication. This can be implemented by using 'modulo n' arithmetic.

For a window 1 system, the next sequence number is calculated using the equation:

next sequence number = (sequence number + 1) mod 2

So, for a sequence of frames, the sequence number will go 0, 1, 0, 1, 0...

Since this sequence numbering scheme requires just 1 bit in the frame, it is extremely efficient.

Although window 1 acknowledgement is used in many networks, there is a problem with it that limits its use. The problem is that the transmitter must wait for the acknowledgement to a frame before it can transmit the next one. Although this makes the link layer software considerably easier to implement and test, it does limit the maximum throughput that can be achieved. This is because the frame takes a certain amount of time to be transmitted to the receiver. The receiver must then check that the checksum is correct, process the frame and produce an acknowledgement to the frame. This must then be sent back to the transmitter before the next frame can be transmitted. Figure 2.5 shows this process. Note that even if the acknowledgement from the receiver is instantaneous the link layer can still not fully utilise the communications bandwidth of the link because of the time taken for the acknowledgement to be sent back to the transmitter. Although this is not serious where the link capacity is very much greater than that required and the response by the receiver is very fast, in most situations it is a limitation, particularly when the bandwidth of the link is not very high in the first place.

What is needed is a mechanism by which the transmitter does not have to wait for the acknowledgement from the receiver before transmitting the next frame. This type of link layer is known as a 'window n' system. X.25 level 2 normally uses a 'window size' of seven. This means that the transmitter can send up to seven frames before an acknowledgement is required from the receiver. Figure 2.6 shows this in action. Note that the response from the receiver can now be quite slow and that it is easy to fully utilise the link capacity even when the receiver is relatively slow.

Obviously, to use a window size of seven, more than one bit is required to encode the sequence number in the frame. To ensure that frames are never lost or duplicated, eight distinct sequences numbers must be used. (The number required is always at least one more than the window size.) The equation for calculating the next sequence number for a window size of 7 is therefore:

next sequence number = (sequence number + 1) mod 8

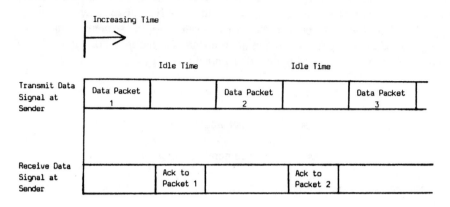

Figure 2.5 Line usage in window 1 system

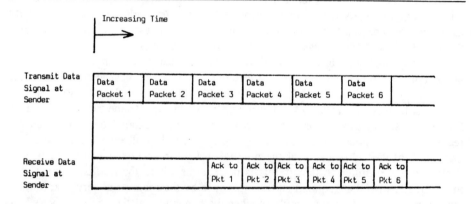

Figure 2.6 Line usage in window 7 system

The sequence numbers then go 0, 1, 2, 3, 4, 5, 6, 7, 0, 1, 2...

Three bits are required to encode this sequence number in the frames.

So far, we have only considered information being transferred in one direction (one device is the transmitter and the other is the receiver). In most cases, it is necessary to transfer data in both directions simultaneously. This is known as 'full duplex' operation. Essentially, full duplex is easily provided by operating different sequence numbers for both directions of information transfer. Each device will then transmit and receive a mixture of information frames and acknowledgement frames.

Some protocols, X.25 level 2 included, allow a frame to be both an information frame and an acknowledgement to an information frame in the other direction. This is often called 'piggybacking'. Although it can often be difficult to implement effectively,

24

piggybacking has the desirable effect of reducing the total number of frames that need to be transmitted and received.

The system of sequence numbering provides the link layer with the ability to detect and correct frames containing errors. The sequence numbering along with a limited window size also provides the other major function of the link layer - flow control. If the receiver is unable to process frames at the required rate at any point in time, all it has to do is to stop acknowledging the received frames. When the transmitter has transmitted as many frames as it can before receiving an acknowledgement, it must stop and wait for the receiver to catch up.

In order for a window n system to operate effectively, the receiver should always be able to receive frames up to the window limit - seven frames in the case of X.25 level 2. If it cannot, this will cause extra re-transmissions of frames and cause a slow down in the rate of information transfer.

2.3.3 The Network Layer

The link layer provides an error free, flow controlled, link between two devices connected together. The network layer provides for communications between devices that are not necessarily connected directly together (i.e., across a network).

In order to set up network layer connections between devices, it is necessary for the devices to be able to refer to each other. This is analogous to the telephone system. In order to make a telephone call to somebody, it is first necessary to know their telephone number. Usually, every device connected to the network has a unique address. A device can use the address of another device to request that a communications path be set up between the two devices.

There are two fundamentally different ways of constructing network layer addresses. The first is to give each device a unique address that is globally significant. This means that, wherever the device is being called from on the network, the address used to refer to it is always the same.

The second method uses the route between devices to construct the address. Figure 2.7 shows the idea. In effect, the address of a device as seen from another is actually a specification of the route that information will take between the two devices. In this case, the links are numbered from 1 to 9. Suppose that end-point device A wants to send information to end-point device B. The route between them could go from link 7 to link 6, then to link 3, then to link 1 and finally on to device B. The address of B as seen from A is then '7631' for this particular route.

Suppose that end-point device C also wishes to send information to end-point device B. The shortest route between C and B is to use link 2 and then link 1 making the address of B as seen from C '21'.

Therefore, using this 'route addressing' system, the address of an end-point device will vary. In the 'global addressing' system, the address for an end-point device always remains the same. Both systems have their advantages and disadvantages as will be seen when we go on to discuss network routing in general. Currently, global addressing is almost always used within packet switched networks. The rest of the examples in this section assume the global addressing system.

Referring to Figure 2.7, how does end-point device A set up a communications path to end-point device B? It does this by establishing a 'virtual call' between the two devices. Device A requests that a virtual call be set up to device B by sending a 'call request packet' down its link to packet switch S4. Whereas information at the link layer is referred to as frames, the equivalent for the network layer are 'packets'. All network layer information is transferred in packets. A call request packet is a special packet that requests that a communications path be set up to the called device. The call request packet contains the address of the device to be called. In many protocols, the call request packet also contains the address of the calling device so that the called device knows where the call originated.

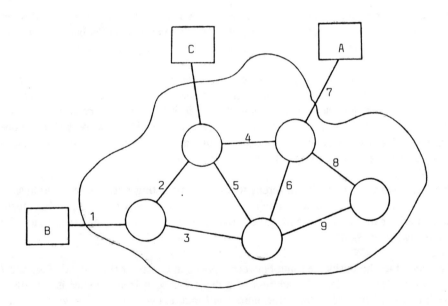

Figure 2.7 Route addressing example

Using its 'routing table', packet switch S4 must decide which of its links the call request should be passed down in order that it reaches the destination device B. It decides to pass the call request packet along to packet switch S2. This goes through the same process as S4 and passes it to S1. Finally, S1 passes the call request packet along to the destination device.

Device B now has the option of accepting the incoming call or rejecting it. If it decides to accept the call request, it sends a 'call accepted' packet back along the route to device A. At this point, a communications path is established between the two devices and end-to-end information can be transferred. The virtual call has now been established and is said to be in the 'information transfer phase'. If device B rejects the call, it sends a 'clear request' packet to indicate to device A that the call is not acceptable.

An important feature of the network level is that it can support many simultaneously active virtual calls. This capability is known as 'multiplexing'. For example, the network layer can support virtual calls to both device B and device C from device A at the same time.

Clearly, some mechanism must be provided that allows the devices to identify to which virtual call packets transmitted and received belong. This is usually done with the aid of a 'logical channel number'. Each virtual call is assigned a unique virtual channel number that is used to refer to that virtual call while it is in existence.

Logical Channel Number	Packet Type	Information

Figure 2.8 Simple network layer packet

Figure 2.8 shows a simple network layer packet structure based on that used in X.25 level 3. The start of the packet contains the logical channel number of the virtual call to which it refers. There then follows a field containing the function of the packet, the packet type. The remainder of the packet contains any extra information that may be required depending on the type of the packet.

When device A wishes to set up a virtual call to another device, device B, for example, it assigns a unique logical channel number to the virtual call. This is carried on the call request packet and tells packet switch S4 that all other packets transferred between packet switch S4 and device A for this virtual call must carry the same logical channel number. The call request packet is then routed across the network to packet switch S1. Packet switch S1 then assigns a unique logical channel number for the link to device B and sends the call request packet to device B using this new logical channel number. This tells device B that all other packets for this virtual call must carry this logical channel number.

Note that the logical channel numbers used at each end of the virtual call will usually be different and that the logical channel number is only significant between an end-point device and the packet switch to which it is connected.

27

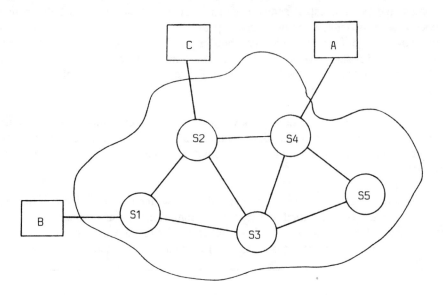

Figure 2.9

An important point to note here is that a distinction has appeared between links from end-point devices to packet switches in the network and links from packet switches to packet switches. In fact, these internal network links may use different or enhanced protocols from those that are presented to the end-point devices. This is very similar to the telephone system. The interface to the subscriber is usually the standard sort of circuit that an ordinary telephone can be plugged into. Inside the telephone switching network, some very fancy communications equipment may be involved, possibly including satellites. At the destination of the call, however, there will probably be just an ordinary telephone again. The point here is that the most important characteristic of any network, as far as the user of the network is concerned, is the interface that it presents to the outside world. X.25 itself is a standardisation of an interface between a network and an end-point device.

When the virtual call is no longer needed, a 'clear request' packet is sent by one of the end-point devices. Usually, the other end-point device has to acknowledge the clear request with a 'clear confirmation' packet.

The transfer of information in the information transfer phase at the network layer is in many ways similar to the transfer of information at the link layer. Generally, the error detection and correction functions of the link layer are not duplicated in the network layer. The network layer must have its own flow control mechanisms, however. This is because the link layer flow control operates on all of the traffic on the link. The network layer flow control, on the other hand, operates on the information relating to a single virtual call operating over the link. If the link layer is flow controlled, then no network layer packets can be transferred. If the link layer is not flow controlled, but a virtual call is, other virtual calls can operate normally, totally unaffected by the temporarily blocked virtual call.

In order to implement flow control at the network layer, the concept of the window n system is used again. Taking X.25 level 3 as an example, the standard sequence numbers for each direction of transfer take up three bits in the packet, allowing sequence numbers from 0 to 7. The maximum window size is therefore seven packets. The most common window size used in X.25 networks is two. Therefore, there can be at most two packets unacknowledged at any one time in each direction of transfer.

The effect of the window size in the network layer is similar to that in the link layer. However, the effects of changing the window size in the network layer are much more pronounced. To see this, consider a virtual call between end-point device A and end-point device B in Figure 2.9. Every packet from device A has to go through packet switch S4, S2 and S1 before reaching B. The packet on this path has to be transferred across four different links. All this adds delay, known as the 'transit time', before device B receives a packet transmitted by device A. Equally, every network layer acknowledge has to follow the same route in reverse to get back to device A.

Putting some figures in for the transit time may help to illustrate the problem. Suppose the transit time for an information packet or acknowledgement is ten milliseconds for every link in the path and that we can ignore the delay added by the packet switches. Since there are four links between device A and B, a packet from device A takes 40 milli-seconds to get to device B. The acknowledgement back from device B takes another 40 milli-seconds making a total of 80 milliseconds for the round trip.

If the window size in use in the network layer is 1, device A can only transmit one packet every 80 milli-seconds giving a maximum packet rate of 12.5 packets per second. If the window size is 2, however, the situation is considerably improved. Figure 2.10 shows what happens. Device A transmits one information packet followed ten milli-seconds later by the next. After 40 milli-seconds, device B receives the first packet and sends an acknowledgement. Ten milli-seconds later, device B receives the second and sends an acknowledgement for that one too. After 80 milli-seconds, the first acknowledgement reaches device A which than sends out the third packet. 10 milliseconds later, device A receives the second acknowledgement which then sends out the fourth packet. Device A can therefore send two packets in every 80 milli-second period of time. Device A can then send 25 packets per second to device B, doubling the rate for the window 1 example.

In this case, because the round trip delay is long compared to the individual link delays, a window size of 7 could be utilised to great advantage. Device A could send seven packets and still be limited by the rate at which it receives acknowledgements from device B. Using a window size of 7 would result in a packet rate of 87.5 packets per second.

With this in mind, why is it that, in practice, a window size of 2 is almost always used in X.25 networks? There are several reasons for this including the fact that most X.25 equipment is delivered with the maximum window size set to 2 and it is never changed! A significant factor is the resources that large window sizes require in both the packet switches and end-point devices. At any time, any device may be required to buffer the entire window size of packets for a virtual call. If that device is supporting a large number of virtual calls, this can place enormous demands on buffer space within the packet switch or end-point device. On occasions, it may be necessary for devices to take drastic action in these circumstances. (This can include clearing virtual calls in order to get some resources back.)

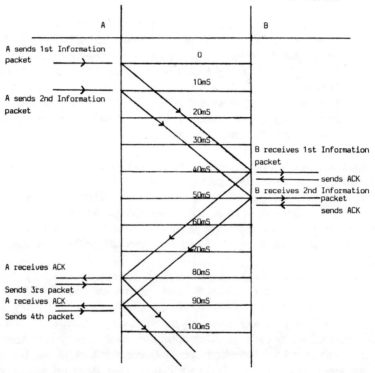

Figure 2.10 Window size 2 example

The window size chosen for a particular virtual call, where the network layer allows different window sizes on a per call basis, should really depend on the delay time of the various links and packet switches in the route between the two end-point devices at the ends of the call. This means that the optimum window size varies depending on which end-point device is being called. Mostly, a compromise window size is chosen, which works reasonably well in all situations. Only those calls that require maximum throughput really need to worry about the window size in use.

So far, we have only considered networks that use the virtual call concept to provide communications paths between end-point devices. There is an alternative possibility seen in some types of packet switched networks. These networks are known as 'datagram' networks. In a datagram network, there is no concept of call set-up and an information transfer phase followed by the call clear down. Instead, each individual packet is merely 'launched' into the packet switched network at any time (in theory, at least). It is up to the network to route the packet to its destination.

Clearly, as there is no call set-up phase, no logical channel number can be allocated in the network layer. Each packet in a datagram network therefore has to contain the explicit source and destination end-point device addresses. Datagram networks do have some interesting advantages over virtual call networks. As there is no concept of a connection between devices in a datagram network (i.e., they are 'connectionless'), the packet switches do not need to keep any records of active calls and can therefore be made extremely simple and very fast. Also, if only very small amounts of data need to be transferred between the devices on the network so that each transfer can be fitted into one datagram packet, information transfer can be extremely efficient. This is because one of the most time consuming operations for virtual call networks is the actual process of setting up the virtual call in the first place. If a virtual call has to be set up for a relatively small period of time with a high call set up rate, a packet switched network can rapidly grind to a halt.

There are also several disadvantages in using datagrams. First of all, there is no explicit flow control mechanism as with the virtual call network. Also, because every datagram packet has explicit addresses in it and the network keeps no records of connections, every packet switch in the packet's path has to look up the explicit address in its routing table to determine where to switch the packet. This can be slower than using a simple logical channel number to identify the route as in a virtual call network. Also, there is no formal acknowledgement system so that, where errors in reception are possible, the sender cannot be sure that the datagram packet was transferred correctly.

It is possible to combine virtual calls and datagrams within the same network. One or other mechanism is used depending on the characteristics of the information transfer. Another approach is to use a datagram network but run a simulated virtual call network over the top of the datagram service. This combines the advantages of the virtual call network with the speed and simplicity of datagram network packet switches. An example of this type of network is given at the end of this section.

2.4 Routing in Packet Switched Networks

In the previous discussion of the network layer, the concept of routing tables was briefly mentioned. When a packet enters the network 'cloud' from an end-point device, it must be routed to the destination end-point device by the packet switches forming the network. There are many different ways of doing this. As usual, there are pros and cons for each different technique. Mostly the trade-off is between the routing functions provided and the complexity of the implementation.

Practical packet switched networks tend to exhibit an architecture known as an 'irregular mesh'. The example network shown in Figure 2.9 is of this type. Packet switched networks tend to grow organically. Bits get added on here and there as dictated by need. The routing strategy needs to be general enough to cope with almost any shape (topology) packet switched network.

There are two fundamentally different types of routing strategy: fixed and dynamic.

2.4.1 Fixed Routing

Fixed routing is the simplest routing strategy in that the packet switches forming the network contain fixed routing tables. These routing tables provide them with all of the information that they need to be able to route packets around the network. Many X.25 networks only provide a fixed routing capability, so it is important to understand how they work.

Figure 2.11 shows a small irregular mesh packet switched network. To illustrate how things work, we will determine the routing tables for packet switch S2.

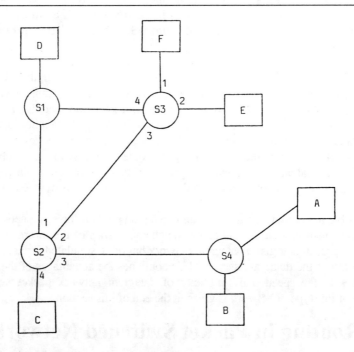

Figure 2.11 Fixed routing example

The routing table consists of a number of entries, one for each end-point device connected to the network. In this example, there are six end-point devices, so the routing table will have six entries. Each entry contains two pieces of information. The first is the address of the end-point device, the second is the link down which packets for that end-point device should be routed. S2 has four links numbered 1 to 4. The routing for S2 in the example network is shown in Table 2.1.

Table 2.1 S2's routing table

Address of end-point device	Link
A	3
B	3
C	4
D	1
E	2
F	2

Note that it is quite possible that packets for more than one end-point device may be routed down the same link. This is true for end-point devices A, B and E, F in the case of packet switch S2. This means that there is at least one more packet switch on the route to the end-point devices.

How do the routing tables get into the packet switches? In the case of fixed routing, pre-constructed tables are loaded into the packet switches when the network is first configured. If a new end-point device is added to the network, the routing tables in the packet switches must be updated to reflect this fact.

It is quite useful to look at the routing table for another packet switch, S3, for example:

Table 2.2 S3's routing table

Address of end-point device	Link
A	3
B	3
C	3
D	4
E	2
F	1

The most important thing to notice when comparing the routing tables for S2 and S3 is that they are different. This is because they are seeing the network from a different point within it.

The fact that, in general, the routing tables in every packet switch are different can become quite a problem, particularly in large networks. Managing a large set of routing tables becomes an onerous task for the people running the network, the network managers.

Clearly, the most important advantage of fixed routing in this form is its simplicity. The disadvantages are the fact that all of the routing tables have to be built manually. This process of building routing tables requires quite detailed knowledge of the topology of the network and the traffic loadings that may be expected. This last point is made because it should be remembered that links in a packet switched network may not all have the same capacity.

Looking at Figure 2.11, there are two routes between packet switch S2 and packet switch S3. There is the direct route between them consisting of a single link. In addition, there is the indirect route through packet switch S1. It could just be that the direct link between the two is slow making the indirect route faster. Equally, it may be that the traffic between the two packet switches is so heavy that the load must be split between the two routes. This can be done by modifying the routing tables. For example, it may be decided that traffic through S2 for end-point device E should go via the direct route and that traffic for end-point device F should go through the indirect route. Decision making at this level requires a deep understanding of how the network is to be used.

Even if a packet switched network is initially very carefully configured, often by the equipment suppliers, adding new end-point devices can upset the whole routing strategy. Often the information and personnel involved in the initial installation are not available making the job of expanding the network even more difficult.

How can this simple strategy be improved? One common method of reducing the routing table problems is to use 'domain addressing'. Where this sort of addressing is used, end-point device addresses contain some of the routing information in them. The concept is not unlike that used in the telephone system. A typical seven digit telephone number within London consists of a three digit area code followed by a four digit code unique to that area code. The area code tells the telephone switching system whereabouts in London the telephone is located, while the last four digits are only used at the destination telephone exchange to choose the particular telephone line.

Figure 2.12 shows a packet switched network that uses domain addressing. In this network, there are four different addressing domains. The end-point devices connected to the network use four digit addresses in this example. The first two digits identify the addressing domain to which the end-point device belongs. The second two digits uniquely identify the end-point device within the addressing domain.

To see how this affects the routing tables within the network, we will construct the routing table for packet switch S2.

Table 2.3 S2's routing table

Address of end-point device	Link
01xx	1
0201	4
0202	5
03xx	2
04xx	3

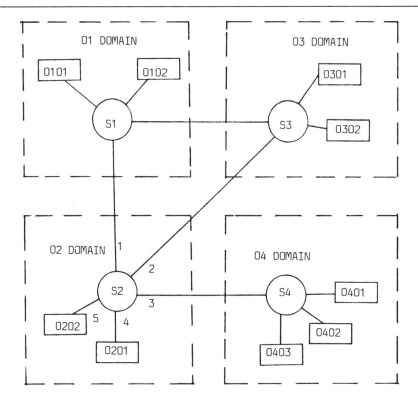

Figure 2.12 Domain addressing

Notice that, although there are nine end-point devices connected to the network, there are only five entries in S2's routing table. Entries of the form '01xx' mean that packets for all devices within addressing domain 01 should be routed down the same link (link 1 in this example).

There are many advantages in using this domain addressing concept. First of all, the routing tables in each packet switch are kept small. This is important as it reduces the time taken to search the table when a call request packet has to be routed and a virtual call path set up, as in the case of a virtual call network, and when datagrams have to be routed, as in the case of a datagram network. The situation is particularly serious with datagram networks as every packet has to be individually routed.

Without the use of domain addressing, each packet switch in the network has to know every end-point device that is connected to the network. With domain addressing, the packet only needs to know where the domains are located, not every end-point device within those domains. The only end-point devices that the packet switch has to worry about are those directly connected to it. This makes expanding the network very much

35

simpler. Instead of having to update every routing table whenever a new end-point device is added to the network, only the routing table of the packet switch to which the end-point device is directly connected needs to be updated.

In very large packet switched networks, it may be necessary to use sub-domains within domains. Again, the telephone system provides a useful analogy. Viewing the telephone system from a global perspective, the domains are the individual countries. The domain is identified by the international dialling code for the country. The domain itself then contains a number of sub-domains represented by the area code. Finally, the remaining digits of the telephone number identify the specific telephone line. The same can be done with packet switched networks. The end-point device addresses can be split into parts analogous to the international dialling code, area code, etc. Depending on where packet switches are located, they may only need information about the major domains without having to know about sub-domains within those domains. The domain addressing technique therefore makes it practical to build very large packet switched networks without having to deal with enormous routing tables.

In practical networks of any kind, it is important to consider the effect of link or packet switch failures on the operation of the network. This is where the fixed routing strategy really falls down. Because the routing tables are fixed, if a link fails for some reason, any routes through that link will not be available until the link is restored. Depending on what the network is being used for, this can either be just about tolerable or completely unacceptable. Even though, in the case of the example network in Figure 2.12, there is more than one route between packet switch S2 and packet switch S3, packets and virtual calls cannot suddenly be routed via an alternate route if the main route fails.

In practice, it is essential that information about network failures and problems be communicated to the network managers as rapidly as possible as they may be able to manually alter routing tables to avoid failed links and packet switches. 'Network management' systems are therefore very important to those responsible for running large packet switched networks.

It is possible to add many refinements to the basic fixed routing strategy to make it more manageable in real life operation. These include load sharing between multiple routes in a way that does provide an automatic fall-back in the case of a failure in the network. Another possibility is to use 'secondary routing' tables. In essence, there may be more than one route to an end-point device from a packet switch. The normal routing table contains the ideal route information. If the ideal route fails, the packet switch can try the alternate route (if one exists) indicated in the secondary routing table. Although this does provide some measure of automatic fall-back, it makes the task of building routing tables even more complicated.

In the final analysis, the only real way to avoid the problems of fixed routing is to use dynamic routing.

2.4.2 Dynamic Routing

In packet switched networks that use fixed routing, all of the decisions that the network takes about routing packets are predetermined by the fixed routing tables in the packet switches. In packet switched networks that use dynamic routing, the packet switches are able to make routing decisions based on conditions in the network when packets are switched. This means that the people responsible for installing and running such a network do not have to have such a deep understanding of the behaviour of the network when it is in use. The network itself should take care of that for them.

There are several other reasons for preferring a dynamic routing strategy to a fixed one. In many networks, availability is very important. Put simply, it is important that the paths between end-point devices should be available as much of the time as possible. To increase availability, the network should be able to automatically use alternate routes between end-point devices in the case of a link or packet switch failure.

Another reason for using dynamic routing is where several routes between end-point devices are available. In order to get the best use out of the network, it is desirable to split the traffic between the various routes. This process is known as 'load sharing'. A dynamic routing strategy may well be able to adjust the loading of each route to ensure that maximum use is made of the links and that the delay to packets is kept as low as possible. In order to do this, the packet switch has to make intelligent decisions when switching each packet in such a situation.

The load sharing capability can also be very useful when some of the links in the network actually belong to public networks meaning that charges will be made for use. A dynamic routing strategy may be able to optimise the use of such links in conjunction with private links so as to provide good throughput at a reasonable cost.

The simplest form of dynamic routing is where each packet switch in the network only has detailed link loading and status about the links connected directly to the switch; they have no detailed knowledge about the status of links and packet switches elsewhere in the network. The simplest piece of information that a packet switch has about a link is whether it is up (active) or down (inactive). If the link is down, the packet switch will have to use an alternate route when routing packets that would normally go down the link that is down.

When two or more routes are available such that the packet switch could route a packet down one of two or more links, only local information is available to the packet switch when making its decision. It's configuration table may contain information about the relative capacities of the links and whether they are chargeable or not. The packet switch will also have information about the relative loadings of the links by keeping track of the packet rates on each link and the size of the queues of packets awaiting transmission down the links.

The chief advantage of this simple dynamic routing strategy is that it does not require any extra mechanisms within the network to transfer routing information between the packet switches. The dynamic procedures are totally contained within each packet switch. This is particularly useful in X.25 networks as little provision is made in the protocol for dynamic routing. If an X.25 packet switch is to present standard X.25 interfaces, it cannot rely on using special dynamic routing mechanisms other than those totally contained within the packet switch.

There are several disadvantages, however. It does nothing to help one of the problems with fixed routing: the routing tables still have to be built manually. In fact, it can make the job more difficult in that, in order to give the packet switch the required information about capacity, etc., even more information must be included in the tables.

Another problem is that, although the packet queue for a link on a particular route might be small within the packet switch, there may be severe delays further along the route. As the packet switch knows nothing about what is going on elsewhere in the network, there is no way that the packet switch can deduce this. Eventually, the backlog may reach the packet switch, causing its queue to build up but by that time severe network congestion may have occurred.

In order to get the full benefits of dynamic routing, it is important that the packet switches in the network have information from other parts of the network if they are to stand much chance of making correct routing decisions. This form of dynamic routing is known as 'distributed adaptive routing'. The packet switches in the network exchange information about the state of the network, modifying their routing strategies as appropriate. Special mechanisms are added to the packet switches to allow this exchange of routing information.

The most famous example of a packet switched network that uses this form of dynamic routing is ARPANET. ARPANET is able to transfer information both about the availability of links in the network and an estimate of the loading of the route to end-point devices.

The routing tables contain an entry for each end-point device attached to the network. When the network is first brought into operation, these entries contain estimates of the route loadings to the end-point devices. The aim of the network is to always use the 'best' route between end-point devices. This is one where the transit delay is as small as possible. When the network is in operation, it can estimate the delay of any one route by combining its own information of queue size with that provided by the packet switches to which it is directly connected.

Every so often a packet switch will send a 'delay table' to every packet switch to which it is directly connected. This delay table contains an entry for every end-point device on the network. When a packet switch receives such a table, it combines it with the packet switch's current routing table to form a new one. For each end-point device, the packet switch compares the delay in its routing table with that indicated in the received delay table, adjusted for the effects of the link on which it was received. If the new delay is smaller than that for the route currently in use, the routing table entry for that end-point device is updated to indicate that a better route has been found.

This mechanism allows changes in network loading to be communicated throughout the packet switched network automatically. If the size of the routing tables is dynamic, new end-point devices added to the network will appear in the routing tables of the packet switches automatically and within a very short time after network connection. Also, when an end-point device goes down, that fact is reflected throughout the network within a short time. Therefore, the availability of every end-point device connected to the network as available at any point within the network.

If a new link is added to the network, possibly to ease loading of existing routes, the network will automatically use the new route where it results in shorter packet transit delay times.

The ability of a packet switched network to dynamically re-configure itself when presented with changing usage and topology gives such a network excellent operational characteristics. The network managers can basically sit back and let the network take care of problems. As the availability of end-point devices is known everywhere within the network, it is very simple to monitor and automatically inform the network managers of problems that are occurring. Expansion is easy as no manual routing table changes have to be made in order to add new end-point devices to the network.

There are two different strategies for controlling the transmission of the delay tables between the packet switches in the network. One method, used by ARPANET, is that every packet switch in the network transfers its delay tables at a fixed rate. In ARPANET, tables are exchanged every two-thirds of a second. Lower rates are used for slow lines. The problem with this is that, most of the time, nothing has changed that warrants the transmission of delay tables. In general, and in particular for large networks, the overhead in processing delay tables can be considerable. Therefore unnecessary transmissions of delay tables waste packet switch and link capacity.

In order to prevent unnecessary transmissions of delay tables, an 'event driven' strategy can be used. In this case, delay tables are only transmitted when something has changed. This could be either a new route or end-point device becoming active or perhaps an indication of increasing delay times on a set of routes. If the network is stable and loading constant, there will be no transmissions of delay tables, and therefore the full packet switch and link capacity is available for switching packets.

Packet switched networks that use distributed adaptive routing are most suited to use as datagram networks as no information about virtual calls needs to be maintained within the packet switches. It is a much more difficult job to use dynamic routing with virtual call networks because the information required to switch packets is localised within the packet switches on the route of the virtual call. In order for packets to take a different route, the virtual call information would also have to be moved.

The best way of using distributed adaptive routing to provide a virtual call network is to run the virtual call protocol above the datagrams (i.e., using datagrams to convey the virtual call information between end-point devices). Only the end-point devices need to have any knowledge of the virtual call protocol. In order to illustrate many of the concepts introduced in this section, we will look at a real network in some detail. The network is the CN-3X network, an example of a network that uses distributed adaptive routing to provide a virtual call network in the way described above.

2.5 An Example - The CN-3X Network

The CN-3X is a real network that uses many of the principles of distributed adaptive routing while providing a virtual call interface very similar to X.25. The CN-3X network was developed at Imperial College, London in the early 1980s. The aim was to provide a packet switched network that had the excellent operational characteristics provided by distributed adaptive routing while, at the same time, keeping the network packet switches as simple (and as cheap) as possible.

The CN-3X link layer is standard X.25 level 2. This protocol is in fact provided by VLSI (Very Large Scale Integration) integrated circuits that can run at up to one million bits per second. X.25 level 2 was chosen because of this and also because it is a well understood protocol that provided all of the functions necessary for the higher level CN-3X protocols. The use of X.25 level 2 also means that standard CN-3X link controller hardware can be used to provide gateways to X.25 networks. All that is required is software to convert the higher level protocols between the CN-3X network and the X.25 network.

The network layer is in fact just a datagram protocol. Above this, at the transport service layer, is the protocol that actually provides the virtual call service. Figure 2.13 shows the structure of the virtual call datagram packets. The five byte header forms the datagram part of the packet. The remainder of the packet consists of the virtual call protocol information. The datagram protocol is called the 'InterNet Protocol' or INP for short. The virtual call protocol is known as the 'Trans Network Control Protocol' or TNCP for short.

CN-3X end-point device addresses are four digit numbers. This is generally split into three groups of digits. The first two digits specify an 'area code' and give a general indication of where the end-point device is physically located. The third digit is an indication of the type of the end-point device and its function. The fourth digit indicates the number of that type of end-point device in that area code.

As an example of CN-3X addressing, consider the address below:

1442

This indicates that the end-point device is in area 14, that the end-point device is of type 4 (a packet assembler/disassembler) and is number 2 in that area.

Although this structured address is in the correct form to allow the use of domain addressing, this was not implemented. The reason for this is that the routing tables within CN-3X are constructed totally dynamically, so that manual building of tables was not necessary. Also, devices from any area can be connected to any packet switch in the network giving complete flexibility in distributing the end-point device links around the packet switches.

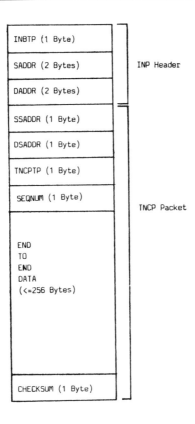

Figure 2.13 CN-3X Virtual call packet

2.5.1 The INP Block Types

This one byte field indicates the function of the packet. There are several types of INP packet in addition to the end-end datagrams. These additional packets allow the CN-3X links to be brought into operation in an orderly way and provide the mechanisms required to allow the network to use dynamic routing. Table 2.4, overleaf, shows the various INP block types.

Table 2.4 INP Block Types

Block type	INPBTP code	Function
TNCPDT	00	End-end virtual call data
TNCPND	01	Undelivered TNCPDT
ACTCON	02	Active configuration
PASCON	03	Passive configuration
DOWN	04	Link down
RESYNC	05	Link coming up
UP	06	Link is up
INPMNT	07	Maintenance packet

The TNCPDT packets contain TNCP virtual call information. These packets are transferred between end-point devices across the CN-3X network. More will be said about these packets later. These are the only packets that have end to end significance; all of the others are transferred between the two devices at each end of a CN-3X link.

The TNCPND packets contain TNCP virtual call information that could not be routed to the destination by the CN-3X packet switches. Usually, this would be because the destination device had been marked as unavailable in the routing tables of a packet switch along the packets path. In fact, this packet was never used as the information was not particularly useful. For example, it could be generated during a period when the network was re-configuring itself. The destination device might only have been temporarily unavailable when the TNCPND packet was generated. If the end-point device that generated the original packet was to process a TNCPND packet as though the destination device was permanently unavailable, the virtual call may be cleared unnecessarily.

Another possible use for this packet would be to indicate that the contents of the original TNCPTP packet would be lost as it could not be routed. Upon receiving the TNCPND, the sender of the original packet could then retry the packet later. In fact, it proved simpler to rely on time-outs at the virtual call level to detect this situation. The packet switches in fact discard unroutable packets rather than keep them flying around the network.

The ACTCON packets are used to broadcast delay tables across the CN-3X links. In CN-3X, the delay tables are known as 'configuration tables'. More will be said about these packets later.

The PASCON packets, along with the ACTCON packets, are used to provide the configuration broadcast protocol.

The DOWN packets are used to indicate that a CN-3X link is DOWN (i.e., not operational). A device transmits DOWN packets every 500 milliseconds until the device at the other end of the link transmits the correct response, indicating that the link should be brought into operation.

The RESYNC packet is the packet transmitted in response to a received DOWN packet when the link is to be brought into operation.

The UP packet is sent in response to a received RESYNC packet to indicate that the link is operational. The UP packets are also used to check the status of a link while it is operational. The devices at each end of the link transmit UP packets approximately once every 500 milliseconds while the link is idle (i.e., TNCPDT packets are not being transferred). If a link is idle for more than 2.5 seconds, the link will be marked as DOWN and DOWN packets transmitted every 500 milliseconds again. This process of transmitting something even when the link is idle is known as 'polling'. It is effective in checking that the link is still operational even when nothing is happening. Otherwise, a link failure might only be noticed when an attempt was made to transmit a TNCPDT packet.

The final packet type, the INPMNT packet, is used to allow a remote network management device to get access to information within the CN-3X about its internal state, the status of its network link and the status of virtual calls. We will not go into this in detail here as it is very specific to this network. Usually, remote management is performed by calling a special address within the device, the remote management facility. In the CN-3X network, the packet switches have, in effect, end-point devices within them. This means that it is possible to call into the packet switches and get access to the remote management facility from any (suitably authorised) point within the CN-3X network.

2.5.2 The CN-3X Virtual Call Protocol - TNCP

TNCP packets are transferred across the CN-3X network in TNCPTP INP packets. The SADDR field of the packet contains the source address of the packet (i.e., the four digit CN-3X address of the sender). The DADDR field of the packet contains the destination address of the packet (i.e., the four digit CN-3X address of the receiver).

The SSADDR and DSADDR fields of the TNCPTP packet contain the source and destination 'subaddresses' respectively. These are effectively the logical channel numbers that have been allocated to the call by the end-point devices at each end of the call. The SSADDR is chosen by the originator of the virtual call and is unique as far as that end-point device is concerned. The DSADDR is chosen by the receiver of the virtual call set up request and is unique as far as that end-point device is concerned. The complete SADDR+DADDR+SSADDR+DSADDR combination is therefore unique to that virtual call within the CN-3X network.

The TNCPTP field of the TNCPDT packet contains the TNCP type code of the packet. This specifies the function of the packet at the virtual call level. Finally, the SEQNUM field contains the sequence number of the packet. All TNCPDT packets carry a sequence number. There is a separate sequence number maintained for each direction of transfer in a virtual call. When the call is first set up, the sequence numbers are initialised to 1. For each packet transferred, the sequence number is incremented modulo 256 (but excluding 0, which has a special meaning).

The valid function codes (in hex) for the various TNCP functions are given in Table 2.5 below.

Table 2.5 TNCP Function Codes

Code	Name	Function
08	CONREQ	Connect request
18	CONACC	Connect accept
28	DISREQ	Disconnect request
38	DISACC	Disconnect accept
48	RESREQ	Reset request
58	RESACC	Reset accept
02	SVCDAT	Virtual call data
22	SVCDET	Virtual call data - end of message
42	SVCDAQ	Virtual call data - qualified
62	SVCDEQ	Virtual call data - qualified and end of message

Every TNCP packet type can have a data field of up to 256 bytes following the TNCP header. The contents of this field depends on the function of the packet.

When an end-point device wishes to set up a virtual call to another end point device, it sends a CONREQ packet with the DADDR field containing the address of the end-point device that is being called. The data field of the CONREQ packet contains any extra addressing required to determine the precise service within the end-point device that is being called. This encoding is very similar to the fragment technique that is used in the 'Yellow Book' protocol.G. This is described in detail in Chapter Seven so it will not be described here.

When an end-point device receives a CONREQ packet, it decides whether or not it wishes to accept the call. If it does, it responds with a CONACC packet to indicate to the caller that the call is successful. When the sender receives the CONACC, the virtual call set up is complete and information may be transferred. If the call set up request is not acceptable to the called end-point device, it responds with a DISACC packet. When the sender receives the DISACC packet, it knows that the call was not accepted and that the virtual call no longer exists.

Assuming that the call has been successfully set up, information in the form of the four data packet types may be sent between the two end-point devices. Up to 256 bytes of data may be sent in each data packet.

It is at the time of the CONREQ/CONACC exchange that the values for the SSADDR and DSADDR fields are established. When the CONREQ is sent, the end-point device chooses one from the range of values 1 to 255 for the SSADDR field. This will be used by that end-point device in all SSADDR fields of packets sent on that virtual call. The only rule is that the end-point device is not currently using that value for some other virtual call.

When an end-point receives a CONREQ and the call is acceptable, the end-point device chooses a number as above and sets in the SSADDR of the CONACC. The SSADDR of the CONREQ goes in the DSADDR of the CONACC. From then on, all packets transmitted by that end-point device on that virtual call will have the same SSADDR and DSADDR fields. When the CONACC is received by the originator of the call, it records the SSADDR field. All packets transmitted by that end-point device on that virtual call have the SSADDR field as originally used on the CONREQ and the DSADDR field set set to that received in the SSADDR field of the CONACC.

The four different types of data packets can be formed into two groups: the unqualified data packets (SVCDAT and SVCDET) and the qualified data packets (SVCDAQ and SVCDEQ). For the unqualified packets, SVCDAT indicates that the data in the packet forms part of a sequence of data packets which together to form a longer unqualified message, consisting of a number of data packets. The SVCDET packet indicates that the data in the packet are the end of an unqualified message. The SVCDAQ and SVCDEQ packets perform the same task for qualified messages.

This distinction between an unqualified message and a qualified message is a useful facility that can be used by higher level protocols. In most cases, unqualified data is used to transfer information from applications in the end-point devices at each end of the call. Qualified messages are often used to transfer control information between the end-point devices that is not actually part of the application information. A good example of the use of qualified messages in this way is the control of the operation of packet assemblers/disassemblers by remote host computers across the CN-3X network. This is similar to the 'triple X protocol' used in X.25 networks described in Chapter Seven.

The RESREQ and RESACC packets are used basically when things go wrong. Should the end-point devices disagree about the state of a virtual call, they can exchange RESREQ and RESACK packets. When one of the end-point devices discovers an error, it sends a RESREQ to the other end-point device. The receiver of the RESREQ then transmits a RESACC in response. This exchange resets the calls to a known state. In particular, the sequence numbers for each direction are reset to 1. The data fields for the RESREQ and RESACC packets are used to contain the reason for the reset sequence. The encoding of these fields is very similar to that used in the Yellow Book protocol.

The DISREQ packet is used to clear a currently active virtual call between two end-point devices. When an end-point device sends a DISREQ packet, this may well overtake and destroy any data packets or RESREQ/RESACC packets currently in transit. When an end-point device receives a DISREQ packet, it transmits a DISACC packets in response and considers the virtual call to have been terminated. When the DISACC is received by the sender of the DISREQ, the virtual call is completely terminated and all resources released. Figure 2.14 illustrates a typical packet sequence for a TNCP virtual call.

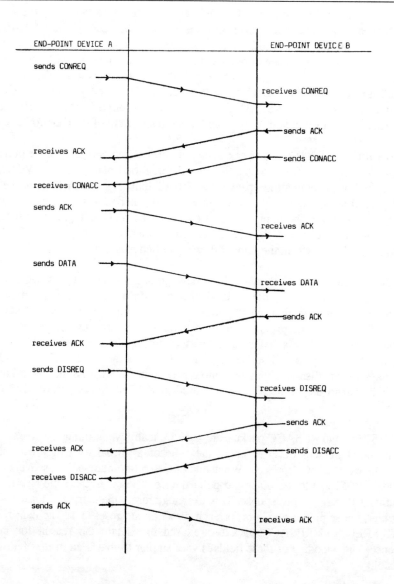

Figure 2.14 Typical CN-3X packet sequence

One of the features of TNCP is that it does not assume that the underlying datagram network guarantees that all packets transmitted will be received, either at all or in the correct order. In fact, while the network is re-configuring itself (after a link failure, for example), it is quite likely that packets in transit will be lost. Therefore, TNCP contains its own mechanism for ensuring that all packets are transferred correctly.

There are three possible fates that might befall a packet in transit across the network. The first possible fate is that the packet is lost. This may be because the network is in the process of re-configuring resulting in some packets in transit getting lost. The second is that a packet may become duplicated. This could occur because a packet was held up somewhere, the sender's timer expired causing the packet to be re-transmitted and then both being delivered by the network to the receiver. Finally, the packet may have become corrupted in transit, possibly by a faulty interface or other faulty hardware within one of the packet switches on the route of the virtual call.

Dealing with the last possibility first, each TNCP packet contains a checksum byte. This is calculated over the entire contents of the TNCP packet and then appended as the last byte of the packet (see Figure 2.13). If the receiver, upon receiving a packet, finds that the checksum is incorrect, it must discard the packet and await a retransmission of the packet.

Lost and duplicated packets are dealt with using sequence numbers and acknowledgement packets. Every packet transmitted on a virtual call must be acknowledged. An acknowledgement to a CN-3X packet consists basically of the nine byte INP and TNCP headers. The main difference is that bit 0 of the TNCPTP field is set to indicate that the packet is an acknowledgement. If an acknowledgement is not received within the sender's timeout period, the packet will be re-transmitted. Usually, this time out period is 500 milli-seconds. The packet will be sent 40 times. If an acknowledgement has still not been received, the virtual call is cleared by sending a DISREQ. The DISREQ itself must be acknowledged by the remote end-point device also or else the same process will occur. However, if a DISREQ is not acknowledged within 40 tries, the virtual call is declared terminated and all resources released.

If a packet is lost, the sender will not see an acknowledgement and will therefore retransmit the packet. If the acknowledgement to a packet is lost, the sender will still retransmit the packet. The receiver, by checking the sequence number that it is expecting next, will be able to deduce that the packet has been re-transmitted. It will therefore acknowledge the packet again and then discard the received packet.

If a packet is duplicated, the receiver will see two copies of the same packet. The receiver will able to deduce what has happened by checking the sequence numbers. The situation looks to the receiver as though the acknowledge that it transmitted to the first packet had been lost.

Special attention has to be paid to CONREQs. They, like all other packets must be acknowledged by the receiver. If the acknowledge to a CONREQ is lost, the CONREQ will be re-transmitted by the sender. The problem is that the CONREQ does not know the DSADDR field to use for the call as the receiver of the CONREQ has not yet accepted the call. The receiver would normally use the DSADDR field to find the 'call channel' allocated to that virtual call. The call channel contains all state information for each virtual call. Therefore a special check has to be made that a CONREQ has not been received from the same end-point device using the same SSADDR. In other words, it must check that specifically that the CONREQ is not a retransmission of a previous one. If this is not done, the second CONREQ will be processed as a second new virtual call request resulting in the setting up of a spurious virtual call.

After the initial call set up phase, TNCP uses a window size of 2 for packets transmitted. This means that up to two packets can be transmitted before an acknowledgement is received for the first packet. Since CN-3X was designed to operate over very fast links with fast packet switches, this window size is perfectly adequate for most situations.

The acknowledgement packets also implement flow control at the virtual call level. Bit 2 of the TNCPTP field is used to indicate whether the transmitter of the acknowledgement can receive any more data packets on that virtual call. If the bit is clear, then more data packets can be received. If it is set, then no more data packets can be received. Any that are will be queued (up to a limit), but the remote end-point device should not transmit any more. When the receiver is able to cope with more data packets, it sends a special packet to inform the transmitter. This is an acknowledgement packet with the sequence number set to 0 as it is indicating a flow control state rather than acknowledging a packet received.

A problem could occur if this special packet was lost. The transmitter would never realise that the receiver could cope with more packets, so that the flow in that direction would be blocked until the call was reset or cleared. In order to prevent this, the transmitter 'polls' the receiver. Basically, it resends the last packet acknowledged, simulating the lost acknowledgement situation, from time to time. In practice, every two seconds was chosen for this function. If the special acknowledgement is lost, the acknowledgement to the poll packet will indicate that the flow control condition has cleared allowing normal flow to resume. If no acknowledgement is received after 40 retries, the transmitter assumes that the receiver has failed and clears the call.

2.5.3 The CN-3X Configuration Broadcast Protocol

The CN-3X network uses a special protocol to transfer network configuration information between the packet switches and the end-point devices forming the CN-3X network. When a device starts up, it knows of no other devices in the network. As soon as links start operating, network configuration information is exchanged. In a very short period of time, every device connected to the network knows of the existence of every other on the network and how to get packets routed to them.

The configuration broadcast protocol uses the ACTCON and PASCON INP block types. Figure 2.14 shows the structure of the two types of packet.

The ACTCON packet contains a sequence number that is used to identify the ACTCON uniquely. This sequence number begins at 0 when the link first becomes operational. The sequence number is incremented modulo 256 for every ACTCON successfully transferred.

When a device receives an ACTCON successfully, it responds with a PASCON containing the same sequence number. Upon receiving the PASCON, the sender can then transmit the next ACTCON, if there are any changes to transmit. Essentially, the protocol is window 1 with a timeout of five seconds. If an acknowledgement PASCON is not received within five seconds of an ACTCON being sent, the ACTCON is re-transmitted. This will occur 20 times before the link is declared as DOWN. The ACTCON packets carry a checksum as their last byte to ensure that the information contained has not been corrupted in any way. This is important as corrupted configuration broadcasts can cause serious mis-operation by mis-routing packets until another configuration broadcast corrects the error. The ACTCON/PASCON protocol is operated in both directions simultaneously: there is no relationship between ACTCONs transferred in different directions across a link.

When a link between a packet switch in the CN-3X network and an end-point device becomes operational, the packet switch knows about the entire network, while the end-point device only knows about itself. The first thing that both devices do is to transfer their entire routing tables to each other. In the case of the end-point device, this is an ACTCON with just one entry, the entry for itself with an estimate of its delay (i.e., an estimate of the delay in the link between it and the packet switch).

The packet switch also sends its complete routing table to the end-point device. This is likely to consist of many entries, a number equal to the number of end-point devices in the network. The entries within the ACTCON are grouped into a number of 'records'. A record may not be split across different ACTCONs. Each record contains all of the entries for a particular area code. The first byte of the area record contains the area code. The second contains the number of entries in that area code. For each entry (i.e., for each end-point device) there are two bytes of information. The first byte contains the last two digits of its network address. This combined with the area code give the complete CN-3X network address. The second byte contains the estimate of the transit delay to that end-point device.

The processing of the configuration broadcast information is similar to that for ARPANET. For every entry within an ACTCON, the current entry for that end-point device is checked. If the end-point device is not found, then it must be a new device on the network. A new entry within the routing table must then be made for that end-point device with an indication that the route to that end-point device is via the link on which the configuration information was received.

To illustrate the processing of ACTCON records, consider the network segment shown in Figure 2.15. We are going to look at how the packet switch at the centre of the diagram processes ACTCON records for a particular area code. We will choose area code 12 for this example. From each of the packet switch's four links, it receives an ACTCON record for the area code 12. The contents of the records received on each link are shown after Figure 2.15.

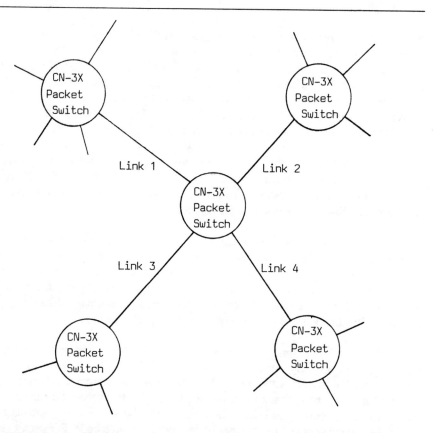

Figure 2.15 Example network segment

Address	Delay
1210	10
1241	8
1242	30
1243	20
1260	12

Link 1

Address	Delay
1210	20
1242	12
1243	20
1260	5
1270	15

Link 2

```
    Address    Delay                        Address     Delay
   +-------+-------+                        +-------+-------+
   | 1210  |  25   |                        | 1210  |  25   |
   | 1241  |  15   |                        | 1241  |  30   |
   | 1242  |  35   |                        | 1242  |  16   |
   | 1243  |  20   |                        | 1243  |  20   |
   | 1260  |  40   |                        | 1260  |  20   |
   +-------+-------+                        +-------+-------+

        Link  3                                  Link  4
```

Note that the ACTCON record from link 2 does not have the same end-point devices as
that from the other links. This may indicate that end-point device 1241 has just come
up and that the network configuration has not settled yet. In fact, as ACTCONs are
only transmitted when a change in the network configuration is detected, this is very
likely to be the cause of the re-configuration. How does the packet switch receiving
these ACTCON records process them? This depends on what the packet switch already
knows about the network configuration. This information is contained in its routing
table, for which the segment for area code 12 is shown below.

```
        Address        Delay          Link
       +----------+------------+------------+
       |   1210   |     20     |     2      |
       |   1241   |     35     |     3      |
       |   1242   |     20     |     4      |
       |   1243   |     20     |     1      |
       |   1260   |      5     |     2      |
       |   1261   |     12     |     3      |
       +----------+------------+------------+
```

The received ACTCON records are processed in sequence to build up the new routing
table. Assume that the received ACTCON records are processed ascending link number
order. For each area code record processed, the packet switch first sets a flag against
each entry for that area code that has a link number of 1 as the best route in its own
routing table. It then checks each entry in the received ACTCON record in turn. The
first entry is for 1210 showing a delay of 10. This is compared with the delay of 20
indicated in the routing table available via link 2. Since 10 is lower, this entry is
updated to shows a delay of 10 and that the route is via link 1. It then moves on to the
entry for 1241. Again, the new route is better, so this entry is changed to reflect the
new delay and the new route. This process continues until there are no more entries in
the ACTCON record. The resulting routing table is shown on the next page.

Address	Delay	Link
1210	10	1
1241	8	1
1242	20	4
1243	20	1
1260	5	2
1261	12	4

Every time an entry that is shown as having the best route via link1 is found in the ACTCON record, the flag against that entry is cleared. After processing the ACTCONs from link 2 and link 3, the routing table within the packet switch looks like this:

Address	Delay	Link
1210	10	1
1241	8	1
1242	12	2
1243	20	1
1260	5	2
1261	12	4
1270	15	2

Note that both link 1 and link 2 shows a delay of 20 to end-point device 1243. In this case, the packet switch makes an arbitrary choice of the best route. In practice, this is the first one encountered, so link 1 is chosen. Also, a new entry has been added to the routing table. The ACTCON record from link 2 contained an entry not previously known to the packet switch.

Finally, the ACTCON record from link 4 is processed. As with the others, a flag is set on every entry in the table that shows link 4 as being the best route to that end-point device. In this example, there is only one entry of this type, for device 1261. In fact, the entries for link 4 do not improve the current delays, so there are no changes to the table for this reason.

Note that end-point device 1261 is not in the ACTCON record received from link 4 even though that link 4 is shown as being the best route. This can be determined by the fact that the flag is still set against this entry in the routing table, even when all entries in the received ACTCON have been processed. This means that end-point device 1261 is no longer available. The packet switch therefore deletes this entry from its routing table.

Therefore, the final routing table after processing all four received ACTCON records is:

Address	Delay	Link
1210	10	1
1241	8	1
1242	12	2
1243	20	1
1260	5	2
1270	15	2

Processing received ACTCON records is only one half of the story; the packet switch needs to communicate to the other packet switches any new information that the packet switch has. Changes that cause the packet switch to transmit ACTCONs are: new end-point devices appearing in the routing table; end-point devices vanishing from the routing table; better routes to existing end-point devices. As we have seen, new end-point devices and new routes are indicated by suitable entries appearing in the ACTCON record for the appropriate area code. End-point devices no longer available are indicated by their absence from the ACTCON record for that area code. Consequently, whenever a change occurs within an area code, the packet switch must send all of the entries that it has in its routing table for that area code to all of the devices to which it is directly connected.

There is one significant exception to this process of including all entries in an area code in the ACTCON record for that area code. If the ACTCON record is to be transmitted down a link which is the best route for any of the entries in that record, then those entries must be omitted. The reason for this is that there is no point telling that device that the entry exists - the information about its existence must have come from that device in the first place.

There is also a more serious reason for removing these entries. Suppose that, at the same time as the ACTCON is being sent, the destination device marks an end-point device that used to be available via that destination device as unavailable (i.e., it removes the end-point device from its routing table). Shortly afterwards, it will process the received ACTCON and find an entry for the end-point device again and think that it has found a new route to it. This is, of course, not the case as the route is the same one. This behaviour is known as 'bouncing' as entries for an end-point device no longer available can fly around the network in the most alarming way. This can consume a lot of resources in the packet switches resulting in the network running very slowly.

Deleting entries from the ACTCON records goes some of the way to solving the problem of bouncing. However, loops in the network (i.e., loops of packet switches connected together) can still display this behaviour if further steps are not taken. The simplest method of doing this is to introduce a time delay before ACTCON records are transmitted after changes have occurred. This time period allows changes to be aggregated together, resulting in less ACTCONs being transmitted and more efficient processing. It also has the effect of slowing down re-configuration, effectively damping

The aggregating time period is obviously a critical variable. If it is too short, the bouncing will not be damped out resulting in inefficiency. If the period is too long, network re-configuration will be very slow. If a link were to fail, routing the traffic through a different path may prove unacceptably slow if the time period chosen is too long. The size of the network is a factor here. The larger the network, the more slowly configuration broadcasts spread across the network requiring a shorter time period.

For the CN-3X network, it was found that by using a window 1 protocol for the ACTCON packets, enough delay is introduced to prevent bouncing as changes are aggregated while waiting for the PASCON response to the previous ACTCON.

2.5.4 The CN-3X Network in Practice

So far, the theory behind the CN-3X network has been described. What are the practical results of using this type of dynamic routing architecture? Perhaps the most noticeable characteristic is the operational flexibility. Since there are no fixed routing tables in the packet switches, almost no manual configuration of the packet switches has to performed. End-point devices and inter-packet switch links can be added at any time, at any point in the network during normal operation without affecting network performance. Due to the dynamic routing, links can be physically moved from packet switch to packet switch with only temporary disruption to virtual calls using that link at the time.

As the entire network configuration is available at every point in the network, it is very simple to see whether end-point devices are available. Real time network monitors for the network managers are very simple to implement.

Given all these desirable operational characteristics for a packet switched network, why is it that few packet switched networks actually use a virtual call over datagram architecture? The reason is that no international standard has emerged for this sort of network. As we will see throughout the remainder of this book, international standards are the driving force behind all communications protocols, packet switched network protocols included. As X.25 is the accepted international standard, this particular protocol dominates so that almost all packet switched networks these days are X.25 networks. A detailed description of the link layer and network layer X.25 protocols can be found in Chapter Six.

2.6 Summary

The OSI seven layer model consists of the following layers:

Layer 1	-	Physical layer
Layer 2	-	Link layer
Layer 3	-	Network layer
Layer 4	-	Transport layer
Layer 5	-	Session layer
Layer 6	-	Presentation layer
Layer 7	-	Application layer

The OSI seven layer model is used as a framework for the basic theories underlying packet switched networks.

Packet switches route packets of information between the network links connected to the packet switch. End-point devices make use of the facilities provided by the network to which they are connected.

When a packet enters the network from an end-point device, it must be routed to its destination by the packet switches which form the network.

There are two basic routing methods. The first is fixed routing. The packet switches contain routing tables which tell them how to route the packets that they receive. The second method is dynamic routing. With this method, the packet switches are able to make decisions on which way to route packets depending on the condition of the network at the time that the particular packet is being switched.

The CN-3X network is used as an example of a real packet switched network that uses many of the principles of distributed adaptive routing. It provides a virtual call layer above the underlying datagram network that is very similar to X.25 level 3 but with improved operational characteristics.

3

Packet Switched Network Components

3.1 Introduction

In this chapter we will look in more detail at the functions of the various components that together form packet switched networks. Each type of component has its own specific set of characteristics. It is necessary to understand the practical aspects of the characteristics of each component if the correct decisions are to be made when putting together a real packet switched network.

3.2 Network Communications Links

Network communications links are the components that join together the other components of a packet switched network. The precise technology used for the network links is independent of the higher level protocols that are run over the links. The purpose of the links is to move the higher level protocol information from one physical location to another with as little distortion to the information as possible.

Packet switched network links, except in special cases, are 'bit serial'. This means that the information being transferred across the link is sent one bit at a time. If information can be sent in both directions simultaneously, the link is said to be 'full duplex'. If information can only be transferred in one direction at a time, the link is said to be 'half duplex'.

In order for the transmitted information to be reconstructed at the receiver, the bit serial information stream must be converted back into information in the memory of the receiver. The receiver must be provided with a 'clock signal' in order to determine precisely what information is being received. This clock signal tells the receiver when to sample the data signal to reconstruct the information. Figure 3.1 shows how the clock signal is used to sample the received data stream.

Depending on the precise type of communications link, there may be a separate clock signal for each direction of transfer, just one clock used for both directions, or else no clock signals at all. In the latter case, the data stream also carries the clock information. Special ways of encoding the data stream allows the clock to be extracted from the data. One technique is called 'Manchester encoding'.

In most cases, there is a distinction between the interfaces at each end of a communications link. One end is known as the 'Data Circuit-terminating Equipment', or 'DCE' for short. The other end is known as the 'Data Terminal Equipment', or 'DTE' for short. Generally, the devices inside the network 'cloud' (i.e., packet switches) present DCE interfaces to the end-point devices outside the network cloud. The end-point devices present DTE interfaces to connect to the DCE interfaces. This is always the situation when connecting to public communications systems: the public network presents a DCE interface while the user equipment must present a DTE interface.

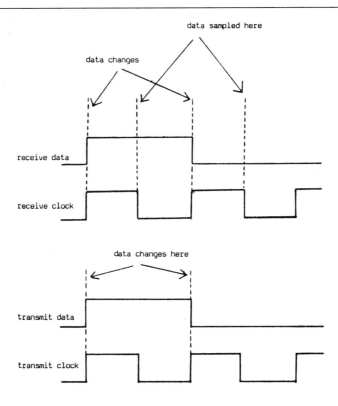

Figure 3.1 Relationship between data and clock signals

What is the distinction between a DCE and a DTE at this level? In almost all cases, the DCE interface provides the clock signals for the link timing. The DTE has to use the timing information supplied by the DCE when sampling received data and transmitting data. There is also a physical distinction between DCE interfaces and DTE interfaces. DCE interfaces always use female connectors while DTE interfaces always use male connectors. This again relates to the public network situation where, for electrical safety reasons, the circuits directly connected to the public network interface must never appear on exposed pins. This would be the case if male connectors were used for DCEs.

The most common medium for packet switched network links are 'twisted pairs' or ordinary multi-core cables. Twisted pairs are a special type of multi-core cable where pairs of wires are twisted around each other down the cables length. For some types of electrical signalling (the interface called 'X.21', for example), the cable used must be twisted pair cable as it is important to the operation of the drivers and receivers at each end of the cable.

This type of wiring can be used at any data rate up to about ten million bits per second over very short distances. Cables up to about one kilometre in length can be used although with much lower data rates. If faster or longer links are required, fibre optic cables are often used. The whole subject of physical interfaces for packet switched networks is dealt with in detail in Chapter Ten.

3.3 Packet Switches

Packet switches are the heart of a packet switched network. They form the 'cloud' part of the networks, as shown in many diagrams of networks, and they give the complete packet switched network many of its most important operating characteristics. Consequently, it is very important to make sure that the packet switches chosen for a network have the correct characteristics and capabilities for whatever the network is to be used.

3.3.1 The Physical Layer Interface

Figure 3.2 shows the key elements in a packet switch. The network communications links into the packet switch connect to the switch's physical interfaces. These provide the physical connections (i.e., the connectors) and electrical connections (the correct drivers and receivers for the electrical signalling in use). As the type of interface can vary, these interfaces are often in the form of plug-in cards. The different types of interfaces used for packet switched networks are covered in detail in Chapter Ten. For the purposes of this section, the interfaces will just be mentioned by name without going into deep detail.

The most common physical interface (i.e., physical layer interface) is called 'X.21bis', or sometimes V.24. In either case, the electrical signalling is usually V.28 - also commonly known as RS-232. This works perfectly well at link speeds up to about 19.2k bits per second, provided that the distance over which the link runs is not too great. It can be run at faster speeds, typically up to 76.8k bits per second, over short cables, but this is not really recommended.

Second in importance (based on numbers of interfaces in use) to X.21bis is the interface known as 'X.21'. This is a high speed physical layer interface that can cope with link speeds up to ten million bits per second over moderate distances. This interface will become more important as time goes on, because the communications links used in packet switched networks are getting faster all the time and require the high speed capability.

The third interface sometimes found in packet switched networks is known as 'V.35'. This medium speed interface is often found on host machine X.25 interfaces. V.35 is specified to run at 48k bits per second, although it is possible to run it at other speeds. These days, V.35 is more of a nuisance than a benefit, and so hopefully, in the fullness of time, it will disappear completely.

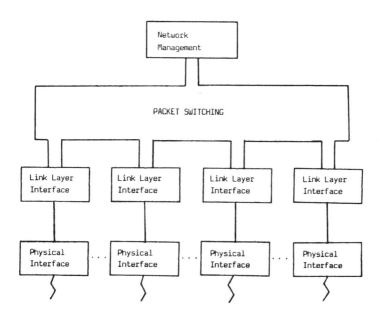

Figure 3.2 Key elements in a packet switch

3.3.2 The Link Layer Interface

The physical interfaces connect inside the packet switch to the link layer interfaces. In an X.25 packet switch, the link layer interfaces may run part or all of X.25 level 2. The extent to which the link layer protocol is run inside the link interface depends on the intelligence of hardware used for this function.

There is one physical layer and one link layer interface for each network link connected to the packet switch, and the packet switching function at the network layer provides the inter-communications between the links.

3.3.3 The Packet Switching Module

The packet switching module takes the packets received by the link layer interfaces, determines the correct outgoing route for that packet, then gives it to the correct link layer interface to transmit out of the packet switch and on to its destination. This is the packet switches network layer module. There are two different forms of the packet switching module, depending on how much checking the packet switch does on packets being switched.

The first performs a 'transparent switch' of packets. This means that received packets are routed, if possible, without checking that their content is meaningful or whether they violate the network layer protocol in any way. This type of switching will usually occur in datagram networks, as the packet switch only looks at the datagram header information. As it has no state information, which it would have in the case of a virtual call network, there is very little checking that the packet switch can do. The advantage of this sort of switching is that it is very fast. The processing overhead per packet can be kept very low, resulting in high switching rates. It also means that the software in the packet switch can be relatively simple.

The disadvantage of transparent switching is that transparent packet switches can let errors propagate throughout the network. This would not be a problem if every device on the network could handle every conceivable error condition. Unfortunately, experience shows that, although devices will perform correctly when presented with normal situations, out of the ordinary situations may show up faults in the software or hardware, resulting in failures which may be very serious indeed. In the worst case, the whole network may collapse in a heap.

In any implementation of networking software, a large proportion of the software is devoted to coping when things go wrong. It is the size of the error checking and recovery software along with the fact that it may be difficult to test all possible error conditions that causes this problem. No doubt, as software writing technology improves, it will be possible to prove that a particular network software product works correctly in all situations. For the moment, it remains a problem.

If the packet switches rigorously check each packet that they switch, errors can be localised and prevented from getting into the network as a whole. This is most effective in virtual call networks. As the packet switches need to maintain the state of virtual calls passing through them, they have all of the information they need to check that a particular packet is appropriate to the state of the virtual call to which it belongs.

To illustrate how this might work, take the case of an end-point device that has suffered a particular type of software failure. The failure is that it does not obey the network layer flow control, resulting in the sending of a continuous stream of packets on a virtual call into the network. If the packet switch to which the end-point device is connected, just switched the packets transparently, a continuous stream of packets will be injected into the network. This could use up a large amount of resources within the packet switches along the path of the virtual call, possibly resulting in packet switch failure, or, at the very least, degraded performance.

As the packet switch has information about the state of the virtual call, it can police the network layer protocol flow control for itself. Should the end-point device disobey the network layer protocol at any time, the packet switch can trap illegal packets and inform the end-point device that it has done something wrong. Consequently, the error is trapped as soon as it reaches the network and cannot propagate through it. This sort of protection is particularly important for public packet switched networks, which must have a very high availability and also cannot allow a particular user of the network to affect others. An example of this situation is British Telecom's Packet SwitchStream (PSS) X.25 network. The packet switches enforce very strict adherence to the X.25 protocol (as defined by British Telecom) and any transgressions are trapped.

The amount of work that the packet switching module has to do depends on the intelligence of the link layer interface. This can vary from very simple hardware, just providing the basic communications functions to a full blown layer 2 protocol implementation. In the former case, the packet switching function has to be combined with supporting the link layer protocol, resulting in lower performance in terms of the number of packets switched and the bit rate at which the network links can be run. In the latter case, the packet switching function is not affected by the link layer at all. The result here is that the packet switching rate will be high and unaffected by the bit rates of the various links.

3.3.4 The Network Management Module

The final important element of a packet switch is the network management module. Network management is dealt with in much more detail later in this section. In general though, the network management element supports functions like packet switch configuration (including any fixed routing tables) and monitoring the performance of the packet switch while in operation. As the size of a packet switched network increases, the network management facilities supported by the packet switches become more and more important. This includes providing information to the network managers about the packet switch's operating state and the availability (or otherwise) of its network links.

3.3.5 Hardware Architecture of Packet Switches

Design philosophy for the hardware architecture of packet switches in current use varies widely. The earliest packet switches used standard minicomputers running packet switching software. The link layer interfaces were simple serial interfaces. The single processor in the minicomputer had to run virtually the entire link layer protocol along with everything else. Usually, the link speed supported by this type of switch is relatively low, 9.6k bits per second being a typical sort of speed that might be expected. A DEC PDP-11 computer might be used in this role.

This simple architecture has the benefit that standard, general purpose hardware can be used. Only the software has to be specially written. Another advantage is that the software development environment supported by the minicomputer can be used to allow the packet switch to be customised for specific network applications.

The disadvantage is that the performance obtained in this way is usually fairly poor and the cost of the hardware can be very high. The performance can be improved by using more intelligent link layer interfaces that offload work from the main processor, but this makes the packet switch even more expensive.

Probably the most common approach used currently is the use of microprocessor-based hardware, usually specially designed for communications applications. In most cases, there is just a single microprocessor doing all of the work, but because the entire hardware and software system is dedicated to packet switching, performance can be much improved. Also, microprocessor hardware tends to be much cheaper than minicomputers resulting in a much better 'price/performance' ratio.

A new approach to packet switch architecture is to use more than one microprocessor within the packet switch. Usually, a self-contained microprocessor system runs the link layer protocol for a number of links (usually between one and four). A number of these 'intelligent' link layer interfaces can be used together to provide larger packet switches. These link layer interfaces plug into the main microprocessor that runs the packet switching and network management modules. Very high packet switching rates can be obtained with this sort of architecture as the load is shared between many microprocessors.

Whatever the architecture, most packet switches allow incremental expansion of the number of network links to which the packet switch can connect. For example, a packet switch may be able to support up to 32 network links. The manufacturer may supply the packet switch with a smaller number of link layer and physical layer interfaces fitted, 16 for example, if the customer only requires 16 links when the packet switch is purchased. The customer could then expand the packet switch at a later date by adding more interface cards to give the required number of link interfaces.

3.3.6 Packet Switch Performance

Two commonly quoted performance figures for a packet switch are its maximum packet switching rate and the maximum speeds at which the network links can be run.

Packet switches can be grouped according to their packet switching capability. A possible grouping is given.below.

Low speed	:	less than 50 packet switches per second
Medium speed	:	between 50 and 500 packet switches per second
High speed	:	more than 500 packet switches per second

The whole subject of what exactly is a 'packet switch per second' in this context is covered in detail in Chapter Eleven. Generally speaking, packet switches are getting faster all of the time. Switching rates of more than 2,000 packets per second are quite possible now.

The maximum speed at which the packet switch can run the network links is another important measure of packet switch performance. Slow links will result in limited throughput and long packet transmission delays. As with packet switching rates, it is possible to define groups of link speeds to characterise packet switches.

Low speed   :   less than 19.2k bits per second

Medium speed   :   between 19.2k bits and 64k bits per second

High speed   :   more than 64k bits per second

As with packet switching rates, there is plenty of room for manoeuvre when quoting the maximum link speeds. Chapter Eleven has all of the details.

Another important piece of information is the number of simultaneous virtual calls that the packet switch can support. Obviously this only really applies to virtual call networks as datagram network packet switches do not need to store the same amount of information as virtual call network packet switches.

This is usually quoted as the total number of virtual calls that the packet switch can support. It may also be true that each link can only support a lesser number of virtual calls. This can be important, as virtual calls are rarely evenly distributed amongst the links connected to the packet switch. In extreme cases, all virtual calls through the packet switch may come in on one link and then be distributed amongst the other links. If the maximum virtual call figure for a single link is lower than the total that the packet switch can support, then the lower figure applies.

Two other figures that are sometimes quoted are the reliability and the availability of the packet switch. The reliability can be split into two parts: the reliability of the hardware and the reliability of the software. In general, modern hardware is very reliable. The same cannot always be said of the software. Significantly, this latter figure is quoted rather less often.

The availability refers to the percentage of time that the packet switch is operating. This takes into account things like the average time to repair hardware faults and recover from software failures.

3.4 PADs

PAD stands for Packet Assembler/Disassembler. PADs are used to connect devices to a packet switched network that cannot be directly network connected. This is because the devices are 'character mode' devices rather than the packet switched network components which are 'packet mode' devices. Basically, character mode means that the devices treat each character as a separate entity. Packet mode devices deal with packets as separate entities. These packets may contain a number of characters.

Typically, PADs are used to connect things like terminals, personal computers, printers, etc., onto packet switched networks. These devices have asynchronous interfaces, often known as RS-232 or serial interfaces that are designed to connect to similar interfaces on other systems. A PAD has a number of asynchronous, character mode, interfaces on one side with a packet mode interface on the other side.

Figure 3.3 shows the key elements in a PAD. The functions of the various elements are described below.

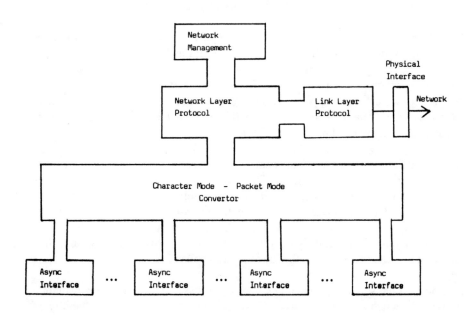

Figure 3.3 Key elements in a PAD

3.4.1 The Asynchronous Interface

The asynchronous interfaces provide the physical interfaces to the character mode devices. In the vast majority of cases, the connector for each asynchronous interface is a 'D25' socket with RS-232 (or V.28) electrical drivers and receivers. This makes the interfaces suitable for connection to the vast majority of character mode devices. V.28 is described in detail in Chapter Ten. Occasionally, RS-422 or RS-423 interfaces may be found. These allow the asynchronous interfaces to run at higher speeds, but relatively few character mode devices support them.

Figure 3.4 shows the D25 connector and the signals usually found in the asynchronous interfaces. TXD is used to carry the data from the character mode device to the PAD. TXD is used to carry data from the PAD to the character mode device. RTS and CTS are normally only used for hardware flow control (see later). DSR is a signal from the

64

PAD to the character mode device that can be used to indicate whether or not the PAD port is active. Frequently, it is used to indicate to the character mode device that a connection across the network has been terminated. DCD is a similar signal from the PAD. DTR is used by the character mode device to indicate to the PAD that it is online and ready to transfer data. The GND pin is the common signal ground.

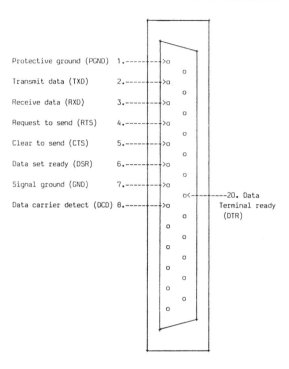

Figure 3.4 D25 connector pin out

The RS-232 asynchronous interfaces found on most PADs run at speeds up to 9.6k bits per second. In some cases, 19.2k bits per second and even 38.4k bits per second may be available. These high speeds are useful when a lot of data has to be transferred over the connection. Graphics terminals and file transfer operation on personal computers often involve the transfer of large amounts of data requiring that the highest possible speed be used.

The interface between the PAD and the character device will usually support flow control for data in each direction of transfer. Flow control of data from the PAD to the character mode device can be useful when the rate would otherwise be too high. A good example of this is when clearing the screen on some terminals. This process can be quite slow causing the data following the screen clear command to the terminal to be lost. If the flow from the PAD is flow controlled, the terminal can turn off the flow of data in this situation and therefore prevent this data loss.

Flow control can be equally important in the other direction (to the PAD). If data is being sent into the PAD at a higher rate than is being achieved on the packet switched network side of the PAD, the PAD has to buffer the received data locally. Sooner or later, the PAD will run out of buffering and will lose data unless it can stop the data being sent using the flow control mechanism.

There are two common methods of flow control in use: software and hardware. Software flow control is usually the 'XON/XOFF' method. When a device cannot accept any more data, it sends an XOFF back to the sender of the data. The sender should stop sending within a defined number of characters, usually quoted as a maximum of 32 characters. When the receiver can handle more data, it sends an XON. This restarts the flow of data. XON/XOFF can be run in both directions at the same time allowing full flow control of the connection.

The second common method is known as hardware flow control. In this case, two of the interface's 'control lines' are used to control the flow of data between the PAD and the character mode device. This is often known as 'RTS/CTS' or 'DTR/CTS' flow control depending on which pair of control lines are used. To the PAD, one of the control lines is an input, while the other is an output. In the case of most PAD interfaces, the input is RTS while the output is CTS. At the character mode device, RTS is an output while CTS is an input. When the PAD cannot accept data from the character mode device, it sets CTS to 'inactive', indicating this to the character mode device. When it is able to receive data again, CTS is set to 'active'. The character mode device uses RTS to control the output of data from the PAD in exactly the same way.

There are advantages and disadvantages in using either method. If XON/XOFF is used, these characters cannot be sent directly as data unless some 'escaping' method is used. Hardware flow control does not take any characters out of use and therefore has improved transparency to data. On the other hand, hardware flow control requires more wires between the PAD and the character mode device. Typically, only four wires are required between the PAD and the character mode device if XON/XOFF flow control is used (TXD, RXD, DTR and GND). If hardware flow control is to be used, two extra control lines must be added to this set, bringing the minimum to six (TXD, RXD, RTS, CTS, DTR and GND). If the DSR output from the PAD is required at the character mode device, the total becomes seven.

3.4.2 The Character Mode - Packet Mode Converter Module

This module does the actual conversion between the character mode device and the packet mode network interface. When a network connection from the PAD port is active, characters received by the PAD from the character mode device are assembled into packet buffers before being sent across the network. In the reverse direction, packets received from the network are stored in packet buffers and then sent character by character to the character mode device.

The character mode - packet mode converter module is probably the most important in the PAD in that the overall capabilities of the PAD are often determined by the capabilities of this module. The module can operate in one of two modes: command mode and data transfer mode.

If a PAD port is in command mode, the character mode device is talking to the PAD itself rather than another end-point device via a network connection. In this mode, the character mode device can instruct the PAD as to the functions that the PAD will provide when in data transfer mode. Status can be obtained about the state of the PAD port and the PAD itself. Network connections (virtual calls in the case of a virtual call network) can be established and terminated while in command mode.

In data transfer mode, the character mode device is communicating with another device across the network via a network connection. In some applications, the PAD will try to look as transparent as possible. Characters from the character mode device will be forwarded as soon as possible to the remote end of the connection, while characters in packets received are sent straight out to the character mode device.

Alternatively, the PAD may be configured so as to play quite a large part in data transfer mode. For example, the PAD may buffer lines of characters internally, only forwarding the line of characters across the network when the appropriate character is received from the character mode device. The PAD can be configured to allow the locally buffered characters to be edited. It can also add linefeed characters to carriage returns received from the network, sent to the network and echoed to the character mode device if required.

There are usually many other functions that the PAD interface can provide. These have been standardised by CCITT in the 'X.3' recommendation, described in detail in Chapter Seven. Another standard, 'X.28' defines a user interface to the PAD. Unfortunately, the X.28 interface is so appalling that most PADs have much more user friendly interfaces, in some cases using menu driven interfaces with help facilities.

In addition to the character mode device being able to configure the operation of the PAD port, the device at the other end of the network connection can re-configure the port while a network connection is active. For X.25 packet switched networks, a CCITT standard called 'X.29' describes how the X.3 parameters of a PAD port may be modified across an X.25 network. Together with the X.3 and X.28 recommendations, this forms the complete 'triple X' or 'XXX' standard for PADs. An X.25 PAD that does not support X.3 and X.29 is not going to be very much use, as when most host computers are called across the packet switched network from a PAD port, they assume that the PAD supports X.3 and X.29.

In many situations, the network managers only want certain PAD ports to be able to call specified destinations. This is often implemented using 'autocall' mode. When the character mode device comes online (i.e., DTR becomes active), a call is automatically set up to the programmed destination. The effect is such that the user may be unaware that the PAD is even there as it is relatively invisible.

PAD ports can usually be configured to be in 'reverse PAD'. This is sometimes known as 'anti-PAD' mode as it reverses the effect of the PAD. Usually, reverse PAD ports are connected to asynchronous ports on host computer systems. PAD users can call in to the reverse PAD ports and therefore gain access to the host computer.

The character mode - packet mode converter module can be a very heavy user of processing power. This is because of the rich variety of functions that the PAD has to support in data transfer mode. Often, each character received or transmitted has to be processed a number of times to determine whether any extra processing is required. An example is to check whether or not a particular character received from the character mode terminal causes forwarding of buffered characters.

3.4.3 The Network Layer Protocol Module

The job of the network layer protocol module is to provide the appropriate network layer support for the packet switched network and to send and receive packets from the character mode - packet mode converter module. The PAD user does not see too much of this module directly. Usually, the user is only aware of this module when things go wrong and a virtual call is cleared unexpectedly for example.

In an X.25 packet switched network, the network layer protocol module supports X.25 level 3. The module must be able to support at least the same number of virtual calls as there are asynchronous interfaces or else not all of them will be usable at the same time.

3.4.4 The Link Layer Interface

The link layer interface provides the link layer protocol appropriate to the packet switched network protocol. Packets are passed between the network layer module and the link layer interface.

In an X.25 network, the link layer interface is the X.25 level 2 protocol.

3.4.5 The Physical Interface

The physical interface provides the electrical drivers and receivers to allow the PAD to be connected to the packet switched network. The same comments as for the packet switch physical interfaces apply here. The main difference is that the physical interfaces are rarely in the form of plug in cards. Almost all PADs provide an X.21bis interface. In addition, some have an X.21 interface. It is often possible to select between the two interfaces by configuring the PAD's software. In other cases, the interface in use may be selected using switches somewhere in the PAD.

3.4.6 The Network Management Module

The final element in the PAD is the network management module. This provides facilities to configure the operation of the PAD's asynchronous ports and also to configure the operation of the network layer, link layer and, sometimes, the physical interface of the PAD. In operation, the network management module may allow a remote network management station to extract performance information from the PAD.

3.4.7 Hardware Architecture of PADs

PADs are usually specially designed systems dedicated to providing the very specific PAD function. The most common approach to PAD hardware architecture is to use a single microprocessor system to support all of the protocol modules. A number of serial interface integrated circuits are used to interface the character mode devices to the PAD. The packet switched network link is provided in the same way.

The microprocessor has to run the character mode - packet mode converter module, the network layer protocol module, the link layer interface module and the network management module. This represents a very heavy processing load for a single processor, no matter how fast it is. X.25 PADs using this architecture are usually limited to running the packet switched network link at a maximum of 19.2k bits per second. The asynchronous ports are usually limited to 9.6k bits per second.

A first step towards improving this situation is throw some more microprocessors at the problem. There are two principle targets for extra microprocessors. The first is to support the character mode - packet mode converter module, as this is a very heavy user of the microprocessor. The second target is the link layer interface. The nature of functional separation between the modules allows these extra processors to operate in parallel with the main microprocessor, which is left to run just the network layer protocol and the network management module.

Another step along this path is to use very large integration (VLSI) integrated circuits that support the entire link layer protocol. For X.25 level 2, at least three different manufacturers make such integrated circuits.

Using VLSI link interfaces and multiple processors, it is possible to provide vastly superior performance than that of PADs using a single processor. Link rates of up to ten million bits per second are possible with asynchronous interfaces operating at 38.4k bits per second.

3.4.8 PAD Performance

Apart from the rate at which the PAD can run the network link and the rate at which the asynchronous ports can operate, the most important performance figure is probably the packet rate that the PAD can support. It is not much use having very fast interface speeds if the packet throughput of the PAD cannot make use of them.

As with packet switches, it is possible to group PADs according to their packet rates:

Low speed	:	less than 10 packets per second
Medium speed	:	between 10 and 60 packets per second
High speed	:	more than 60 packets per second

Here, 'packets per second' refers to the number of packets containing 128 bytes of data processed per second. This particular packet size is the usual maximum X.25 packet size and has therefore become a standard way of measuring PAD (and packet switch) performance. We will have more to say about all this in Chapter Eleven.

The figure of 60 packets per second is significant. If an X.25 PAD can support a throughput of 60 128 byte packets per second, it can fully utilise a 64k bits per second communications link such as a British Telecom KiloStream link.

An obviously important piece of information about a PAD is the number of simultaneous network connections it can support while running continuous data on each connection. This usually has to be discovered by experiment as this is rarely quoted. This should really be equal to the number of asynchronous ports on the PAD although this is not always found to be the case. In the case of PADs that can support more than one network connection per asynchronous port, this information becomes even more important.

Often, PADs can be supplied with different numbers of asynchronous ports, depending on requirements. The ultimate extreme is the single port PAD. This provides just one asynchronous PAD port and one network link interface. The usual number of ports found on a PAD is 16 which seems to fit the vast majority of requirements. Some PADs can be easily upgraded by adding two or four ports at a time, so that the number of ports on the PAD can be expanded as demand increases.

In addition, some PADs allow more than one packet switched network link interface to be fitted. This allows 'daisy chaining' of the PADs. This is where a PAD's network connection is via the link interface of another PAD. This PAD is then either connected into a packet switch or else another daisy chained PAD.

As with packet switches, reliability and availability are very important, as if the PAD fails, a large number of network users may be affected. Of course, the failure of a packet switch is likely to be even more disruptive.

3.5 Host Interfaces

Host interfaces provide the mechanism for connecting host computer systems to packet switched networks. A host computer system is one that provides some sort of computing service. In many cases, this will be a large VAX computer running a time-sharing service. PAD users can get access to the host computer across the network if the host computer is fitted with the appropriate packet switched network interface.

Figure 3.5 shows the key elements in a host interface. The physical interface is usually one of the standard interface types, X.21bis, X.21 or possibly V.35. The link layer interface and the network layer protocol modules implement the layer 2 and layer 3 protocols respectively.

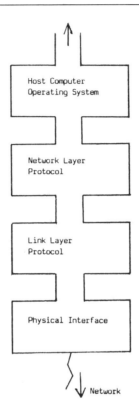

Figure 3.5 Key elements of a Host Computer Interface

The final module is the host computer operating system interface module. This allows applications running on the host computer to gain access to the network facilities via the appropriate operating system functions. In some implementations, the result is that it is possible to access files in other host computer systems in the network as though they were on the local host computer. This can be done if the operating system is able to map standard file access functions into the appropriate network file access functions. Perhaps the best example of this sort of use of a packet switched network by host computers is Digital Equipment Corporation's DECNET.

In some implementations, the network connection is not integrated into the operating system. This means that applications have to interface to the packet switched network interface directly, something that can cause problems in a multi-user environment. This 'bolted-on' approach is often used when the operating system supplier for a particular host computer does not support the network interface and does not provide suitable facilities for doing so.

3.5.1 Host Interface Hardware Architecture

Generally, a packet switched network host interface will be fitted as an optional plug-in card that fits into the host computer's hardware bus system. The intelligence of these cards can vary widely.

In the simplest case, the card can provide little more than the most basic elements, the physical interface and a serial interface. The link layer, network layer and operating system interface modules have to be run by the host computer's processor. As running these modules for most packet switched networks is going to be quite a burden, performance obtained by this sort of interface is very poor. If the host computer is very heavily loaded, the network interface may grind to a complete standstill.

The first step to improving this situation is to put the link layer protocol onto the network interface card. This offloads some of the processing from the host computer but still leaves the network layer and operating system interface modules in the host computer. However, putting the link layer onto the card is a major improvement. This is because the link layer has to deal with data being received at quite a rapid rate and in the form of a stream of bytes (the bit stream is converted to a byte stream by the serial interface). The host computer then only has to deal with complete network layer packets which arrive at a much lower rate than the layer 2 frame bytes.

Another improvement in performance is obtained if the network interface card can place network layer packets directly into the host computer's memory. This is often referred to as a 'DMA' (direct memory access) interface. The DMA part actually refers to the hardware that copies packets to and from the host's memory at very high speed.

One more step on the road is to move the network layer protocol module onto the network interface card. This once again reduces the overhead of running the network connection as far as the host computer's processor is concerned. In some cases, it may also be possible to move the host computer operating system interface module onto the network interface card. In this extreme case, the network interface places virtually no burden on the host computer.

A slightly different approach is to use a 'front end processor' to provide the host computer's interface to the packet switched network. The front end processor is usually a quite powerful processor in its own right. The front end processor supports the physical, link and network layer interfaces. The front end processor is then connected to the host computer over a very high speed interface, so that information can be moved between the two processors very efficiently.

3.5.2 Host Interface Performance

Until recently, the performance of most host interfaces has been very disappointing. Host interfaces have been of the very simple kind resulting in very low data rates and packet throughputs. Typically, such an interface might run at a maximum of 9.6k bits per second with accordingly low packet rates. Since the host computer is usually a multi-user system and requires that many connections to remote users run through this interface, clearly the throughput that any one user sees will be very limited.

This situation is improving as host interface cards get more intelligent. Bit rates of 64k bits per second and above are becoming available as the network layer protocol moves onto the interface card. Even so, if there are 32 users with active network connections using such a link, the data rate per user is only 2k bits per second. In practice, however, most connections will be idle at any one time, so that the apparent capacity is much higher than this.

Front end processors provide the best way of obtaining high speed links to host computers from packet switched networks. Link rates up to two million bits per second (up to ten million bits per second in the near future) are possible with suitably high packet rates to enable these high link speeds to be utilised.

3.6 Gateways

The purpose of gateways is to join together two different networks in such a way as to allow network connections to be made between end-point devices in the different networks. All of these inter-network connections must pass through this gateway.

Figure 3.6 shows the key elements of a gateway. The physical interface, link layer interface and network layer protocol modules are much the same as those in a PAD or host interface. In a gateway, these elements are duplicated on the other side of the gateway. There is a physical interface, a link layer interface and a network layer module to permit connection to the second network.

The final element of the gateway is the 'switching module'. This moves packets between the network layer protocol modules on each side of the gateway. The work that this module has to do depends on the particular characteristics of the networks on each side of the gateway and the particular purpose of the gateway. If the networks are very different in concept, the switching module may have to perform extensive processing of the packets to reformat them between the two network layer modules.

In most cases, the protocols run on each side of the gateway are different. A typical example would be where an X.25 packet switched network is connected, via a gateway, to an Ethernet network. In this case, the network protocols are very different on each side of the network. The gateway provides a protocol conversion between the two networks. Ideally, devices connected to each network should be able to communicate with devices in the other network as though they were part of the same network. This may not always be possible as facilities provided by one network may not have no analogue in the other network.

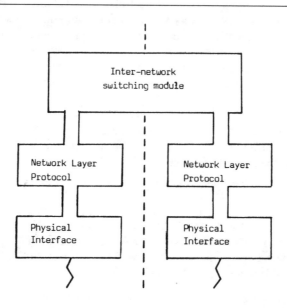

Figure 3.6 Key elements in a gateway

Another problem which may occur in joining networks together is that the two different networks may use different addressing concepts. It is the job of the switching module to convert between the two different types of addressing. Often, this involves the use of address mapping tables within the gateway.

In the case of X.25 and Ethernet, Ethernet has the concept of a 'broadcast'. Essentially, it is possible to broadcast a message to all devices on the Ethernet network by transmitting one special packet. There is no analogue of this in X.25. If the gateway was to try and duplicate this function, it would have to set up a call to every end-point device on the X.25 network, send it the message, then clear the calls again. Since this is not, in general, a practical thing to do, the broadcast facility will be lost across the gateway.

Sometimes, gateways are used to connect together two networks using the same protocols and technology. There are three reasons why this might be done. First of all, the purpose of the gateway may be to limit the size of a single network to a manageable level. For example, if a particular network has limited capacity in its routing table management system, there may be a limit to the number of end-point devices which can be supported on a single network. A gateway would then be required to split up the network if this limit is to be exceeded.

A second situation where such a gateway might be used is when it is not desirable for one of the networks to be generally accessible. A typical example of this would be where the use of one of the networks is, in fact, a public network that levies a charge on its use. In this case, the gateway will be a 'validation gateway'. Attempts to connect to the protected network have to stop first at the gateway, which then ascertains whether or not the caller is permitted to use the protected network. If not, the connection is aborted.

There are two common mechanisms that can be used to validate connection attempts. The first is to check that the address of the caller is one of the addresses allowed to use the protected network. The second method, commonly used to prevent access from PADs, is to ask the caller to supply a password. This can then be checked against a list of valid passwords maintained in the gateway to determine whether or not the connection should proceed.

Another use of a gateway is to connect together similar networks where the purpose of the gateway is to collect information about usage with an aim to charging callers for use of the gateway. This is generally combined with a validation gateway to form a validation/charging gateway. The result is that only validated users can get access to the protected network and that they can be charged for usage of the protected network.

An example of the use of a validation and charging gateway is where a private X.25 network is connected to a public X.25 network like PSS. It may be desirable to share a single PSS account amongst a number users. Only a single bill from PSS would be issued and the problem then is to apportion the cost amongst the users. A validation/charging gateway could be used here to solve the problem. First of all, only validated users could get access to the PSS connection. Secondly, as the gateway keeps usage records, these could be used to break down the PSS bill into smaller bills to each of the users.

3.5.1 Gateway Hardware

Obviously, the particular hardware chosen for a gateway depends very much on the nature of the two networks to be connected together. Quite often, minicomputers are used to perform this function. This is because it is usually possible to obtain interface cards for both networks that plug into the minicomputer. All that needs to be added is the switching module, so that packets can be routed between the two interface cards.

A lower cost solution is to use a PC to provide the gateway. Plug-in interface cards for most networks are available for the PC family. Again, all that needs to be added is the switching module that moves packets between the interfaces.

There are also gateways that use special purpose hardware to perform the gateway function.

3.6.2 Gateway Performance

It is difficult to generalise too much about gateway performance, because requirements vary so much depending on the nature of the two networks on each side of the gateway. It is certainly true to say that it would be better if gateways were not needed and should be avoided wherever possible. All connections between the networks on each side of the gateway have to pass through the gateway. Although this is also true of packet switches in a packet switched network, the gateway has to perform rather more processing on each packet. This is because the gateway is performing a protocol conversion function rather than a simple switching function. Gateways very often represent a performance bottleneck.

Gateways may also be less reliable than some of the other elements in a network. This is because a gateway usually has to run two, sometimes very different, protocols at the same time. Since the implementation of even one protocol is difficult, the implementation of two within a single device is even more difficult. There is the added complication of the switching module. This has to map facilities on one side of the gateway to facilities on the other side. If this mapping is incorrect in any way, it will be another source of problems.

3.7 Network Management Systems

Network Management Systems (NMSs for short) are essential tools for the managers of any kind of network. Networks have a terrible ability to keep important information about availability and performance to themselves. It is the job of the NMS to extract the information that is available and present it to the network managers.

There are three important aspects to the network management function. The first is configuration management. The NMS may be responsible for looking after the various device configurations within the network. In the case of a packet switched network with fixed routing tables in the packet switches, the NMS may be responsible for loading the routing tables into the switches and providing facilities for the network managers to build and modify the routing tables. PAD configurations may also be maintained on the NMS. If there is a validation/charging gateway in the network, then validation tables may be built and stored within the NMS and then downloaded to the gateway over the network when required.

A second aspect of network management is 'real-time network management'. This aspect deals with the operational state and performance of the network. While the network is operational, the NMS is continually checking the state of the network and the devices in it. A very important part of this is to be able to determine, in the event of a network failure, which devices have become unavailable and where precisely the fault lies. The NMS may also be able to monitor the performance of the network's communications links and inform the network managers if the link loading is getting above a certain level or if the error rate on a link is exceeding a certain threshold.

The third aspect of network management is 'billing' or 'accounting'. The use of certain services or gateways in the network may involve a charge to the user. In the case of a validation/charging gateway, the gateway will record information about usage. Obviously, something must be done with this information. There are two choices here. Either the gateway itself can store the information and perhaps print it out from time to time. Alternatively, the information can be sent to the NMS. The NMS can then record the information for later processing. The use of the NMS for this function is desirable as the network managers will often be responsible for producing billing information.

The ideal situation is where all three functions can run simultaneously on the same system. For example, while the configuration editor is being used, messages about network failures should still be displayed and billing information still received from the network devices. This requires quite sophisticated software so that some NMSs do not have this capability. If 24 hour real-time network management is required, a separate machine would have to be provided for the configuration management function.

3.7.1 The NMS - Network Manager Interface

The interface presented by the NMS to the network managers is very important. In many cases, the network managers will be responsible for running several different networks. It is essential that the NMS be easy to use and not require extensive knowledge of the network being managed.

Dealing first with the configuration management aspect, this can be split into two parts. The first is the actual building and editing of configurations inside the NMS itself. This often takes the form of a special purpose screen editor for the particular type of network device to which the configuration belongs. The configurations will be stored on disk, either floppy disk or hard disk, so that they can be retrieved at a later date. The second part is the process of downloading a network device with its configuration (i.e., sending the configuration from the NMS to the target device). In some cases it may be useful to upload the configuration (i.e., the NMS retrieves the configuration form the target device). This is useful when the configuration of a device has been modified using some other facility, such as the device's own management facility, so that the NMS's record is out of date.

The real-time network management aspect is probably the most important as it gives the network managers up to date information about the state of the network. By real-time we mean that this process is carried out continuously (i.e., on a 24 hour basis) so that a complete record of network state is recorded.

Device availability is perhaps the most important part of real-time network management. Depending on the application for which the network is being used, rapid detection of failure within the network may either be very important or absolutely critical. In the case of packet switched virtual call networks, there are two basic approaches which can be used.

The first is 'polling'. This means that every device on the network is called in turn. If it is possible to call the device, then it must be available. The advantage with this approach is that only one call is active at any one time, placing minimal strain on the

NMS and the network itself. Also, the called devices only have to maintain a call to the NMS for a very short period of time. Sometimes, it is not even necessary for the target device to accept the call. In the case of X.25 networks, it is possible to deduce from the information returned when a call fails whether or not the call failed because the device was unavailable, or merely because the call was unacceptable to the device. The major disadvantage with this method is that it may take a significant amount of time to poll around all devices in the network.

Take the case where the NMS polls one device every five seconds. This is a low enough rate so that the call set up rate does not affect the operation of the network and that the NMS can process any information returned by the device (polling is often used to collect performance information at the same time as determining the availability of the device). This rate allows the NMS to poll 12 devices every minute. This means that the NMS would take around eight minutes to poll a network consisting of 100 devices. In the case of a very large network consisting of 1000 devices, this polling operation would take around 80 minutes, unlikely to be acceptable for any application.

An alternative method for virtual call networks is to maintain a call from the NMS to every device in the network. This has the advantage that, should a device fail, the call will be cleared by the network. In this way, the NMS will be informed almost immediately. In order to check that the devices are still operating correctly, a background polling operation is useful to ensure that everything is all right. The rate at which this occurs is less important as the primary indicator is the continuous call to each device.

The disadvantage with this method is the number of calls that the NMS has to maintain simultaneously. Although it is possible for a single device to support up to 100 or possibly 200 calls at one time (the calls are idle almost all of the time), it is very unlikely that 1000 calls could (or should) be maintained to a single end-point device on the network. Very large networks can be managed by using helper NMSs distributed around the network. The main NMS maintains a single call to each helper NMS, which then maintains a call to every device that is in its domain. Effectively, this allows a large number of management calls to be 'multiplexed' across the single call between the main NMS and the helper NMS. Using this enhancement, even very large networks can be managed with almost instantaneous indication of device failure anywhere in the network.

Performance information is usually obtained from the packet switches within the network. They have access to all information about information flowing on each link connected to them. Packet switches can maintain error counters for each link along with packet, byte and virtual call counters. This information can be sent to the NMS in one of two ways. Either the NMS can poll the packet switch for the information periodically, or else the packet switch can send the information unsolicited to the NMS when it has something interesting to send.

The first method is useful in large networks, otherwise it is possible that the NMS can become totally saturated with information from packet switches. If the packet switches are only allowed to send information to the NMS when asked for it, the NMS can easily control the rate at which the information is going to arrive. The problem with the latter method is that, in the case of a large network, it may take the NMS a while to poll around all of the packet switches. The packet switches may therefore need to buffer information internally and then send the whole lot when polled by the NMS.

Obviously, since the packet switch can only have a finite buffer for network management information, it is possible that the buffer will fill up before the NMS polls for it. This is particularly likely if either the NMS itself is unavailable for a while, or if the path between the NMS and the packet switch is unavailable, possibly due to a link failure. In such a situation the packet switch will have to make an intelligent decision as to what to do. The most sensible action is to discard the oldest information in the buffer.

Moving on to billing information, the same comments apply as for performance information as described above. The problem in the event of a charging information buffer overflow is rather more serious, however. Losing charging information is possibly the ultimate sin, but there may be no alternative if the packet switch, or charging gateway (as gateways are also relevant here), cannot get access to the NMS to dump the billing information. If the packet switch or gateway has a disk attached it may have considerable buffering capacity. However, in most cases there will not be a disk available for this purpose.

Clearly, an NMS failure can be a very serious event. Depending on how long the NMS is unavailable, billing information throughout the network may be lost and the network managers will be totally unaware of the state of the network, apart from users telephoning them and complaining! Duplication of the NMS is the obvious way to solve this problem, particularly if it is operating in a 'hot standby' mode. This is where the standby NMS is kept in the same state as the main NMS. Should the main NMS fail, the standby can be brought in to use immediately with almost no discontinuity. Due to the extra cost and complexity of the hot standby solution, it is likely only ever to be used for very large networks.

3.7.2 NMS Hardware and Software

NMSs are usually general purpose computer systems with the appropriate host interface for the network to be managed. Usually, a small minicomputer or PC is used. The hardware itself does not matter too much, it is the software that really counts for network management. Ideally, the NMS should have a hard disk and a high resolution colour graphics display. Depending on the style of user interface, a mouse may be provided for selecting menu options.

The operating system used needs to be real-time multi-tasking if all three management functions are to be performed simultaneously. In the case of PCs, this is done by providing a special 'kernel' outside of the PC's operating system as the operating system is not able to support real-time multi-tasking.

A 'windows' display manager is very useful as it allows several windows of information to be displayed simultaneously on the screen. For example, one window may be being used for configuration editing while another is being used to display alarm messages from the real-time network management component of the NMS. Colour is very useful, particularly when there is a lot of information on the screen, for highlighting important information. A graphics capability is also useful as it allows network layout diagrams to be displayed, giving the network managers a good idea of how the network is configured. Such a diagram could be annotated with real time information about link loading etc providing a very understandable view of the state of the network at any one time.

A NMS will usually provide some sort of audible warning when certain events are detected. The NMS interface provides the network managers with the ability to request alarms when serious events occur. These could include devices becoming unavailable, link loading exceeding a preset threshold or a link error rate exceeding a threshold. Alarms of this sort would be displayed in the alarms window on the screen accompanied by an audible alarm to attract the attention of the network managers. This latter feature is necessary, as it is rare for the network managers to be staring at the NMS screen all day. Without an audible alarm, alarms might go unnoticed for some considerable time before someone happens to look at the screen.

3.8 Summary

There are six basic components which can go together to make up packet switched networks. All six components are not necessary to make up a packet switched network, but communications links and packet switches are always involved.

Communications Links are used to join the other components of the network together.

Packet Switches form the heart of the packet switched network. They provide the connections between other network components such as PADs and host interfaces.

PADs provide the connection to a packet switched network for devices which cannot be directly network connected.

Host Interfaces provide the connection to a packet switched network for host computer systems.

Gateways are used to join two different networks together so as to allow connections to be made between end-point devices in the two different networks.

Network Management Systems collect information about availability and performance for the network manager. They present the information to the network manager in a meaningful form. Network management systems cover areas such as validation and charging, real-time management and configuration management.

Packet Switched Protocols

Part 2 covers *Packet Switched Network Protocols*. This is a brief introduction to the contents of this part.

International Standards

International Standards are becoming increasingly important in packet switched networks. The move is towards standardisation which will mean that different manufacturers equipment can be mixed and matched to suit requirements.

Standards used in the UK

There are some standards which are not International Standards but are standards used in the UK (or, at least, areas in the UK). One area of the UK which has a lot of standards is the UK Academic Community.

X.25 - A Packet Switched Network Protocol

X.25 is an International Standard and is a packet switched network protocol. Most packet switched networks use X.25 or are based on X.25 in some way. X.25 is covered in detail in Chapter Six. It goes into the gory detail and readers not interested in this may wish to skip this chapter. Readers requiring more details should, of course, refer to the relevant standard documents. A list of International Standards relevant to packet switching can be found in Appendix B.

Higher Level Protocols

Chapter Seven deals with higher level protocols. These are protocols which are often found running on packet switched networks. This section introduces a fair amount of jargon. A lot of this jargon is covered in Appendix C - Glossary of Terms.

Security in Packet Switched Networks

The last section in this part of the book covers security. it goes into encryption methods, reasons for requiring security and different types of security.

4

International Standards

4.1 Introduction

The purpose of this section is to take a good look at International Standards. This includes the need for them and who makes them. Then we are going to look at possibly the most important standards work in the area of communications - the Open Systems Interconnection Standards (OSI).

4.2 The Need for International Standards

Standards of some sort are needed in a very large number of situations. A very commonplace standard is the design of a UK 13 amp power socket and plug. Although the fine detail of the designs may differ from manufacturer to manufacturer, they should hopefully all fit together correctly and operate safely with each other.

Another example is the design of telephones that can be used connected to the public telephone network. They are tested for conformance to the required standard before they are given approval for connection to the telephone system. Part of this is to ensure that they satisfy safety requirements, but a very important part is to check that the telephone will use the telephone network correctly and perform the required functions adequately.

The situation with computers is currently rather different. Different computer systems from different manufacturers are usually very different. The hardware is usually totally incompatible with each other, meaning that special peripherals and add-on cards have to be specially designed for each system. The same is true of operating systems and the interfaces presented to users. Each one is incompatible with each other and users moving from one system to another often have to learn a completely new set of commands and possibly even a quite different style of working.

The situation with communications was exactly the same. Manufacturers produced their own communications equipment that suited their applications and requirements. Since most of these solutions were completely different, it was very difficult to transfer information between computer systems from different manufacturers. The only easy solution was for a particular customer to buy equipment from only one manufacturer; very nice for the manufacturer but somewhat limiting for the customer.

The use of standard protocols for communications has two substantial advantages. The first is that manufacturers offer communications support for their computer systems that allow connection with a range of other manufacturer's machines. The second is that the customer can choose from a wide range of communications equipment rather than that offered by just one manufacturer.

National standards have been around for some time. For example, the 'Colour Book' protocols, widely used by UK academic institutions, have attained some sort of national standard status. Many computer system manufacturers can supply software to support the Colour Book protocols, and indeed have to if they intend to sell their systems to the academic institutions. National standards are not really good enough, as there is a general need for international communications. Although gateways between different national networks could conceivably be produced, there would need to be so many different types that the whole thing would be a complete mess. The only real solution to this problem is to use standard protocols wherever possible and avoid protocol converters and gateways as often as possible.

The need for a standard set of protocols for all communications requirements is now very strong indeed. The best solution to date is the OSI set of protocols. Although it is still not clear to what extent the OSI protocols will be implemented, they are becoming more and more important. Nearly all specifications for large networks require conformance either immediately, or within some specified timescale, to the OSI standards. This is forcing manufacturers to conform to OSI standards if they wish to win large contracts.

4.3 The International Standards Bodies
4.3.1 ISO - International Organisation for Standardisation

The most important standards body as far as OSI work is concerned is ISO (the International Organisation for Standardisation). ISO is based in Geneva and co-ordinates the activities of a variety of smaller standards bodies, the British Standards Institute (BSI) being one of them. A very important contribution to the OSI work, particularly in the area of local area networks, is the IEEE (the Institution of Electrical and Electronic Engineers) which is based in the United States. ISO consists of a large number of committees working in different areas. The committee responsible for OSI work is 'TC97', the technical committee for information processing systems.

As so many different organisations are involved in the standardisation process, it can take an awfully long time to get anything done. ISO meetings only take place every nine months or so and the process can take a number of these meetings to get anywhere. A standard first appears as a draft proposal (DP), followed by becoming a draft international standard (DIS), and then finally becoming a full international standard (IS). There is a voting process at each step so that all parties involved can decide whether the standard is in an acceptable form. Eventually, a consensus will be reached and the standard can go forward to the next stage.

In fact, it is the length of this process that has caused a lot of criticism of the OSI effort. OSI began life in 1979 and even now is not complete. Changes and developments are still going on. This makes things a bit difficult for implementors as they are trying to hit a target that keeps on moving.

4.3.2 CCITT - International Telephone and Telegraph Consultative Committee

As its name may suggest, the CCITT is mainly concerned with telephone and telecommunications systems. The full members of CCITT are normally the PTTs (the Post, Telegraph and Telephone authorities, providers of telecommunications systems such as British Telecom). CCITT standards are known as recommendations. The CCITT works rather differently to ISO in that its recommendations are published every four years at set times. In 1980, the recommendations had yellow covers and are consequently known as 'yellow book' (not to be confused with the Yellow Book Transport Service protocol which is one of the Colour Book protocols). In 1984, the recommendations had red covers and so are called, not surprisingly, 'red book' (again, not to be confused with Red Book, the Colour Book Job Transfer and Management Protocol). There will be a new set of recommendations published towards the end of 1988.

One problem with publishing the recommendations at fixed times is that this schedule may not fit the development of the recommendations very well. Recommendation X.32 is a good example. The phrase 'for further study' covers major areas of the recommendation. Clearly, this recommendation is at a very early stage.

4.3.3 The Rest

Although CCITT and ISO are the major players in OSI, there are number of other standards bodies milling around. ECMA, the European Computer Manufacturer's Association, is one of these, but only represents a limited point of view. Two other names that come up are CEN/CENELEC and SPAG. These European bodies are working on 'functional standards'. The full OSI standards, designed to cover almost every eventuality, are very large and complex. Most implementations will only have a subset of the total number of functions that could be implemented. The idea of functional standards is to define a subset of the full standards that can always be implemented. This guarantees that there will always be some common ground to allow interworking between any two OSI systems even if not all of the capabilities are available.

4.4 Open Systems Interconnection

The most basic OSI standard is the OSI 'reference model' standard known as ISO 7498. This, like many other ISO standards, is also published by the BSI. The BSI number for this standard is BS6568. This provided the basic structure for the OSI protocols by breaking up the effort into seven well defined layers. The basic concept is shown in Figure 4.1. The idea is that the lowest levels deal with the low level aspects of the connection (physical interface, etc.) while the higher levels deal with a more abstract view of the network and provide support for the application using the network.

Each layer uses the services provided by the layer below and presents a defined service to the next higher layer.

```
+--------------------------------+
|      LAYER 7: APPLICATION      |
+--------------------------------+
|      LAYER 6: PRESENTATION     |
+--------------------------------+
|        LAYER 5: SESSION        |
+--------------------------------+
|       LAYER 4: TRANSPORT       |
+--------------------------------+
|        LAYER 3: NETWORK        |
+--------------------------------+
|         LAYER 2: LINK          |
+--------------------------------+
|        LAYER 1: PHYSICAL       |
+--------------------------------+
```

Figure 4.1 Seven layer model

Each layer consists of two basic parts. The first part is the layer protocol. This defines the procedures used between itself and the similar layer in another device. The second part is the service that the layer provides to the next higher layer in the stack.

The boundary between the Network Layer and the Transport Layer is very important as it marks the point at which the real network (below the boundary) becomes hidden by an abstract view of the network above. This division occurs at the Network Service interface, the service provided by the Network Layer to the Transport Layer above. In principle, any network technology could be used below this point as long as it is capable of supported the OSI Network Service.

Figure 4.2 shows how two end-point devices, using OSI protocols, communicate across a network. The dashed, horizontal lines represent the interaction between the protocols in each layer. As each layer only interacts with another similar layer having the same status, the protocols are known as 'peer to peer' protocols. The intermediate systems are the nodes in the networks. These could be packet switches or perhaps gateways in the case of packet switched networks.

There are two different types of networks that are covered by the OSI standards. The basic type is known as 'connection-orientated'. The virtual call packet switched networks we have described earlier fit into this category. The second type is 'connectionless' and is similar in concept to the datagram networks described earlier. The connectionless mode was not in the original OSI standard and had to bolted on at a later stage. As we have seen, it is possible to run virtual call services over a datagram network illustrating the fact that that connectionless and connection-orientated modes can be used together but within different layers.

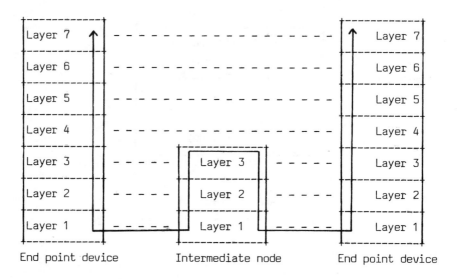

Figure 4.2 End to end communications in an OSI network

Figure 4.3 is a composite diagram showing the important standards at each layer in the seven layer stack. We will be concentrating primarily on the connection-orientated protocols as they are the most appropriate to packet switched networks.

4.5 Layer 1 - The Physical Layer

Layer 1, the physical layer, deals with the lowest level aspects of communications. These include bits of wire and signal drivers and receivers, the basic requirements to transfer information from one place to another.

As far as packet switched network protocols go, the most important layer 1 standards are the CCITT X.21 and X.21bis recommendations. These are described in more detail in Chapter Ten.

The other possibilities at this layer are the local area network standards. These are all from work by the IEEE '802' committee which produces standards for local area networks. The most famous of these is the 802.3 protocol. This is the international standard form of Ethernet. The standard is published by ISO as ISO 8802/3. The next standard, ISO 8802/4, describes a 'token bus' network and uses a single cable to implement a token-passing network. Another interesting standard is ISO 8802/5, which describes a 'token ring' network. This protocol is used by IBM for its local area network and is therefore very important for that reason alone!

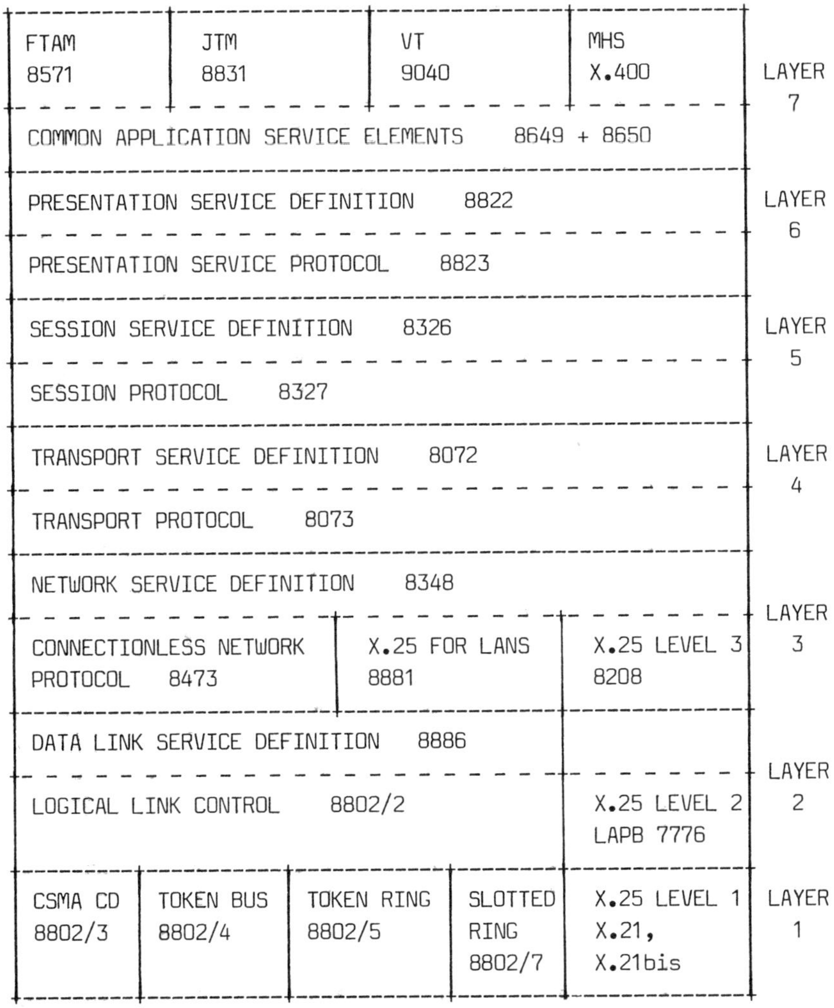

FTAM 8571	JTM 8831	VT 9040	MHS X.400	LAYER 7
COMMON APPLICATION SERVICE ELEMENTS 8649 + 8650				
PRESENTATION SERVICE DEFINITION 8822				LAYER 6
PRESENTATION SERVICE PROTOCOL 8823				
SESSION SERVICE DEFINITION 8326				LAYER 5
SESSION PROTOCOL 8327				
TRANSPORT SERVICE DEFINITION 8072				LAYER 4
TRANSPORT PROTOCOL 8073				
NETWORK SERVICE DEFINITION 8348				LAYER 3
CONNECTIONLESS NETWORK PROTOCOL 8473		X.25 FOR LANS 8881	X.25 LEVEL 3 8208	
DATA LINK SERVICE DEFINITION 8886				LAYER 2
LOGICAL LINK CONTROL 8802/2			X.25 LEVEL 2 LAPB 7776	
CSMA CD 8802/3	TOKEN BUS 8802/4	TOKEN RING 8802/5	SLOTTED RING 8802/7	X.25 LEVEL 1 X.21, X.21bis	LAYER 1

Figure 4.3 Standards in the OSI model

4.6 Layer 2 - The Link Layer

The service and protocol used at layer 2 for packet switched networks is basically that provided by the X.25 LAPB protocol. This is described in more detail in Chapter Six. The ISO version of this is published as ISO/DIS 7776 and by BSI as BS 5397:Part 7.

4.7 Layer 3 - The Network Layer

The Network Service has to present a uniform interface to the transport layer above and copy with a variety of network layer protocols and lower layers below. There are two types of Network Service: connection-mode and connectionless-mode. We are only interested in the connection-mode Network Service here. The Network Service itself is an abstract concept, so, in addition, to the Network Service definition, there is also a Network Service protocol definition. As there may be many different types of network used to provide the Network Service, so there are different standards for each different type. These standards define the mapping of the Network Service primitives onto real network layer packet protocols.

4.7.1 The Connection-Mode Network Service

The connection-mode Network Service, often referred to as 'CONS', is published by ISO as ISO/DIS 8348 and by BSI as DD119. The network connection can be modelled as a queue of information in each direction of transfer. Figure 4.4 shows this 'queue model' concept. 'NSAP' stands for Network Service Access Point. This is the point at which the transport layer gains access to the Network Service.

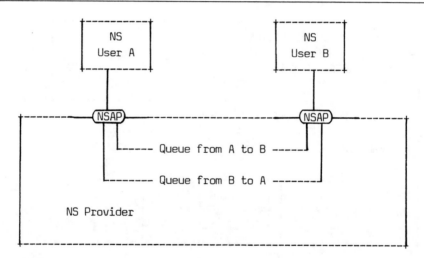

Figure 4.4 Queue model

The queues between two NSAPs come into existence when one of the two NSAPs wants to set up a connection. To do this, the NS user passes an 'N-CONNECT' primitive down to the NSAP below. The queues then remain in existence until the connection is terminated by an 'N-DISCONNECT' primitive being entered or removed from a queue at an NSAP.

Associated with this queue model are a set of rules about ordering of information in the queues while in data transfer phase. For example, a disconnect removes all data in front of it as it moves between the NSAPs. Normal data is transferred in the order in which it is entered into the queue. A special type of data, 'expedited data' is allowed to jump over ordinary data in front of it in the queue.

Network Connection Establishment Phase

The purpose of this phase is to establish a network connection that provides communications of the required quality between two NSAPs. There are four Network Service primitives involved with this phase. These are the N-CONNECT request, the N-CONNECT indication, the N-CONNECT response and the N-CONNECT confirm. Figure 4.5 shows the sequence of primitives involved in successful network connection establishment attempt.

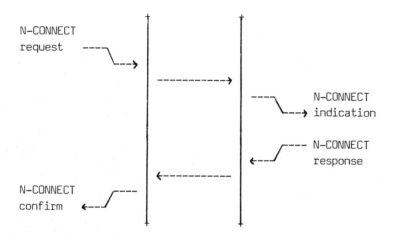

Figure 4.5 Network connection attempt

The N-CONNECT request and indication primitives carry a number of parameters. These include the address of the called NSAP and the address of the NSAP trying to establish then call. There is also a parameter indicating whether 'receipt confirmation selection' is required. Receipt confirmation is a process that informs the sender of the data that the receiver has actually received the data. It is an optional facility in the Network Service and so may not be generally available. Another parameter indicates whether or not expedited data is to be used as this is another optional feature of the Network Service.

The 'QOS parameter' defines the quality of service required for the connection. There are a number of subparameters within the overall QOS parameter. The first if these is 'throughput'. This allows the caller to specify a target throughput and a lowest acceptable throughput for each direction of data transfer individually. The 'transit delay' subparameter allows the caller to specify both a target and lowest quality (i.e., highest transit delay) acceptable.

The N-CONNECT response and N-CONNECT confirm primitives also contain a number of parameters. The first of these is the 'responding address'. This is the address of the called NSAP that is responding to an incoming N-CONNECT indication. Then follows the response to the receipt confirmation use indication and the response to the expedited data use indication. The final parameter contains the responses to the throughput and transit delay requests. These indicate the quality of service allocated to the connection.

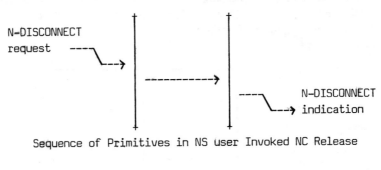

Sequence of Primitives in NS user Invoked NC Release

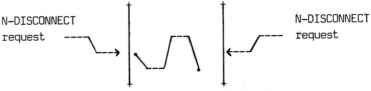

Sequence of Primitives in Simultaneous
NS User, Invoked NC Release

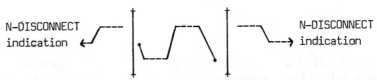

Sequence of Primitives in NS Provider Invoked NC Release

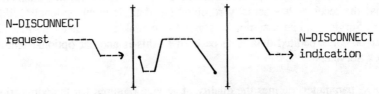

Sequence of Primitives in Simultaneous NS User and
NS Provider Invoked NC Release

Figure 4.6 Connection release phase

Network Connection Release Phase

There are two primitives involved in the termination of a network connection. These are the N-DISCONNECT request and the N-DISCONNECT indication. Figure 4.6 shows the four possible version of the connection release phase. Four parameters are may be carried. The 'originator' parameter gives the origin of the primitive and may be 'NS user', 'NS provider' or 'undefined'. The 'reason' parameter indicates why the N-DISCONNECT was generated. Then follows 'NS User data'. This is data which may be included by the NS user generating the N-DISCONNECT. The final parameter, which only occurs on N-DISCONNECTs generated in response to N-CONNECTs is the 'responding address' of the NSAP that generated the N-DISCONNECT.

Data Transfer Phase

The data transfer primitives allow the NS-users to transfer data across the network connection. The NS user data is carried in primitives called Network Service Data Units or NSDUs. There are two types of primitives involved: N-DATA request and N-DATA indication. Figure 4.7 shows the two types of sequences for the normal N-DATA primitive and for the N-DATA primitive with receipt confirmation requested. An alternative way of conveying NS user data is to use the N-EXPEDITED DATA primitive. This, as was mentioned earlier, is able to jump over N-DATA primitives ahead of it. The sequence of primitives for N-EXPEDITED DATA is exactly the same for the normal N-DATA transfer.

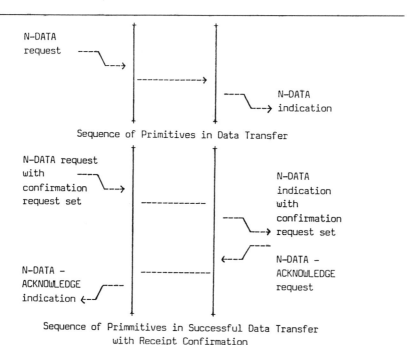

Sequence of Primitives in Data Transfer

Sequence of Primmitives in Successful Data Transfer
with Receipt Confirmation

Figure 4.7 N-DATA transfer

It is sometimes necessary to reset a connection back to an initial state. This might be required after a serious error has been detected and it is necessary to start again. The N-RESET primitive is used to convey this situation. The sequence of primitives is shown in Figure 4.8 for the four possible situations.

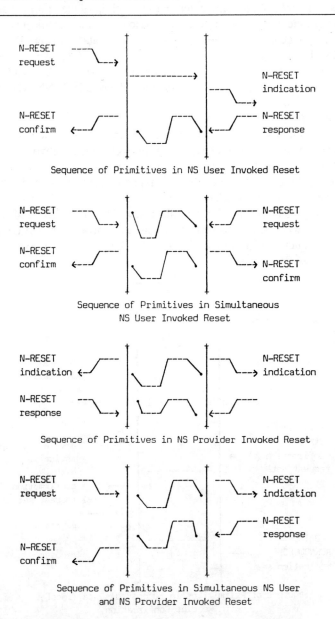

Figure 4.8 N-RESET exchange

4.7.2 Use of X.25 to Provide the CONS

There are several ways of providing support for the CONS. In this book we are going to look at the use of X.25 to provide the CONS as it is the most important for packet switched networks. The standard specifying the use of X.25 to provide the CONS is published by ISO as ISO/DP 8878 and by BSI as DD122.

This standard is in two parts. The first specifies how to map the Network Service primitives onto the X.25(84) network layer protocol. The second part describes how the X.25(80) protocol can be used to also provide support for the CONS. X.25(80) cannot be used directly, because it misses out some important features (such as extended addressing as described in Chapter Six) which are essential for supporting the CONS. The second part of the standard defines a protocol effectively run over the top of X.25(80) that adds the necessary functionality. Here we are only going to look at the basic standard that concerns itself with the use of X.25(84) to support the CONS. The X.25(84) protocol is described in detail in Chapter Six. If the reader is not familiar with this protocol at all, the description of the use of X.25(84) to provide the CONS below should be skipped until Chapter Six has been read. The mapping between the CONS primitives for the network connection establishment phase and X.25(84) packets is shown in Table 4.1.

For the network connection release phase, the N-DISCONNECT primitive maps into the clear request packet. The N-DISCONNECT indication primitive can be mapped into either a clear indication, restart indication or clear request depending on the precise reason for the N-DISCONNECT.

In the data phase, N-DATA packets are mapped into X.25(84) data packets. If the receipt confirmation option is requested, this is mapped into the use of the D-bit in the X.25(84) data packet. N-EXPEDITED DATA primitives are mapped into X.25(84) interrupt packets with the NS user data carried in the interrupt user data field. Note that this limits the size of the NS user data to 32 bytes maximum.

Finally, the N-RESET request primitive is mapped into the X.25(84) reset request packet and the N-RESET indication primitive is mapped into the X.25(84) reset indication packet or reset request packet. There is no mapping for the N-RESET response or N-RESET confirm primitives as they only have local significance between the NSAP and the NS user.

4.7.3 Network Layer Addressing

As part of the OSI standards, ISO has produced a standard for NSAP addresses, the network layer addresses. The standard is published as by ISO as ISO/DIS/DAD2 and by BSI as DD134. Global addressing is used, so that an NSAP address is the same anywhere within a group of interconnected OSI networks.

Table 4.1 CONS to X.25 mapping for connection establishment phase

CONS	X.25
Primitives:	Packets:
N-CONNECT request N-CONNECT indication N-CONNECT response N-CONNECT confirm	CALL REQUEST INCOMING CALL CALL ACCEPTED CALL CONNECTED
Parameter:	Fields (Including Facilities)
Called Address	Called DTE Address Field Called Address Extension Facility
Calling Address	Calling DTE Address Field Calling Address Extension Facility
Responding Address	Called DTE Address Field Called Address Extension Facility
Receipt Confirmation Selection	General Format Identifier
Expedited Data Selection	Expedited Data Negotiation Facility
QOS Parameter Set	Throughput Class Negotiation Facility Minimum Throughput Class Negotiation Facility Transit Delay Selection And Indication Facility End to End Transit Delay Negotiation Facility
NS-User Data	Call and Called User Data Field Fast Select Facility

The standard recognises that some sort of control over the allocation of NSAP addresses is required in order to provide sensible routing arrangements and to ensure that NSAP addresses are not duplicated. The concept of network addressing domains is used. Addresses within each domain are allocated by an 'addressing authority' of which there is only one permitted per domain. Figure 4.9 illustrates how the global addressing domain, containing all of the domains, is split up into domains. These smaller domains can be split up into subdomains and so on.

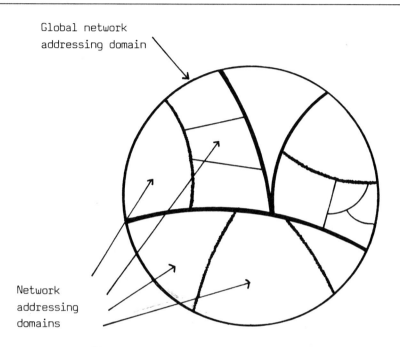

Figure 4.9 Domain addressing

The standard then goes on to specify the specific encoding rules for NSAP addresses. We will not worry too much about this here, except to say that the process of building addresses within the domain structure is similar to that described in Chapter Two.

4.8 Layer 4 - The Transport Layer

Put very simply, the purpose of the transport layer is to hide as much of the underlying network as possible from the higher layers. In order to do this, the transport layer may have to perform extra error detection and correction if the underlying network has an unacceptable uncorrected error rate. If the underlying network has a tendency to lose information, the transport layer may be required to detect this and cause the lost information to be resent. If the network layer connection fails for some reason, the transport layer may be required to handle this transparently so that the layers above do not notice what has happened. In effect, the transport layer is acting as a 'quality of service improver' in that it adds quality of service to the network layer in order to match the requirements of the higher layers.

Clearly, if every transport layer had to provide all of the capabilities mentioned above, even for high quality underlying networks, transfers would be very inefficient, due to a considerable overhead from the transport layer. For example, X.25 networks generally have a very low uncorrected error rate and a very low connection failure rate. In this case, only a very simple transport layer is required. In other types of network, where there is a significant uncorrected error rate or connections are prone to failure, a more powerful transport layer is required.

In order to cope with these different requirements, the transport layer can offer one or more of five different classes of service. Particular implementations only need to implement a subset of the total number of classes. This opens up the possibility that two systems may not be able to interwork, because they do not support compatible transport layer service classes.

4.8.1 The Connection-Mode Transport Service

As with the previous layers, there are two versions of the transport layer and we will be dealing here with the connection-orientated layer, sometimes called the 'COTS' for Connection-Orientated Transport Service.
The Transport Service is the interface that the transport layer provides for the session layer to use. In common with the Network Service, there are three distinct phases of operation: connection establishment, connection release and data transfer phase. It will be seen that the general style of operation in the Transport Service is very similar to that in the Network Service.

Transport Service Connection Establishment

A connection at the transport layer is between 'TS users'. When a TS user wants to set up a transport layer connection to another TS user, it issues a T-CONNECT request primitive containing the TSAP address of the called TS user and the quality of service required for the connection. The TSAP has the same meaning for the transport layer that the NSAP does for the network layer. If the underlying TS provider (i.e., the transport protocol and the layers below) can cope with the quality of service requested and the called TSAP exists, the T-CONNECT is passed to the called TS user as a T-CONNECT indication. If the called TS user can accept the connection and can provide at least the minimum quality of service required, it accepts the connection by responding with a T-CONNECT response primitive. This is passed back to the caller as a T-CONNECT confirm.

There are rather more quality of service parameters in the Transport Service than in the Network Service. The TS user can specify the maximum Transport Service connection delay (the time it takes to set up the connection) and the connection establishment failure probability. The TS user can also specify the throughput and transit delay required for the connection. Also specified is the maximum residual error rate required and the maximum transfer failure probability.

The TS user can also specify the maximum acceptable release delay and the maximum acceptable release failure probability. Finally, there is the ability to request protection of the data transferred.

Transport Service Connection Release

When a TS user wishes to terminate a transport layer connection, it issues a T-DISCONNECT request to the TS provider. This is passed through to the other TS user as a T-DISCONNECT indication at which point the connection is terminated. The TS provider itself may terminate the connection for several reasons. One possibility is that the quality of service has fallen below the minimum specified when the connection was set up. If this happens, the TS provider issues a T-DISCONNECT indication to both TS users.

Data Transfer Phase

TS user data is transferred using the T-DATA primitive. There are two forms of this primitive: one for normal data and another, T-EXPEDITED DATA, for expedited data. In principle, the size of the T-DATA primitive is unlimited. Since the N-DATA primitives are limited in size to the maximum that the network layer protocol can handle, the Transport Service has to split up T-DATA primitives and then recombine them in order to overcome this limitation.

4.8.2 Transport Layer Protocol

The transport layer protocol provides a method of implementing the abstract Transport Service described above. The transport layer protocol makes use of the Network Service in order to do this. The OSI transport layer protocol is published by ISO as ISO/DIS 8073 and by BSI as DD116.

Network Connection Types

As mentioned earlier, there are five different classes of transport layer. The particular type required depends on the characteristics of the underlying Network Service. The standard defines three types of underlying network.

Type A network connections have an acceptable uncorrected error rate and an acceptable rate of signalled errors (those signalled by a disconnect or reset).

Type B network connections have an acceptable uncorrected error rate but an unacceptable signalled error rate.

Type C network connections have an unacceptable uncorrected error rate.

Transport Classes

The class of transport layer chosen depends on which of type of network connection is available.

Class 0 provides the most basic type of transport connection and has been designed for use with type A network connections.

Class 1 provides a simple transport connection with the ability to recover from a network reset or disconnect. This class has been designed for use with type B network connections.

Class 2 provides the ability to multiplex several transport connections onto a single network connection. As no error recovery is included, this class is designed for use with type A network connections. Class 2 includes a flow control mechanism for the transport connections, so that a single transport connection cannot block the single network connection. This is somewhat analogous to the explicit flow control of network layer connections over a single link layer connection.

Class 3 is similar to class 2 except that it includes the ability to recover from a network reset or disconnect. Class 3 has been designed for use with type B network connections.

Class 4 provides all of the functions of class 3, except that it also has the ability to detect and correct errors left uncorrected by the network layer. It is able to detect and correct for loss, duplication, corruption and delivery out of sequence of transport protocol data units (TPDUs). Class 4 has been designed for use with type C network connections.

All of this means that a class 4 transport layer can cope with a raw underlying datagram network. Class 4 is also able to split the TPDUs from a single transport connection among a number of network connections and then recombine them at the other end. Clearly, class 4 is really quite clever and is therefore quite a large protocol.

4.9 Layer 5 - The Session Layer

The session layer is, as usual, split into two parts: the Session Service and the Session Protocol.

4.9.1 The Session Service

The purpose of the Session Service is to provide the SS user (the user of the Session Service) with the means for organised and synchronised exchange of data with other SS users. It provides the means for them to set up a connection with another SS user and exchange data with that user in a synchronised manner, then release the connection in an orderly manner. It also allows the SS user to negotiate for the use of 'tokens' to exchange data, synchronise and release the connection. It allows the connection to be either half duplex or full duplex. The Session Service also provides the means to establish synchronisation points so that, in the event of serious problems, the dialogue can be resumed from a known point. Finally, it allows a dialogue to be interrupted and then restarted at a prearranged point. The OSI Session Service standard is published by ISO as ISO/DIS 8326 and by BSI as DD111.

A central concept in the Session Service is the 'token'. A token is dynamically assigned to an SS user and gives that SS user exclusive use of a particular service. There are four types of token: the data token, the release token, the synchronise-minor token and the major/activity token.

A token can be either *available* or *not available*. In the latter case, neither SS user can have exclusive use of a service, the service is either available or unavailable to both. If the token is available, it can is *assigned* to one SS user, who then has exclusive use of the service and *not assigned* to the other SS user.

There are two types of synchronisation points that the SS user may insert into the data being transmitted, major and minor. A dialogue is completely contained between major synchronisation points. Within a single dialogue there may also be a number of minor synchronisation points.

Session Connection Establishment Phase

The style of the various phases of the Session Service is very similar to that of the previous two layers. When an SS user wants to call another SS user, it issues an S-CONNECT request. This is conveyed by the Session Service provider (SS provider) to the called SS user as an S-CONNECT indication. If the called SS user is able to accept the connection, it responds with an S-CONNECT response, which is conveyed by the SS provider to the calling SS user as an S-CONNECT confirm.

The S-CONNECT carries various parameters. The first of these is the 'session connection identifier'. This allows the two SS users to uniquely identify the Session Service connection. This is followed by the calling and called SSAP addresses in S-CONNECT requests and indications and just the called SSAP address for S-CONNECT responses and confirms. In the latter case, the called SSAP address is followed by the 'result'. This indicates whether or not the connection is acceptable by the called SS user. This is followed by quality of service negotiation parameters.

The next parameter is slightly different in that it allows the calling and called SS users to specify their session requirements. This is in the form of a set of 'functional units'. Each functional unit provides a specific set of functions that are either available or not available. Two examples of functional units are the 'half-duplex' functional unit and the 'full-duplex' functional unit.

The final three parameters are the 'initial synchronisation point serial number', the 'initial assignment of tokens' followed by SS user data, which can be up to 512 bytes in length.

Data Transfer Phase

Before going on to describe the primitives involved in the data transfer phase, it is necessary to understand the various types of services that are available.

The *Normal Data Transfer* service allows the transfer of normal Session Service data units (NSSDUs) over a session connection.

The *Expedited Data Transfer* service allows the transfer of expedited SSDUs (XSSDUs) over a session connection. This is free from any flow control constraints imposed on other types of data.

The *Typed Data Transfer* service allows the transfer of typed data SSDUs (TSSDUs). The difference between this and NSSDUs is that the token normally required before data can be transferred is not needed in order to transfer TSSDUs. The idea is that TSSDUs can be used by the higher layers to transfer protocol information, using NSSDUs for application information.

The *Capability Data Exchange* service is provided to allow a limited amount of information to be exchanged while not within an activity (an activity is a collection of one or more dialogue units).

The *Give Tokens* service allows an SS user to give one or more tokens to the other SS user.

The *Please Tokens* service allows an SS user to request tokens from the other SS user.

The *Give Control* service allows an SS user to surrender all available tokens to the other SS user.

The *Minor Synchronisation Point* service allows an SS user to establish a minor synchronisation point in the dialogue. Its use is controlled by the synchronise-minor token.

The *Major Synchronisation Point* service allows an SS user to define the end of a dialogue. Its use is controlled by the major/activity token.

The *Resynchronise* service is used either to wind back the connection to a previous synchronisation point or else establish a new one. It also reassigns tokens to the SS users.

The *Provider-Initiated Exception Reporting* service allows SS users to be notified of errors detected by the SS provider.

The *User-Initiated Exception Reporting* service is used by the SS user to report an exception condition when the data token is available but not assigned to the SS user.

Finally, the *Activity Start*, *Activity Resume*, *Activity Interrupt*, *Activity Discard* and *Activity End* services are used, as you may well imagine, to control activities.

NSSDUs are issued by an SS user in the form of S-DATA requests. These are conveyed by the SS provider to the other SS user as S-DATA indications. XSSDUs are carried in S-EXPEDITED DATA request and indication primitives in the same way. TSSDUs are similar and are carried in S-TYPED DATA request and indication primitives.

Capability data is carried in S-CAPABILITY DATA primitives which exist in four forms as it is a confirmed data transfer. An SS user issues an S-CAPABILITY DATA request which is conveyed by the SS provider to the other SS user as an S-CAPABILITY DATA indication. The response (confirmation) is issued as an S-CAPABILITY DATA response which finally reaches the original SS user as an S-CAPABILITY DATA confirm.

The token primitives are S-TOKEN GIVE, S-TOKEN PLEASE and S-CONTROL GIVE which appear in the request and indication forms.

The major and minor synchronisation primitives are the S-SYNC MAJOR and S-SYNC MINOR primitives. This is a confirmed service, so that the request, indication, response and confirm forms exist.

The S-RESYNCHRONISE primitive is similar, in that it exists in all four forms. The request and indication forms carry the resynchronisation point serial number at which the dialogue is to resume.

The S-P EXCEPTION REPORT primitive, used to provide the SS provider exception reporting service, only exists in the indication form. This is because, when the SS provider generates this primitive, it issues one to each of the SS users. There is no response to this primitive.

The S-U EXCEPTION REPORT primitive is used to provide the SS user exception reporting service. This primitive exists in the request and indication forms.

The S-ACTIVITY START and S-ACTIVITY RESUME primitives only exist in the request and indication forms whereas the S-ACTIVITY INTERRUPT, S-ACTIVITY DISCARD and S-ACTIVITY END primitives exist in all four forms as they are confirmed services.

Session Connection Release Phase

There are three ways of terminating a session connection. The S-RELEASE primitive is used to terminate a connection in an orderly way. All data in transit is delivered and the service is confirmed, so that both SS users can be sure that the connection has been terminated correctly. This means that the S-RELEASE exists in the request, indication, response and confirm forms.

The second way to terminate a connection is to use the S-U ABORT primitive. This is issued by an SS user when an immediate termination of a connection is required. In-transit data is lost.

Finally, the S-P ABORT primitive allows the SS provider to terminate a connection. The primitive only exists in the indication form as no response is required by the SS users when they receive this primitive from the SS provider.

4.9.2 The Session Protocol

The Session Protocol is published by ISO as ISO/DIS 8327 and by BSI as DD112. The document specifies precisely how the Session Service primitives are mapped onto the Transport Service. There is not too much point in going into the detail of this here, as it does things like specify precisely which bits mean what and does not really assist with an understanding of what is going on.

The session layer is often described in rather vague terms. Hopefully, it will be clear from the description of the Session Service that the Session Protocol is not a trivial thing and provides a large number of very important facilities. These facilities make life a lot easier for the higher layers by providing a very well defined environment in which to operate.

4.10 Layer 6 - The Presentation Layer

The task of the presentation layer is to ensure that the information content of Presentation Service data units (PSDUs) is preserved across a network. The Presentation Service standard is published by ISO as ISO/DIS 8822 and by BSI as DD101.

The Application Protocol data units (APDUs) along with an application protocol go together to form an 'abstract syntax'. Two application layer entities must agree on an abstract syntax before any communication takes place. The presentation layer entities agree on a 'transfer syntax' to use for the communication between the application layer entities.

The abstract syntax is 'converted' into the transfer syntax by applying a set of 'encoding rules'. Rather than go into great detail of the concepts in the Presentation Service, which are largely the same as in the Session Service anyway, we are going to take a very brief look at the only abstract notation and set of encoding rules that is currently defined. This is known as 'Abstract Syntax Notation 1' or ASN.1 for short.

4.10.1 ASN.1

ASN.1 is basically a language for specifying how data is structured. Associated with it is a set of encoding rules for generating the transfer syntax. This effectively defines how the data structuring mechanisms are actually transmitted (i.e., it defines the encoding of the information down to the bit level). ASN.1 is, in fact, very useful in a wide range of situations where complex data structuring is necessary.

The ASN.1 standard is published by ISO as ISO/DIS 8824.2 and by BSI as DD103. The ASN.1 encoding rules are published by ISO as ISO/DIS 8825.2 and by BSI as DD104.

Most high level languages, like C and PASCAL, have a variety of methods for structuring data. Complex data types can be constructed from simple types. The problem with using these languages for communication between applications is that there is no standard for how the structured data is actually represented at the bit level. In other words, there is no standard set of encoding rules to take a C 'struct' definition and generate its layout in the computer's memory.

The encoding rules provide a generalised method for encoding data structures. The standard form consists of a header byte, or bytes, identifying the type of data following. This is then followed by a length byte, or bytes, giving the length of the data following. Next comes the data itself. These encodings are joined together to form the complete data structure.

4.11 Layer 7 - The Application Layer

The application level is split into two different types of 'Application Service Elements', or ASEs: 'Common Application Service Elements' (CASEs) and the 'Specific Application Elements' (SASEs).

CASEs provide the types of facilities that many applications will want to use. Like subroutine libraries, they provide some handy predefined functions.

The most important CASE is known as 'CCR'. This stands for Commitment, Concurrency and Recovery. There are many situations where the CCR facilities are required, as they provide the ability to recover from system failures in such a way that distributed databases are always consistent. A classic situation in which this might be important is where some money is being moved from one bank account to another. First, one bank account must be debited, then the other one credited. Supposing something nasty happens and one of the processes (debiting or crediting) is not performed correctly, the result could be that money is lost or gained somewhere in the process (not very desirable if you are the person lost the money).

CCR provides mechanisms that ensure that a number of databases can be kept in step. If a system failure should occur, it provides mechanisms whereby the databases are 'rolled back' to a point at which they were consistent and then the extra transactions are replayed to reach the desired state.

The most fundamental SASE is 'FTAM'. This is the OSI file transfer protocol and is described in Chapter Seven. Another of the SASEs, Job Transfer and Manipulation (JTM), uses FTAM to move processing tasks between computer systems. Another SASE is X.400, the OSI electronic mail protocol. This is also described in Chapter Seven. Finally at this level, there is VT, the Virtual Terminal protocol. This is the OSI version of 'triple X'. It takes a different approach to triple X in that it uses the concept of a virtual terminal; a standard terminal type that is mapped into a real terminal driving protocol.

4.12 Security in OSI

The description of the OSI security architecture is published by ISO as ISO 7498/PDAD2 and by BSI as DD148. Security in general, is described in Chapter Eight, so we will not discuss techniques here. The standard largely defines what security measure can be taken at each layer in the seven layer model to achieve the desired type of security.

5

Standards Used in the United Kingdom

5.1 Introduction

The purpose of this section is to describe in general terms the most important standards currently in use in the United Kingdom but excluding OSI protocols. Of course, in the future it is very likely that OSI standards will dominate, but at this point in time there are not many networks that actually use them. This is particularly true at the higher layers where the protocols used are fairly new.

There are a large number of manufacturer-specific packet switched network protocols still in use, which no doubt will remain in use for some time to come. The most used 'open protocols' (i.e., non-manufacturer specific) used at the moment are the 'Colour Book' protocols. These were developed within the UK, mainly by people from the academic community together with a number of people from industry. Use of the Colour Book protocols are pretty well mandatory within the academic community, and so have been widely implemented. Implementations have been made both by the academics themselves and manufacturers, who wish to sell their equipment into the academic community.

5.2 The Colour Book Protocols

There are a number of Colour Book protocols in the set. Each protocol is usually known by the colour used on the outside cover of the standard, hence the name 'Colour Book' protocols. The lower level protocols for packet switched networks are not covered by a Colour Book, as X.25(80) is used up to layer 3 (i.e., X.25 level 2 and X.25 level 3).

5.2.1 Green Book

The Green Book is actually titled 'Character Terminal Protocols on PSS' but nobody knows it as that! Green Book is really a recommendation on the use of X.3, X.28 and X.29, the 'triple X' protocols (described in detail in Chapter Seven) that define the operation of PADs. It was prepared by Study Group 3 of the British Telecom PSS User Forum.

Green Book defines a small subset of the possible modes of operation of a triple X PAD so as to provide standardised modes of operation which are useful for the PAD user and easy to use from the point of view of host computer systems driving the PAD port.

Green Book defines three modes of operation: MESSAGE, TRANSPARENT and NATIVE.

MESSAGE mode can be described as a 'line at a time' mode of operation. The user of the PAD port can type in a line of characters, edit the characters and then, when the line has been completed, send it to the host computer system. Normally this would be with a carriage return, the standard way of completing a line. Somewhat quaintly, Green Book suggests that EOT (CTRL + D) is a jolly good end of line character and the recommended forwarding conditions do not include carriage return. Needless to say, most implementations of MESSAGE mode do, in fact, forward on carriage return.

There are two interesting characteristics of MESSAGE mode. One is that it has separated input and output. For example, if the user is in the process of entering a line, any characters received from the host computer system are held inside the PAD. Only when the line is forwarded (or deleted) are the characters from the host computer system sent to the user's terminal. Equally, if the user starts typing while characters from the host computer are being sent to the PAD, echoing of the user's characters is held back until the host computer has completed a line. In this way, the user's characters and the host computer system's characters are interleaved on a line by line basis. This is much better than the standard way of doing things which causes characters to be interleaved making the whole thing unreadable.

The second interesting characteristic of MESSAGE mode is in its handling of linefeeds sent to the user's terminal. When the user forwards a line with a carriage return, the PAD sends a line feed to the user on the basis that the host computer system is going to do that when it has received the line from the user. This is known as a pre-emptive linefeed. When the host computer system receives the line, it assumes that it must send a linefeed to the user to avoid overwriting the line on the user's terminal. As the PAD has already sent a linefeed, the PAD absorbs the linefeed from the host computer system. The result for the user is that a linefeed is sent to the terminal almost immediately. This is much better than having to wait for the host computer system to get around to it.

Although the characteristics of MESSAGE mode are much more ergonomic than that defined by the triple X protocol, this does mean that PAD software has to be specially written to support the Green Book style of interface.

TRANSPARENT mode is similar in many respects to MESSAGE mode except that no modification of the characters from the host computer takes place. In other words, characters from the host computer system are passed transparently to the user's terminal.

NATIVE mode is a much more interactive style of working. Put simply, NATIVE mode causes the PAD to emulate a piece of wire as closely as possible. Characters from the user are forwarded to the host computer system as soon as possible without modification or echoing at the PAD. Characters from the host computer system are passed transparently to the user's terminal. The result is a mode that is suitable for screen editing over the packet switched network. The disadvantage with this mode is that it can generate very high packet rates across the network. Also, as echoing of characters is done by the host computer system, any delays in the network will be easily (and annoyingly) visible to the user. Therefore, NATIVE mode is only really usable over high speed packet switched networks.

As well as defining the three modes of operation of the PAD user interface, Green Book also provides recommendations on how host computer systems should operate. This is important because a Green Book PAD will not allow the host computer system to change operating parameters in the PAD in all situations. There are many situation where attempts by the host computer system to change parameters will be rejected.

5.2.2 Yellow Book Transport Service

The Yellow Book Transport Service is often known as 'YBTS' for short. In terms of the OSI seven layer model it is layer 4, the Transport Service layer. YBTS is used extensively by the higher layer protocols to provide a convenient interface to the underlying network. YBTS is only a very basic Transport Service protocol, providing the same sort of functionality as the OSI Transport Service Class 0. It cannot improve the quality of service of the underlying network, as it has no error correction capability, and cannot split a connection across several network connections. The protocol is described in detail in Chapter Seven so we will not go any further into YBTS here.

5.2.3 Blue Book FTP

The Blue Book protocol is an example of a File Transfer Protocol (FTP). It is often known as 'NIFTP' which stands for Network Independent File Transfer Protocol. In reference to the OSI seven layer model, the Blue Book protocol covers the top three layers (the application, presentation and session layers) and therefore directly accesses the Transport Service. The Blue Book protocol is described in detail in Chapter Seven.

5.2.4 Grey Book Mail

The Grey Book protocol is the Colour Book electronic mail protocol. It is used extensively within the academic community and provides a very effective electronic mail system. As time goes on, it will be replaced by X.400, the OSI electronic mail protocol.

There are three aspects to Grey Book mail: the mail presentation format, the mail transfer format and the mail transfer protocol itself.

The mail presentation format defines how electronic mail is presented to the user and the format in which the user enters electronic mail into the system. A very important part of this is the specification of the intended recipient's address and the sender's address.

The mail transfer format specifies how the electronic mail messages are transferred between Grey Book mail host computer systems. The mail is transferred as a single body of text. The first part is the address of the recipient (or recipients, as the address list can contain more than one address). There then follows a blank line to separate the address list from the mail text. Then, completing the mail message, is the mail text itself.

The mail transfer protocol specifies how mail in the mail transfer format is actually moved between host computer systems. Grey Book mail specifies the use of Blue Book FTP to provide the transfer capability.

5.2.5 Red Book

Red Book is more commonly known as 'JTMP'. This stands for Job Transfer and Manipulation Protocol. It is roughly analogous to the OSI JTM protocol in function. This is the largest and the most complicated of all of the Colour Book protocols.

There are three stages involved in the running of a job (i.e., a computing task). These are the initial acceptance and queuing of the job for later execution, the actual execution of the job and disposal of any output files that the job may have generated. In addition, the user who submitted the job may wish to enquire or change the status of a job.

The purpose of JTMP is to allow these various activities to be spread around a network of host computer systems. For example, the job may be submitted from one computer for execution on another computer with the output delivered to yet another computer.

JTMP allows a user submitting a job to specify the target host computer system on which the job is to be executed. JTMP then moves the 'job description' to the target host computer system. The job description may reference files that are held on the target host computer system. JTMP also allows a job to be executed in stages by more than one host computer system if required. As each one completes its part of the job, the job description is then transferred on to the next host computer until execution has been totally completed.

JTMP also allows for operation in a 'store and forward' mode. Here, if the target host computer system is not directly accessible from where the job was submitted, the job can first be sent to another JTMP host computer system that can forward it at some later point to the target host computer system. The job may also pick up files held within the 'store and forward' host computer system.

A job may produce a number of output files that have to be routed somewhere, possibly to different destinations. JTMP provides the capability to do this output file distribution.

JTMP includes a facility that allows significant events to be reported back to some 'monitor point'. This is usually the host computer system at which the job was originally submitted. These can then be distributed to the user who originally submitted the job. A significant event might be the completion of execution at a particular host computer system for example. This is very useful as there is nothing worse than feeling that a job has vanished down a black hole somewhere in the network.

As well as automatically reporting significant events, a user can make a status enquiry about the job. This can determine whether or not execution has been started or completed, whether output files have been produced and where they have been routed. The user is also able to 'hold' a job (i.e., not let it proceed), hold an output file, delete a job or output file or change the route of an output file.

As with Grey Book mail, JTMP uses Blue Book FTP to move jobs around the network.

5.2.6 Fawn Book

Fawn Book contains the Simple Screen Management Protocol or 'SSMP' for short. SSMP is another applications layer protocol but this time it is providing a Virtual Terminal Service. SSMP provides a protocol for managing a screen image, usually in or attached to a PAD, in such a way that many simple operations can be performed locally without using the host computer system or the network.

As mentioned earlier in the description of Green Book, NATIVE mode operation and other modes that forward characters in small packets can have a serious effect on network loading and produce visible delays for the user. SSMP, on the other hand, does as much as possible locally. This considerably reduces the network loading and also reduces the delays seen by the user. The result is that effective screen editing can be performed over slow packet switched networks.

In order to avoid problems where both the user and the host computer system are updating the screen image simultaneously, SSMP has the concept of an 'access token'. Normally, the host computer system sets up the screen image and then hands over the token to the SSMP module at the user end of the connection. The token remains there, allowing local modification of the screen image, until a function is requested that requires the intervention of the host computer system. The token is then returned to the host computer system so that the function can be performed.

5.3 BT's PSS X.25 Protocol

It might seem a bit surprising that British Telecom's PSS protocol is singled out as being a special case in any way. The reason for this is that, apart from being the most important public X.25 network, it is actually a very specific X.25 implementation.

X.25, as defined by CCITT, is a rather vague protocol, particularly in the area of error handling. Since these are very important considerations for PSS where guaranteed interworking is absolutely necessary, British Telecom have tied down the vague areas and made precise statements about how equipment connected to PSS is to behave. As part of the process of obtaining approval to connect equipment to PSS (something done by the equipment manufacturers), the equipment is checked for conformance with the PSS version of X.25(80). This is defined in British Telecom's Technical User Guide 17.

6

X.25 - A Packet Switched Network Protocol

6.1 Introduction

In this chapter we will discuss some of the technical detail of a very important packet switched network protocol. Readers who are not interested in the gory details may wish to skip to the next chapter.

The protocol is the CCITT X.25(84) protocol - possibly the most important of all of the packet switched network protocols. The '(84)' after the 'X.25' refers to the particular X.25 recommendation document published in 1984. CCITT produce a new version every four years, although this does not necessarily mean that the protocol is changed greatly every four years. X.25(80), the version published in 1980, is the basis of most X.25 implementations to date. This is largely due to the fact that the national networks (BT's Packet SwitchStream, for example) have standardised on X.25(80).

X.25(84) has some new features not present at X.25(80). In most cases, these new features have been included in order to support the Open Systems Interconnection connection-orientated Network Service (more about all of this later). Almost all new implementations will be X.25(84) which is why this protocol has been chosen.

ISO also have a version of X.25(84) level 3. This is published by ISO as ISO/DIS 8208 and by BSI as DD117. The ISO version of the protocol is basically the same as the CCITT version, except that it allows DTE to DTE operation at the packet level whereas CCITT only considers DTE to DCE operation.

At the end of the chapter we take a quick look at X.75. This is a version of X.25 that is used to interconnect X.25 networks and includes a few extra features and different packet formats.

6.2 X.25(84) Level 1 - The Physical Level

The physical level of the protocol specifies things like the electrical signalling to be used and the type of connectors to be used. Two main types of interfaces are allowed. These are known as X.21 and X.21bis. The recommendation also allows the use of V series interfaces when required. Since we are mainly interested in the higher levels of the protocol here, details of the physical level interface will be left to Chapter Ten.

6.3 X.25(84) Level 2 - The Link Level

Put simply, level 2 provides an error-free, flow controlled communications path between the two ends of a communications link. This enables the higher levels to operate without having to worry about corrupted data and low level flow control problems. The link level protocol uses some of the concepts from a protocol known as the HDLC (High level Data Link Control) protocol.

Just to confuse the issue, there are two versions of the X.25 level 2 protocol: LAP and LAPB. LAP stands for Link Access Procedure while LAPB stands for Link Access Procedure Balanced. LAPB is something of an improvement on LAP and is the version used by almost everybody.

In order to confuse the issue even more, there are two versions of the LAPB protocol. The most common form of LAPB is the SLP version. The SLP stands for Single Link Procedure and means that the protocol between the DTE and the DCE uses just one communications link. The new form of LAPB that was introduced at X.25(84) is the MLP version. The MLP stands for Multilink Procedure. This allows the use of multiple communications links between the DTE and DCE. If any one of the links fails, the others can take over with no loss of data. This allows for load sharing between multiple links and automatic recovery from the failure of one or more links.

In this section, the SLP version of LAPB will be described. Those readers interested full details of the different types of X.25 level 2 should get hold of a copy of the CCITT recommendation (see Appendices A and B).

6.3.2 The LAPB Frame Format

The unit of information in the LAPB protocol is the 'frame'. Figure 6.1 shows the structure of the LAPB frames. The 'F' field contains a 'flag' byte. When frames are not being transmitted, continuous flag bytes are transmitted (binary pattern 01111110).

The 'A' field contains the 'address' of the packet. This field can contain either 00000011 (the A address) or 00000001 (the B address). The use of the A and B addresses will be described later, so don't panic.

The 'C' fields contains the 'control field' of the frame. This is used to specify what the frame contains. Note that in (a) and (b) of Figure 6.1 the control field is always 8 bits long while in (c) and (d) the control field may be either 8 or 16 bits long. This is because there is yet another variation of the protocol that has not been mentioned yet. The standard version of LAPB allows for a maximum window size (see Chapter Two for an explanation of protocol windows) of 7 requiring sequence numbers from 0 to 7. A 3 bit field was required for this, which fits quite happily in the control field. There are situations where a larger window size would be nice. To allow for this, there was defined an 'extended' version of LAPB, which can support window sizes up to 127. This requires a 7 bit field. Hence the variable length control field. Incidentally, many implementations of X.25 do not support the extended mode of operation.

Bit order of
transmission   12345678   12345678   12345678   16 to 1   12345678

Flag	Address	Control	FCS	Flag
F 01111110	A 8 bits	C 8 bits	FCS 16 bits	F 01111110

(a)

Bit order of
transmission   12345678 12345678 12345678   16 to 1 12345678

Flag	Address	Control	Information	FCS	Flag
F 01111110	A 8 bits	C 8 bits	Info N bits	FCS 16 bits	F 01111110

(b)

Bit order of
transmission   12345678   12345678   1 to *)   16 to 1   12345678

Flag	Address	Control	FCS	Flag
F 01111110	A 8 bits	C *) bits	FCS 16 bits	F 01111110

(c)

Bit order of
transmission   12345678 12345678 1 to *)   16 to 1 12345678

Flag	Address	Control	Information	FCS	Flag
F 01111110	A 8 bits	C *) bits	Info N bits	FCS 16 bits	F 01111110

(d)

*) 16 for frame formats that contain sequence numbers; 8 for frame
formats that do not contain sequence numbers.

Figure 6.1 Frame Formats

In the case of (b) and (d) of Figure 6.1, there is an 'I' field. This is used to convey higher level protocol information, the X.25 level 3 packets.

The 'FCS' field contains the 'frame check sequence'. This is used by the receiver of the frame to check that it has been received without error. The transmitter of the frame adds on the FCS, the value of which was calculated from the contents of the frame.

Finally, there is another 'F' field. This flag defines the end of the frame. It is quite possible that another frame may follow directly after this flag, so that there is only one flag between frames.

One question arises from this frame structure. Suppose the contents of the frame between the 'F' fields contains the bit pattern 01111110, the flag bit pattern. Since a flag marks the end of the frame, this would mean that the frame could not be received correctly.

To get around this 'data transparency' problem, the data is transmitted in a special way. If the contents of the frame contains five or more 1s in a row, the transmitter adds a 0 bit after the five 1s. This ensures that six 1s in a row can never occur in the middle of a frame. The receiver is aware of what the transmitter has done so that, if it sees five 1s followed by a 0, it knows that the 0 bit must be stripped out as it has been added by the transmitter. This technique is known, somewhat indelicately, as 'bit stuffing'.

6.3.2 The LAPB Frame Types

The LAPB protocol defines a number of legal frame types that are used to transfer LAPB protocol information and the higher level protocol information.

The frame type is specified in the control field. Table 6.1 shows the valid control fields in LAPB. Due to the option of the extended LAPB mode, there are two different forms for some of the frame types. The functions of the frames remain the same whatever. Only the non-extended ones are shown in the table.

There are two fundamentally different types of frames: command frames and response frames. Responses are transmitted to acknowledge the reception of a command. For example, I frames are commands. When an I frame (or frames) is received, a response must be sent to indicate that the frame (or frames) was received correctly. Note that the 'S' frames may be either commands or responses. This is because they can be used in either role, depending on the circumstance.

Commands and responses are distinguished by the value in the 'A' field of the frame. Remember that this field can contain either the A address or the B address? The response transmitted to a command received always has the same 'A' field as that of the command. If the DCE sent the command, the A address is used. If the DTE sent the command, the B address is used. Actually, at the link level, this is the only really major difference between the DTE and DCE.

Table 6.1 Control field formats

Format	Command	Response	1	2	3	4	5	6	7	8
							Encoding			
Information transfer	I (information)		0	N(S)			P	N(R)		
Supervisory	RR (receive ready)	RR (receive ready)	1	0	0	0	P/F	N(R)		
	RNR (receive not ready)	RNR (receive not ready)	1	0	1	0	P/F	N(R)		
	REJ (reject)	REJ (reject)	1	0	0	1	P/F	N(R)		
Unnumbered	SABM (set async balanced mode)		1	1	1	1	P	1	0	0
	DISC (disconnect)		1	1	0	0	P	0	1	0
		DM (disconnected mode)	1	1	1	1	F	0	0	0
		UA (unnumbered acknowledge-ment)	1	1	0	0	F	1	1	0
		FRMR (frame reject)	1	1	1	0	F	0	0	1

It is now time to describe the different types of frames.

The 'I' frame is an 'information frame'. This frame is used to convey higher level protocol information.

The 'S' frames are the so called 'supervisory' frames. There are three types of S frames, the RR (receiver ready), RNR (receiver not ready) and REJ (resend frame) frames. These are concerned with controlling the flow of the I frames and recovering from communications link errors causing corruption of frames.

The 'U' frames are the so called 'unnumbered' frames. They are called this because they do not contain sequence numbers. These frames are used to initiate and close down the link (SABM, SABME, DISC, DM, and UA) and report protocol violations (FRMR).

The SABM (Set Asynchronous Balanced Mode) and SABME (Set Asynchronous Balanced Mode Extended) commands are used to set the link into the information transfer state (i.e., to an 'up' state). The only difference between the two is that SABM requests the normal mode of operation (max window size 7), while SABME requests the extended mode of operation (max window size 127).

The DISC command (DISConnect) frame is used to set the link into the link down state and is therefore the opposite, to some extent, of the SABM and SABME commands.

The DM (Disconnected Mode) response can be used in response to a received SABM or SABME if the transmitter of the DM does not wish to bring the link into the information transfer state.

The UA (Unnumbered Acknowledge) response is used to confirm that a DISC or SABM command has been received.

The FRMR (FRaMe Reject) response is used to indicate the the last command or response was not valid in some way. The FRMR carries information describing the reason (see Figure 6.2).

6.3.3 The N(R) and N(S) Fields

The N(R) field is used by the transmitter of the frame to tell the receiver the sequence number of the next I frame that it expects to receive. The RR and RNR frames use this field to confirm the reception of I frames with sequence numbers up to N(R). The REJ frame is used to request retransmission of I frames with sequence numbers beginning at N(R). The N(S) field indicates the sequence number of an I frame.

6.3.4 The P Bit

The P (or poll/final) bit is generally used to indicate that a frame has been retransmitted. When used in a command, the bit is called the 'poll' bit. When used in a response, the bit is called the 'final' bit. When a response is made to a command, the final bit of the response must be equal to the poll bit of the command.

In general, the first time a command is transmitted, the poll bit is clear. Since a command has been transmitted, a response is required. If no response is received within a specified time, the command will be retransmitted, this time with the poll bit set. The specified time interval within which a response must be received is known as

'T1'. This is one of several parameters that need to be configured for particular links. More about this later in the 'System Parameters' section.

```
                     Information field bits
  12345678  9  10 11 12   13  14 15 16   17  18  19  20  21  22  23  24
+----------+--+---------+----+----------+---+---+---+---+---+---+---+---+
|Rejected  |0 |  V(S)   |C/R |  V(R)    |W  |X  |Y  |Z  |0  |0  |0  |0  |
|frame     |  |         |    |          |   |   |   |   |   |   |   |   |
|control   |  |         |    |          |   |   |   |   |   |   |   |   |
|field     |  |         |    |          |   |   |   |   |   |   |   |   |
+----------+--+---------+----+----------+---+---+---+---+---+---+---+---+
```

- Rejected fram control field is the control field of the received frame which caused the frame reject.

- V(S) is the current send state variable value at the DCE or DTE reporting the rejection condition (bit 10 = low order bit).

- C/R set 1 indicates the rejected frame was a response. C/R set to 0 indicates the rejected frame was a command.

- V(R) is the current receive state variable value at the DCE or DTE reporting the rejection condition (bit 14 = low order bit).

- W set to 1 indicates that the control field received and returned in bits 1 through to 8 was undefined or not implemented.

- X set to 1 indicates that the control field received and returned in bits 1 through 8 was considered invalid because the frame contained an information field which is not permitted with this frame or is a supervisory or unnumbered frame with incorrect length. Bit W must be set to 1 in conjunction with this bit.

- Y set to 1 indicates that the information field received exceeded the maximum established capacity.

- Z set to 1 indicates the control field received and returned in bits 1 through 8 contained an invalid N(R).

Figure 6.2 FRMR information field

6.3.5 The Link Level in Operation

There are two fundamental phases of operation: the link down phase and the information transfer phase. In the formal specification of the protocol, the two phases are broken down into a large number of states. The protocol is then defined as a 'state table'. This says 'if this event occurs in this state, take this action and go into this new state'. State tables are really only of interest to someone implementing the protocol, so we are not going to worry about state tables here.

The two phases of the link will be described below. Operation is the same for the DTE and DCE. Therefore the generic term 'DXE' will be used to mean either the DTE or the DCE.

The Link Down Phase

When a DXE first wakes up, it is in the link down phase. In this state, it is common to send DISC frames periodically. This is basically to say 'I am down'. If no response is received within the T1 period, the DISC is resent with the P bit set. This is written as DISC(P). Figure 6.3 illustrates this condition.

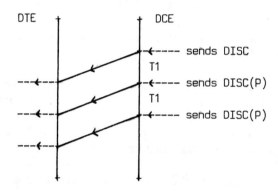

Figure 6.3

If a DXE receives a DISC or DISC(P) and wishes to start up the link, it responds with a UA or UA(F) (i.e., a UA with the final bit set). The DXE receiving the UA or UA(F) will wait for a period of time known as T3. If a SABM or SABME is received within this period, a UA response is sent and the link goes into the information transfer phase. If a SABM(P) or SABME(P) is received, a UA(F) is transmitted and the link goes into the information transfer phase. Note that if the latter happens, the implication is that a SABM or SABME was lost as the poll bit being set indicates that the frame has been retransmitted.

The Information Transfer Phase

Figure 6.4 shows a link set up, taking the link into the information transfer phase, followed by a link clear down back to the link down phase. In the information phase, I, RR, RNR and REJ frames are used to control the transfer of higher level protocol data across the link. If an I frame is received correctly and the DXE can accept more, it responds to the I frame with an RR response frame. If the DXE cannot accept more, it responds with an RNR response which tells the other DXE that it is now busy and can accept no more data for the moment. The REJ response is used to request the retransmission of one or more I frames when the DXE suspects that one or more I frames have got lost (possibly discarded because an FCS error occurred during reception).

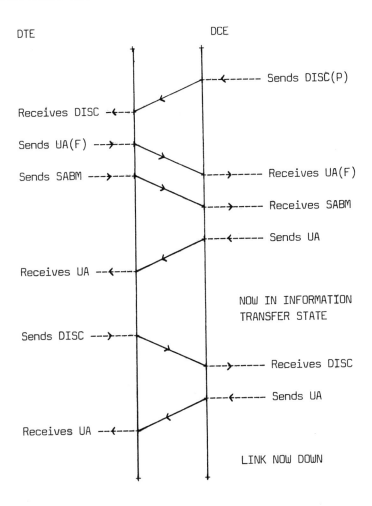

Figure 6.4 link setup followed by link clear down

The RR, RNR and REJ frames used to respond to I frames are responses. The command form of the RR, RNR and REJ frames are used to 'poll' the other DXE for its current state or tell it if the state of the DXE has changed. When used as commands, the RR, RNR and REJ frames always have the poll bit set. Thus the responses generated by the receiver always have the final bit set.

As an example of how this works, suppose that a DXE has responded to an I frame with an RNR response because it can accept no more data. When it can accept more data, it can send an RR(P) command to the other DXE, informing it of the new state. The receiving DXE can then respond with an RR(F), RNR(F) or REJ(F) response (depending on its state) and resume sending I frames. This is shown in Figure 6.5.

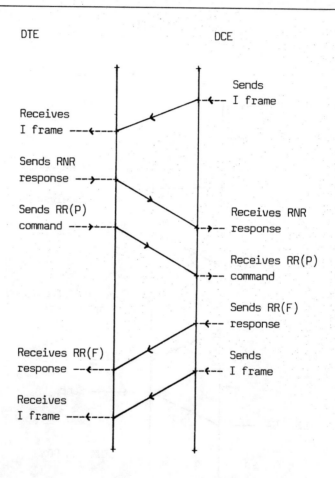

Figure 6.5 Example of use of RR(P)

Either DTE or DCE may put the link back into the link down phase by sending a DISC command at any time. If a DXE requires the link to be reset, it does this by sending a SABM or SABME command. Again, this can occur at any time. The receiver sends a UA in response and the link goes straight back to the information transfer phase.

The Frame Reject Condition

The frame reject condition is entered when an invalid frame is received. This means that a frame was received with either the A or B address in the A field and without an FCS error, but the contents of the frame are still incorrect or inappropriate for the state of the receiver. Clearly, this is a fairly serious condition, possibly indicating a protocol violation, and requires the link to be reset. Although the link could be reset just by sending a SABM or SABME command, this would not tell the other DXE why the link was restarted. A DXE that receives an invalid frame therefore sends an FRMR response telling the other DXE what has gone wrong. This is basically an accusation - 'you have sent me a frame that is wrong and this is why'.

The FRMR response is a bit special because it is the only response that can be sent in response to a response - good isn't it? Once in the frame reject condition, the link can be restarted with an SABM or SABME command.

6.3.6 The System Parameters

The system parameters are the configurable parameters that define certain aspects of the operation of the link level.

The T1 value is the period of time that the transmitter of a command frame will wait for a response before re-transmitting the command with the poll bit set. This is sometimes known as the 're-try period'. T1 should be longer than the time it takes to transmit a maximum length frame and receive a response to the frame, which may itself be a maximum length frame. This is dependent on the rate at which bits are sent on the communications link and the processing delay at the receiver.

There is another timer, known as T2, which is defined as the maximum time taken before a receiver of a frame transmits a frame acknowledging reception of the frame. This must always be less than T1. It is good practice to transmit a frame acknowledging reception of a frame as soon as possible.

The T3 timer defines how long a DXE will wait for a link set up command before starting to transmit DISCs when in the link down phase. The value of T3 is T1 x N2.

N2 is the maximum number of times that a command frame will be re-transmitted before the link has to be restarted. Essentially, if T1 has expired N2 times, the transmitter gives up and restarts the link with a SABM or SABME. PSS uses the value of 20 for N2. Different networks may specify different values for N2 but they are all fairly similar to PSS.

N1 is the maximum number of bits that may be in an I frame. This includes the I A, C, I and FCS fields. For example, if the maximum I field size for a link is 128 bytes, N1 would be 1064.

The system parameter, k, is the maximum number of sequentially numbered I frames that a DXE may have transmitted but not acknowledged at any time (i.e., the window size). PSS defines the value of k as 7 as it does not support the extended mode of operation.

6.4 X.25 Level 2 - Some Practical Hints

Most of the problems that occur when trying to connect two pieces of equipment together is finding a cable that works and providing a clock for the link level (i.e., Physical Level problems)! Having done that, the next step is to get the Link Level going. A DTE will only talk to a DCE; DTEs will not talk to DTEs and DCEs will not talk to DCEs. So the first thing to do is to make sure that one device is a DCE and the other is a DTE. Once this has been sorted out, the Link Level should come up with no further messing about.

The most important configurable parameter is the T1 timer value. This should be set correctly for the rate at which the link is being clocked. Don't forget that the T1 must be set in both the DCE and the DTE.

What happens if T1 is set incorrectly? If T1 is not big enough, there may not be enough time for a long frame to be transmitted and acknowledged before the T1 timer expires. This results in a lot of unnecessary frame retransmissions resulting in inefficient data transfer. If T1 is too big, then serious delays may occur when frame retransmissions are required. In both cases, nothing terribly fatal happens, but it is good practice to get the link as efficient as possible and this requires that T1 be set correctly.

The other major configurable parameter for the link level is N2. This is effectively the number of times that a frame will be re-transmitted before the link is reset. A value of 20 is fairly reasonable; N2 is not dependent on link speed.

T1 and N2 are linked in the sense that T1 x N2 is the maximum time that it may take the link to recover from a serious error. If this value is too large, the time may run into many minutes. Hopefully, this should not occur too often, though.

If the communications link between the DTE and DCE is of good quality, FCS errors should almost never occur. If the link is noisy, causing many FCS errors, frames with errors may start getting through the FCS check. The FCS is not foolproof; it only rejects most of the frames with errors. This is quite a serious condition as corruption of the Network Level data may occur which may not be detected by the higher level protocols.

Even if the problem is not that serious, frequent FCS errors will make the link inefficient, because of the large number of frame re-transmissions that will occur as a result.

6.5 X.25(84) Level 3 - The Network Level

X.25 level 2 provides a method for transferring higher level protocol information (in the I frames) between the two ends of a communications link guaranteeing correct, flow controlled transfer of the data. X.25 level 3 provides the data to be transmitted within the I frames. The unit of data at the network level is the 'packet'. Figure 6.6 shows an example of a network level packet fitted into a frame level I frame.

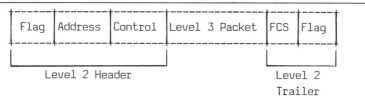

Figure 6.6 Network level in packet in link level frame

The network level protocol basically specifies the operation of 'virtual calls' over the link level protocol (virtual calls were described in Chapter Two). Each virtual call provided by the network level to the higher level protocols is a flow controlled link between the local DXE and a remote DXE across a network.

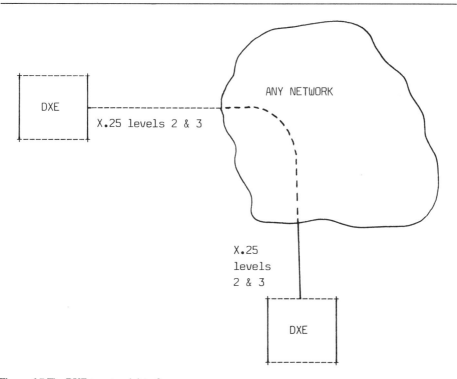

Figure 6.7 The DXE to network interface

X.25 level 3 is actually defined as a protocol between a DTE and a DCE directly

123

connected over a communications link. The DTE might be something like a PAD while the DCE might be an X.25 packet switch. There may be completely different types of networks being used to provide the link between the two DXEs. The important point, however, is that the network level interface between the DTE and DCE remains the same whatever networks are involved in the route between the local DXE and the remote DXE. This is shown in Figure 6.7

6.5.1 Network Level Packet Formats

Every network level packet has the same three byte header format. This is shown in Figure 6.8. The General Format Identifier (GFI) field is a four bit field used to indicate the general format of the rest of the header. The coding of the GFI field will be described once the packet types have been described.

The second field in the first byte of the packet is the Logical Channel Group Number (LCGN). This along with the second byte, the Logical Channel Number (LCN) forms a 12 bit number that is used to uniquely identify a particular virtual call. The third byte is the Packet Type Identifier (PTI) field which specifies the function of the packet.

```
+----------+------+------+----------------+
|GFI       | LCN  | PTI  | REMAINDER OF    |
|+ LCGN    |      |      | PACKET          |
+----------+------+------+----------------+
```

Figure 6.8 Network level packet format

6.5.2 Network Level Packet Types

Table 6.2 shows the network level packet types. Note that the same packet may be called a different thing depending on whether the DCE is sending it or the DTE is sending it. In either case the coding of the PTI field remains the same because, when it comes down to it, the packets are the same. Unlike the link level, however, the DCE is allowed to do some things that the DTE cannot so that the distinction is important.

Note that the call set up and clearing packets are only valid on Switched Virtual Calls (SVCs) while the others are valid on both SVCs and Permanent Virtual Circuits (PVCs). PVCs are like SVCs except that, as soon as the link level comes up, PVCs go straight into the information transfer phase, skipping the call set up. PVCs are rarely used, so we will not discuss them any further.

Call Set Up and Clearing Packets

The Incoming call/Call request packet is used to request that a virtual call be set up between the DXE transmitting the packet and the DXE receiving the packet.

124

Table 6.2 PTI Field Values

PACKET TYPE		BYTE 3
		-----bits------
FROM DCE TO DTE	FROM DTE TO DCE	8 7 6 5 4 3 2 1
Call set-up and clearing		
Incoming call	Call request	0 0 0 0 1 0 1 1
Call connected	Call accepted	0 0 0 0 1 1 1 1
Clear indication	Clear request	0 0 0 1 0 0 1 1
DCE clear confirmation	DTE clear confirmation	0 0 0 1 0 1 1 1
Data and interrupt		
DCE data	DTE data	X X X X X X X 0
DCE interrupt	DTE interrupt	0 0 1 0 0 0 1 1
DCE interrupt confirmation	DTE interrupt confirmation	0 0 1 0 0 1 1 1
Flow control and reset		
DCE RR (modulo 8)	DTE RR (modulo 8)	X X X 0 0 0 0 1
DCE RR (modulo 128)	DTE RR (modulo 128)	0 0 0 0 0 0 0 1
DCE RNR (modulo 8)	DTE RNR (modulo 8)	X X X 0 0 1 0 1
DCE RNR (modulo 128)	DTE RNR (modulo 128)	0 0 0 0 0 1 0 1
	DTE REJ (modulo 8)	X X X 0 1 0 0 1
	DTE REJ (modulo 128)	0 0 0 0 1 0 0 1
Reset indication	Reset request	0 0 0 1 1 0 1 1
DCE reset confirmation	DTE reset confirmation	0 0 0 1 1 1 1 1
Restart		
Restart indication	Restart request	1 1 1 1 1 0 1 1
DCE restart confirmation	DTE restart confirmation	1 1 1 1 1 1 1 1
Diagnostic		
Diagnostic		1 1 1 1 0 0 0 1
Registration		
	Registration request	1 1 1 1 0 0 1 1
Registration confirmation		1 1 1 1 0 1 1 1

The Call connected/Call accepted packet is used in response to a Call request/Incoming call packet to indicate that the connection attempt is acceptable and that the call is now active.

The Clear indication/Clear request packet is used either to reject a call set up request (i.e., in response to a Call request/Incoming call packet) or to terminate an active connection.

The Clear confirmation packet is used to confirm that a preceding Clear indication/Clear request packet was received.

Data and Interrupt Packets

The Data packet is used to convey higher level protocol data between the two DXEs connected by the virtual call.

The Interrupt packet is used to convey a small amount of data (up to 32 bytes) between the two DXEs with very high priority. The interrupt packet is able to 'overtake' data packets and are independent of the network level flow control.

The Interrupt confirmation packet is used to acknowledge the receipt of an Interrupt packet. There can only be one unacknowledged Interrupt packet at any one time.

Flow Control and Reset Packets

The RR and RNR packets are used to acknowledge the reception of data packets. The RR packet is used when the receiver is able to receive more data packets. The RNR packet is used when the receiver has temporarily become busy and cannot receive more data.

The REJ packet can be used by the DTE to request the retransmission of data packets. The REJ facility is not necessarily supported on all DCEs, as it is not actually required for correct operation of the protocol. The use of the REJ packet implies that a data packet correctly received by the link level has been 'lost' in some way by the DTE, maybe because it ran out of buffer space for the received packet.

The Reset indication/Reset request packet is used to return the virtual call to the state that it was in when the call was first set up. All data outstanding is thrown away, sequence numbers are set to zero and flow control conditions are cleared. The packet is usually used when a protocol error is detected or else in order to clear 'stuck' data on a call without actually having to clear the call.

The Reset confirmation packet is used to acknowledge the receipt of a Reset indication/Reset request packet and that the reset procedures have been carried out.

Restart Packets

The Restart indication/Restart request packet is used to clear all active virtual calls and return the entire network level to its initial state. This packet is the first packet sent by the network level when the link level goes into the information transfer phase.

The Restart confirmation packet is used to acknowledge the receipt of a Restart indication/Restart request packet and to indicate that the network level is now active.

Diagnostic and Registration Packets

The Diagnostic packet is sent by the DCE to the DTE when the DCE receives a packet which is seriously in error. For example, if a packet with an incorrect GFI field is received, the DCE may send a Diagnostic packet to the DTE containing an appropriate diagnostic code. Not all DCEs will generate Diagnostic packets.

The Registration request packet can be sent by the DTE to the DCE in order to request the availability or non-availability of certain facilities for a certain period of time. The facilities in question will be described later.

The Registration confirmation packet is sent by the DCE to the DTE in response to a Registration request packet from the DTE.

6.5.3 Network Level Sequence Numbers

In common with the link level, certain packet types carry with them sequence numbers. These numbers are used to ensure that data packets are conveyed without loss and in the correct order. There are two sequence numbers that may be carried, the P(S) sequence number and the P(R) sequence number.

The P(S) sequence number is carried only on Data packets and is used to identify the particular Data packet.

The P(R) sequence number is carried on the Data, RR, RNR and REJ packets. The P(R) fields in these packets convey the sequence number of the next Data packet which is expected by the sender to the receiver.

As with the link level, there is the normal sequence numbering scheme, which uses 3 bit fields and has sequence numbers from 0 to 7, and an extended sequence numbering scheme which uses 7 bit fields, and has sequence numbers from 0 to 127.

6.5.4 The General Format Identifier Field

Having gone through the various network level packet types, now is the time to go into the coding of the GFI field. Table 6.3 shows the values that the GFI field may take. The 'Q' bit, which may only appear on data packets, is used to separate the data packets into two different classes, normal data packets and 'qualified' data packets. The qualified data packets are often used to allow the transfer of higher level protocol control information without affecting the higher level protocol data, which is sent in normal data packets. An example of such a protocol is X.29, which is described in detail in Chapter Seven.

Table 6.3 GFI Field Values

GENERAL FORMAT IDENTIFIER		BYTE 1 --bits-- 8 7 6 5
CALL SET-UP PACKETS	Sequence numbering scheme modulo 8	0 D 0 1
	Sequence numbering scheme modulo 128	0 D 1 0
CLEARING, FLOW CONTROL, INTERRUPT, RESET, RESTART, REGISTRATION, AND DIAGNOSTIC PACKET	Sequence numbering scheme modulo 8	0 0 0 1
	Sequence numbering scheme modulo 128	0 0 1 0
DATA PACKETS	Sequence numbering scheme modulo 8	Q D 0 1
	Sequence numbering scheme modulo 128	Q D 1 0
GENERAL FORMAT IDENTIFIER EXTENSION		0 0 1 1
RESERVED FOR OTHER APPLICATIONS (* undefined)		* * 0 0

The 'D' bit is the delivery confirmation bit. This bit may appear on the call set up packets, but its function is actually relevant to the transfer of data packets.

Bits 5 and 6 of the GFI field are used to indicate which sequence numbering scheme is to be used. The extended sequence numbering scheme is one of the options known as a 'subscription option'. This means that the numbering scheme used must be decided when the X.25 link is set up. All virtual calls on the link must use the numbering scheme subscribed to. If the Registration facility is available, however, it may be possible to change the numbering scheme 'online' under certain conditions. In the vast majority of cases, the normal numbering scheme is used as very few implementations support the extended numbering scheme.

6.5.5 The Restart Phase

Once the link level is in the information transfer phase, the network level must be 'restarted'. A Restart indication/Restart request is sent by the DCE or DTE which is then confirmed by a Restart confirmation packet. Since it is common practice for a Restart indication/Restart request packet to be sent as soon as the link level comes up, a 'restart collision' often occurs. If, when a DXE is waiting for a Restart confirmation, it receives a Restart indication/Restart request, then a restart collision has occurred and the received packet is treated as though it was a Restart confirmation.

Figure 6.9 shows the format of the Restart indication/Restart request and Restart confirmation packets. Note that the LCGN and LCN fields are coded as all 0s. The complete logical channel number 000000000000 may not be available for use by a virtual call in all implementations and should be avoided wherever possible.

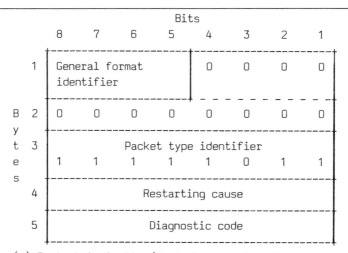

(a) Restart indication/Restart request packet

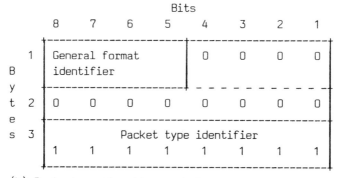

(b) Restart confirmation packet

Figure 6.9

Table 6.4 shows the various possible values for the restarting cause field in the Restart indication packet. When used in a Restart request packet, bit 8 must be set to 1 instead of 0. Incidentally, this is a considerable improvement over X.25(80) which said that this field in the Restart request packet must be coded all 0s. This often meant that, when using multiple X.25 links, the reason for the restart was lost. The diagnostic field can be used to provide more information about the reason for restarting.

Table 6.4 Coding of the restarting cause field in restart indication packets

	bits 8 7 6 5 4 3 2 1
Local procedure error	0 0 0 0 0 0 0 0
Network congestion	0 0 0 0 0 0 1 1
Network operational	0 0 0 0 0 1 1 1
Registration/cancellation confirmed	0 1 1 1 1 1 1 1

The only other packet relevant to this phase is the Diagnostic packet. Figure 6.10 shows the format of this packet. The diagnostic explanation field contains the first three bytes of header information in the packet causing the transmission of the Diagnostic packet. If there were less than three bytes, only what was received is included.

Bytes	Bits 8	7	6	5	4	3	2	1
1	General format identifier				0	0	0	0
2	0	0	0	0	0	0	0	0
3	Packet type identifier 1	1	1	1	0	0	0	1
4	Diagnostic code							
5	Diagnostic explanation							

Figure 6.10

6.5.6 Setting Up Virtual Calls

The Incoming call/Call request packet requests that a Switched Virtual Call be set up between two DXEs connected by the network. Figure 6.11 shows the format of this packet.

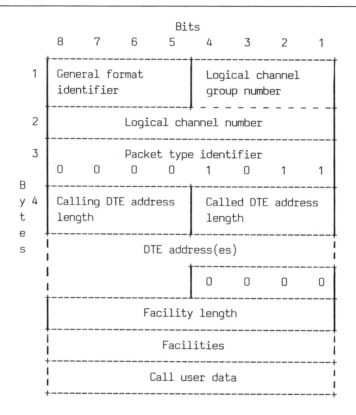

Figure 6.11 Incoming call/Call request packet

Note that bit 7 of the GFI is labelled 'D'. If this bit is set then the caller is requesting use of the 'D bit facility' (see the Information Transfer Phase subsection in this chapter for what this is). If it is clear, then the caller does not intend to use it.

The DXE sending the Incoming call/Call request packet must choose a Logical Group Channel Number (LCGN) and Logical Channel Number (LCN) to uniquely identify the particular call. Obviously, this should not be one that is already in use by an existing call. The PSS service splits the total channel number range into a number of separate groups. The different groups are identified by the LCGN field. The groups are:

LCGN	Type	Name	Use
0000	PVCs	PVC	Only available for Permanent
0001	PVCs	only	Virtual Circuits.
0010	SVCs	SVC Incoming	Only available for SVCs
0011	SVCs	only	from the DCE to the DTE.
0100	SVCs	SVC	Available for use by the DTE
0101	SVCs	Bothway	and the DCE.
0110	SVCs	SVC Outgoing	Only available for SVCs
0111	SVCs	only	from the DTE to the DCE.

It is usual for the DCE to allocate LCNs from the lowest channel number upwards while the DTE allocates LCNs from the highest channel downwards. A very common situation is for both DCE and DTE to be using the SVC Bothway range. For example, if only 16 logical channels are required, LCGN 4 may be used with LCNs from 0 to 15. The DCE will start allocating channel numbers from 0 upwards, while the DTE will start allocating channel numbers from 15 downwards.

There are two fields called the Called DTE address and the Calling DTE address. Each address may be up to 15 digits in length, each digit being 0 to 9. Usually, only a maximum of 14 digits are used. These 14 digits are divided into a 12 digit address, with the last two digits as a subaddress. The X.25 network usually routes on the basis of the first 12 digits; the last two digits are available to address a particular entity within the addressed DXE. Really, the fields should be called Called DXE address and Calling DXE address. The reason why DTE is used is that the specification takes the DTE as the devices connected to the network with the DCE being the interface to the network. The DCEs themselves are therefore never called. In real life, however, either DTEs or DCEs may be called.

The addresses are set into the packet using Binary Coded Decimal (BCD) format. This means that two digits are in each byte: the top four bits (8-5) for the first digit with the low four bits (4-1) for the second digit. The first address is the Called DTE address, which is the address of the device to which the caller wishes a virtual call set up. The second address is the Calling DTE address, which is the address of the device originating the packet. The specification allows the DTE not to include the Calling DTE address, although the DCE must always include it. Since most X.25 implementations can be either DCEs or DTEs, the Calling DTE address is almost always included.

A small problem occurs when the total number of digits in the Called and Calling DTE address fields is odd as only half of the last byte is used. The specification says that a 0 digit is added to fill out the last half byte.

Following the DTE addresses there is the Facility field preceded by the Facility length byte. The length is the total number of bytes in the facility field that follows (its length is variable). The maximum length of the facility field is 109 bytes. The facility field is used to encode extra information about the call and to request certain facilities for the duration of the call. These facilities are described later.

The final field of the packet is the Call User Data (CUD) field. The CUD field contains optional data that is transmitted unmodified between the Calling and Called DXEs. On normal Incoming call/Call request packets the CUD field can be a maximum of 16 bytes in length. If the 'fast select' facility is used, the field may be up to 128 bytes in length. The fast select facility is one of the facilities that may be requested in the facility field of the packet.

The CUD field may be used for many different purposes depending on the application. A common one is to provide extended addressing capability when part of the route includes non-X.25 networks.

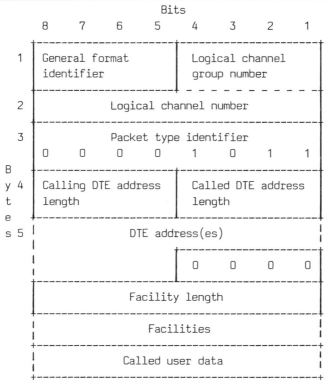

Figure 6.12 Call connected/Call accepted packet

If the call is acceptable to the receiver of an Incoming call/Call request packet, then a Call connected/Call accepted packet is sent in response. Figure 6.12 shows the format of the Call connected/Call accepted packet. Note that there are two forms of the Call connected/Call accepted packet. The normal format can consist of a minimum of three bytes and cannot include a Called User Data field. The 'extended format' format must be at least 5 bytes long (if no address or facilities are present, the address and facility lengths must still be present) and may include a Called User Data field if the Incoming call/Call request packet specified the use of the fast select facility.

Again, the GFI field has bit 7 labelled 'D'. If the caller has requested the facility and the called DXE is able to provide it, it should set this bit in the packet. If it cannot, then the bit should be cleared.

The alternative response to an Incoming call/Call request packet is the Clear indication/Clear request packet. Figure 6.13 shows the format of this packet. Again, there are two variations as for the Call connected/Call accepted packet. The rules for use of the address, facility and Clear User Data follow from those for the Call connected/Call accepted packet.

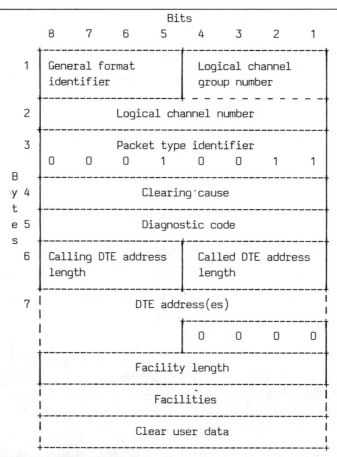

Figure 6.13 Clear indication/Clear request packet

The Clearing cause field is used to indicate the reason why the call is being cleared. Table 6.5 shows the possible values for the Clearing cause field (the Authors' favourite is definitely 'Ship absent'). Note that the DTE can set this field as long as bit 8 is set. As for the restarting cause field, this is one of the important new features of X.25(84) (at X.25(80), the DTE had to code this field all 0s). The diagnostic code can be used to supply more information about the cause.

134

Table 6.5 Clearing Cause Field Values

	bits 8 7 6 5 4 3 2 1
DTE originated DTE originated	0 0 0 0 0 0 0 0 1 X X X X X X X
Number busy	0 0 0 0 0 0 0 1
Out of order	0 0 0 0 1 0 0 1
Remote procedure error	0 0 0 1 0 0 0 1
Reverse charging acceptance not subscribed	0 0 0 1 1 0 0 1
Incompatible destination	0 0 1 0 0 0 0 1
Fast select acceptance not subscribed	0 0 1 0 1 0 0 1
Ship absent	0 0 1 1 1 0 0 1
Invalid facility request	0 0 0 0 0 0 1 1
Access barred	0 0 0 0 1 0 1 1
Local procedure error	0 0 0 1 0 0 1 1
Network congestion	0 0 0 0 0 1 0 1
Not obtainable	0 0 0 0 1 1 0 1
RPOA out of order	0 0 0 1 0 1 0 1

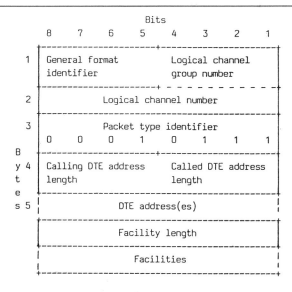

Figure 6.14 Clear confirmation packet

135

The Clear confirmation packet is used to acknowledge receipt of a Clear indication/Clear request packet. Its format is shown in Figure 6.14. Yet again, there are two variations of the packet. This time, the normal format is almost always used. The extended format packet can only be sent by a DCE to a DTE and is only used in conjunction with the 'charging information' facility, another of the optional facilities.

Figure 6.15 shows two possible scenarios for call set up attempts. In (a), the call set up attempt is accepted, data flows and the call is then cleared. In (b), the call set up attempt is rejected.

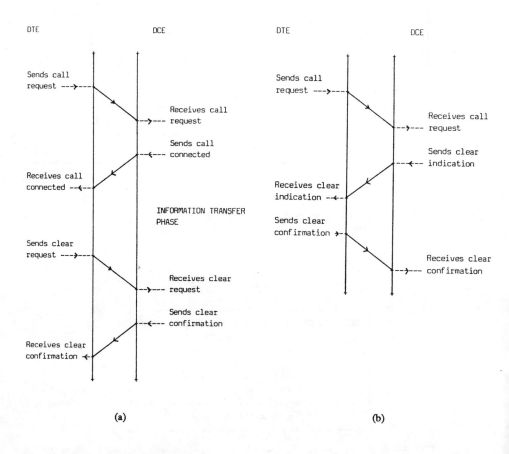

(a)   (b)

Figure 6.15 Call set up followed by clear down

6.5.7 The Information Transfer Phase

A virtual call will spend most of its time in the data transfer phase. Data packets are exchanged between the DXEs at each end of the call.

Figure 6.16 shows the format of the Data packet. Note that, yet again, there are two possible formats. This time, however, this is caused by the normal and extended sequence numbering.

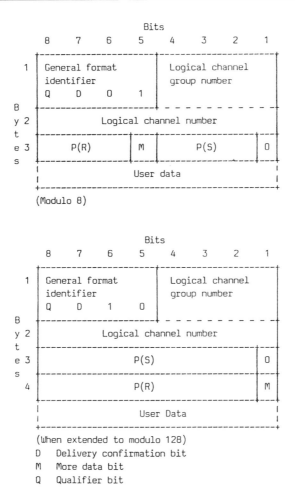

Figure 6.16 Data packet

The 'M' bit is the 'More Data' mark. This is used to provide an ability to send 'data messages', which are longer than a single network level packet. The message is split

137

into network level packets, with all but the final packet having the M bit set. The last packet without the M bit set denotes the end of the sequence.

When a DXE receives a Data packet, it must send an acknowledgement back to the other end of the call. There are two possible packets, the RR or the RNR. Figure 6.17 shows the format of the these packets. The RR is sent when the DXE is able to receive more Data packets. The RNR is sent when the DXE is not able to receive more packets, usually because it has run out of resources.

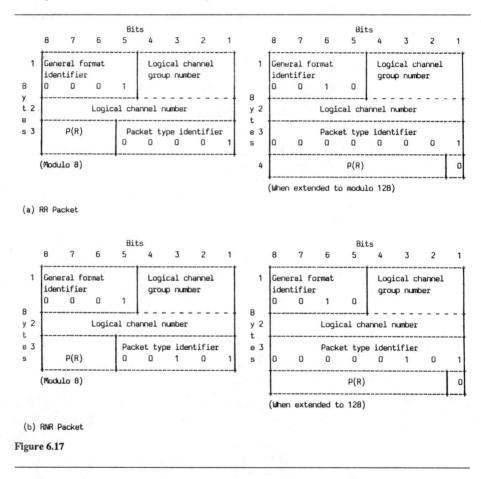

(a) RR Packet

(b) RNR Packet

Figure 6.17

As was mentioned earlier, a DTE may send a REJ packet to the DCE to request re-transmission of Data packets. Its format is shown in Figure 6.18.

The D bit present on the Data packet can be used to ensure that the DXE at the remote end of a call has actually received the Data packet. Why is this necessary? The problem is that, although the DXE sending the Data packet may see an RR or RNR acknowledging the packet, it does not know precisely where this has come from. If the

138

D bit is set, requesting use of the 'delivery confirmation' facility, then the network should not send an acknowledgement until the remote DXE has received the Data packet and acknowledged it.

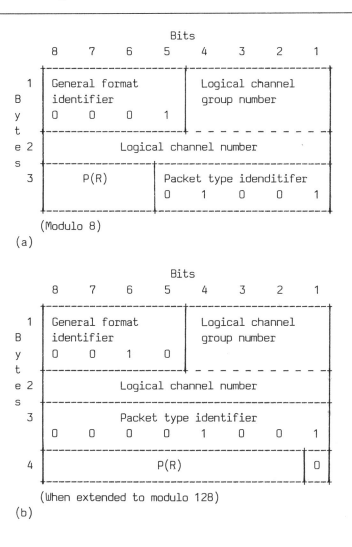

Figure 6.18 REJ Packet

Figure 6.19 shows the format of the Interrupt and Interrupt confirmation packets.

The last packets relevant to the Information Transfer Phase are the Reset indication/Reset request and Reset confirmation packets. Figure 6.20 shows the format of this packet. Table 6.6 shows the possible codings of the resetting cause field. Again, the DTE can set the field as long as bit 8 is set. The diagnostic codes provide more information about the cause of the reset.

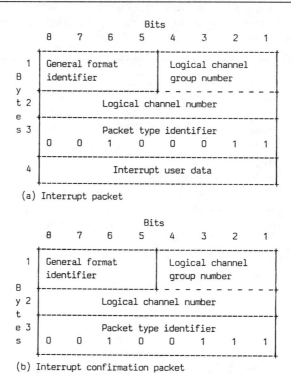

(a) Interrupt packet

(b) Interrupt confirmation packet

Figure 6.19

Table 6.6 Resetting cause field values

	bits 8 7 6 5 4 3 2 1
DTE originated	0 0 0 0 0 0 0 0
DTE originated	1 X X X X X X X
Out of order	0 0 0 0 0 0 0 1
Remote procedure error	0 0 0 0 0 0 1 1
Local procedure error	0 0 0 0 0 1 0 1
Network congestion	0 0 0 0 0 1 1 1
Remote DTE operational	0 0 0 0 1 0 0 1
Network operational	0 0 0 0 1 1 1 1
Incompatible destination	0 0 0 1 0 0 0 1
Network out of order	0 0 0 1 1 1 0 1

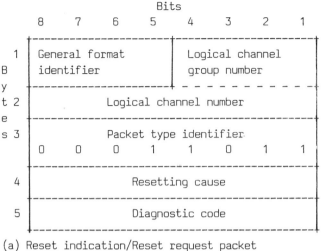

(a) Reset indication/Reset request packet

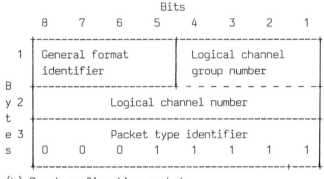

(b) Reset confirmation packet

Figure 6.20

The format of the Registration request and the Registration confirmation packets is shown in Figure 6.21. The details of the online registration process will not be described in this book (check the CCITT specification for the full details).

6.5.8 The Facility Field

Several of the network level packets have a 'facility field' included in them. The facility field allows the calling DXE to request that certain facilities be available for the duration of the call.

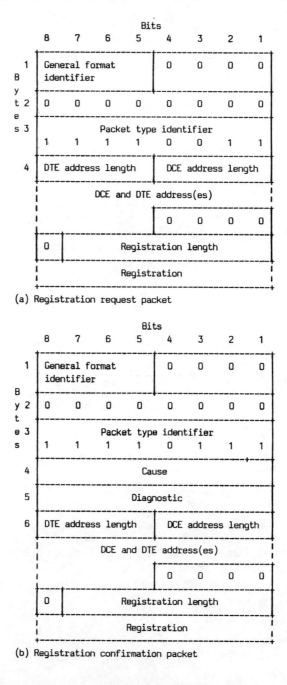

(a) Registration request packet

(b) Registration confirmation packet

Figure 6.21 Registration request and registration confirmation packets

The facility field is made up of one or more 'facility elements'. There are four basic forms of these facility elements (these are shown in Figure 6.22). Bits 7 and 8 of the first byte of the facility element encode the element type. There are, in fact, quite a large number of facility element codes. The ones chosen here are those of most interest in supporting the OSI network service.

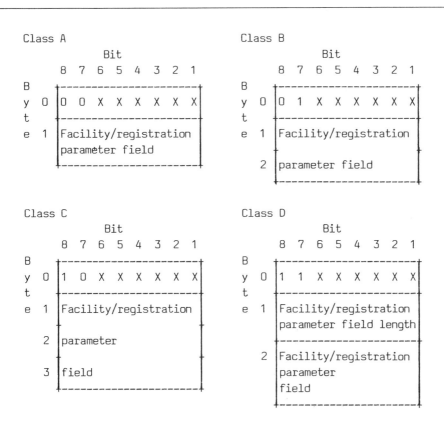

Figure 6.22 Facility elements types

The first byte, which identifies the element type, is followed by one or more bytes that constitute the 'facility parameter field'.

Called Address Extension

This facility was added specifically to support the OSI NSAP (Network Service Access Point) address which requires more space than the Called DTE address field. The first byte after the facility code field is the length of the parameter field in bytes. It is one greater than the number of bytes required to hold the address extension. The first octet of the parameter field is split into two fields. Bits 1 to 6 indicate the number of digits in the address extension (each digit requires 4 bits). Bits 7 and 8 encode the use of the address extension as follows:

Bit 8	Bit 7	Use of Called Address Extension
0	0	To carry an entire called OSI NSAP address.
0	1	To carry a partial called OSI NSAP address.
1	0	To carry a non-OSI called address extension.
1	1	Reserved

The maximum number of digits allowed is between 32 and 40 depending on what is regarded as the maximum legal length of the OSI NSAP address (CCITT and ISO disagree)! The digits of the address extension are packed into the parameter field in the same way as the DTE addresses.

Calling Address Extension

This is exactly the same in structure as the previous facility except that all the 'called' words must be changed to 'calling'.

Reverse Charging and Fast Select

This facility has a one byte parameter field. The various bits in the parameter field request the use of certain facilities. The bits are defined as follows:

Bit number	Facility requested if set
1	Reverse charging. If the network in use charges for use (e.g. PSS), then reverse charging requests that the charges be assigned to the called DXE rather than the calling DXE.
7	Restricted response. The only response if this bit is set is to clear the call.
8	Fast Select. This specifies that the extended Call User Data field and Clear user Data field are available for use.

All of the other bits in the byte should be set to 0 as they may be assigned to new facilities in a future version of the protocol.

Packet Size Negotiation

The first byte of the parameter field is the maximum size for Data packets from the called DXE while the second byte is the maximum size for Data packets from the calling DXE. The possible values for this field are:

00000100	=	16 bytes
00000101	=	32 bytes
00000110	=	64 bytes
00000111	=	128 bytes
00001000	=	256 bytes
00001001	=	512 bytes
00001010	=	1024 bytes
00001011	=	2048 bytes
00001100	=	4096 bytes

If a connect includes this parameter in its facility field, then the calling DXE is requesting the use of the maximum packet sizes indicated. The called DXE has the opportunity to negotiate the values by returning this facility element on the Call connected/Call accepted packet (if the call is to be accepted). If it can support the values requested, then it can return the same values. If it cannot, then it can negotiate the values down to a size that it can manage. Note that it cannot increase the values except in one special case.

All implementations must be able to support a packet size of 128 bytes; many can only support this size. If a request is made for a maximum packet size of less than 128 bytes, the called DXE is allowed to respond with the value for 128 bytes. If the Call connected/Call accepted packet does not contain a response to an attempt at packet size negotiation, this implies that the called DXE can support the packet sizes requested. Although this facility allows different packet sizes to be negotiated in each direction, normally the two sizes are the same.

Window Size Negotiation

This parameter is very similar to the previous one. The first byte of the parameter field is the window size for Data packets from the called DXE. The second byte is the window size for Data packets from the calling DXE.

Where the normal sequence numbering scheme is used, this window size may be from 1 to 7. Where the extended sequence numbering scheme is used, the window size may range from 1 to 127.

The negotiation system for this parameter is much the same as for packet size. Again, the called DXE can only negotiate to the same value or less except where a window size of 1 is requested. All implementations must support a window size of 2 but not necessarily 1. The protocol allows the called DXE to return a value of 2 in response to a request for a value of 1 if it cannot support this window size.

Minimum Throughput Class Negotiation

This allows the calling DXE to request a certain level of throughput for the call. The parameter field is a single byte encoding the (potentially different) throughput class for each direction.

End to End Transit Delay

This allows the DXEs to establish the end to end packet delay likely on the call. The first byte of the parameter field indicates the number of bytes following: this can be 2, 4 or 6. An Incoming call/Call request packet can contain all 6 bytes while a Call connected/Call accepted packet can only contain 2 bytes.

The first two bytes are the cumulative delay between the two DXEs. The next two bytes contain the requested transit delay. The final two bytes contain the maximum acceptable end-to-end transit delay. All values are expressed in milliseconds.

Expedited Data Negotiation

This facility can be used to determine whether the expedited data facility is available; expedited data is carried in Interrupt packets, so this determines whether Interrupt packets can be used.

The parameter field could not be simpler. Bit 1 is 0 if the facility is not available or bit 1 is 1 if the facility is available. The other bits 'may be assigned to other facilities in the future' as the specification says. At the moment, they should be coded all 0s.

6.6 X.25 Level 3 - Some Practical Hints

As with X.25 level 2, if a DTE and DCE are going to talk to each other they must be configured correctly. It is fairly unusual to be able to plug an X.25 PAD into an X.25 switch port and have it work first time!

The main culprit, once it is established that one device is a DCE and the other device is a DTE (remember that in most cases devices can be either and need to be set to one or the other), are the LCGN and LCN values. Many devices define a range of 'assigned logical channels'. An Incoming call/Call request packet with a channel number outside of this range may well fall down a black hole with no indication as to why.

Ideally, the channel ranges to be used by the DTE and DCE should be the same. The DCE will then start allocating channels from the low end of this range with the DTE allocating channels from the high end of this range. A good rule of thumb is to start at LCGN 4 and LCN 0. The end of the range will depend on the maximum number of logical channels that will be required. Suppose that a maximum of 32 logical channels are required. The high end of the range would then be LCGN 4 LCN 31.

Another thing to establish is whether the fast select facility is supported by both devices. If one is generating fast select Incoming call/Call request packets and the other does not support the facility, all attempts to set up calls will be rejected.

6.7 X.75

X.75 is a version of X.25, which has been modified to provide an interexchange signalling system for international packet switched networks. Rather than have DTEs and DCEs, X.75 has STEs. STE stands for Signalling TErminal. The STEs at each end of a link are identical in status. For the purpose of identification, the recommendation calls one STE-X and the other STE-Y.

6.7.1 The X.75 Physical Level

The X.75 physical level interface specified is G.703 for 64k bits per second links. It is a bit vague about other speeds except to say that it is up to networks to agree if they are using interfaces other than G.703. The G.703 interface is described in Chapter Ten.

6.7.2 The X.75 Link Level

The X.75 link level is similar to X.25 level 2. There is a single link form (SLP) and a multilink form (MLP).

6.7.3 The X.75 Network Level

As with the link level, the network level bears a lot of similarity with X.25 level 3. The packet formats are much the same as in X.25 level 3. The main difference in operation is that any DTE/DCE asymmetry in X.25 is eliminated in X.75. This is illustrated by the fact that there is only a Call request packet rather than a Call request packet and an Incoming call packet. The same is true of the other packets; there is only one type of each.

In addition to the facilities field on Call request, Call connected and Clear request packets, there is an extra field for network utilities. This is used for signalling by the network authorities rather than the DTEs involved in the call.

7

Higher Level Protocols

7.1 Introduction

In this section of the book we are going to look at some higher level protocols. By higher level protocols we mean the protocols often to be found running on packet switched networks. The idea is not so much to give a very detailed account but instead to give sufficient information to create an impression of what the protocol is all about. Additionally, most protocols have their own jargon without which it is difficult to talk sensibly about the protocol. So expect lots of jargon to be introduced! The first higher level protocol to be described is the 'Triple X' or 'XXX' protocol. This is a protocol that defines the operation of Packet Assemblers/Disassemblers. It defines the presentation functions that should be provided by PADs and also the mechanism by which remote host computers can control the operation of a PAD port.

The second higher level protocol is rather different. It is the 'Yellow Book' protocol, a Transport Service layer protocol. Yellow Book is used extensively in the academic community as a vehicle for several other higher level protocols.

The third protocol is an example of a protocol that uses the Yellow Book protocol to provide a uniform network interface. This protocol is the 'Blue Book' Network Independent File Transfer Protocol, also known as NIFTP.

Moving on to OSI protocols, the next protocol to be looked at is FTAM, the File Transfer, Access and Management protocol.

Finally, we take a look at X.400 (this is the OSI electronic mail protocol). This is likely to be very important in the future, as it may become the standard method of transferring information across networks.

7.2 The Triple X Protocol

First of all, where does the rather bizarre name of 'Triple X' come from? Rather than coming from some sort of Australian lager, it is actually short for the 'X.3/X.28/X.29' protocol. These are three CCITT specified recommendations that together form a fairly complete specification for the operation of PADs.

7.2.1 The X.3 Recommendation

The X.3 recommendation specifies a set of parameters defining the operation of a PAD port. There are actually 22 parameters in total. It is worth going into these in some detail as they are always cropping up when using PADs in real life.

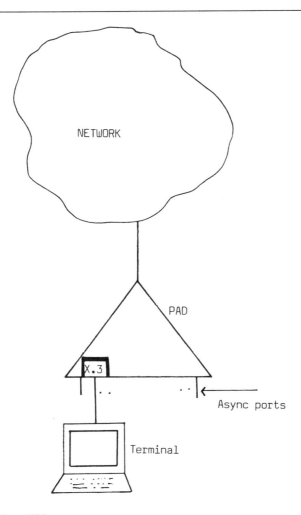

Figure 7.1 User's view of X.3

Figure 7.1 shows the point of view from which we shall be looking at the X.3 parameters. A terminal is shown connected to one port of a PAD which is in turn connected to a packet switched network. The terminal could of course be a personal computer or some other computer.

There are two basic states in which a PAD port can be. The first is the 'command' state. In this state, the terminal talks to the PAD itself. From this state, it can manage call set up and clear down, reconfigure the port's X.3 parameters, etc. In 'data transfer' state, the terminal is talking to the device at the other end of an active call. When a call is set up, the port goes into data transfer state. When the call is cleared, the port goes back into command state. It is usually possible to go from data transfer state back to command state to change a port parameter and then return to data transfer state without affecting the state of the active call.

The control character DLE (generated by <CTRL+P>) has a special meaning for PAD ports. It is often part of a two character sequence which causes something special to happen in the data transfer state. For example, DLE followed by E in the data transfer state often causes the echo state to be toggled for one line.

Having given the necessary background, we can now go on to describe the X.3 parameter set. Note that all numbers given in this section are decimal.

Parameter 1 - Data transfer escape

Parameter 1 defines whether or not it is possible to go from data transfer state to command state by typing the appropriate character (or characters) without clearing the call first. Possible values for this parameter are:

0	:	No escape
1	:	DLE causes escape
32-126	:	Character defined by value causes escape.

If this parameter is set to 1, the PAD port may well actually require a two character sequence to escape to command state. Usually, this will be <CTRL+P>A (i.e., DLE followed by 'A'). This is done, so that the PAD command state prompt (typically, 'PAD>') does not appear as soon as the DLE is entered.

Parameter 2 - Echo state

This parameter determines whether or not the PAD port will echo characters sent to the PAD port.

Possible values are:

0	:	Characters are not echoed
1	:	Characters are echoed

Parameter 3 - Data forwarding characters

This parameter defines when characters from the terminal are forwarded on the active call. The PAD will normally buffer characters from the terminal within the PAD until something happens to forward the buffered characters. This parameter controls which characters cause forwarding.

Possible values are:

0	:	No characters cause forwarding
1	:	Alphanumeric characters (A-Z, a-z, 0-9
2	:	CR (carriage return)
4	:	ESC, BEL, ENQ and ACK characters
8	:	DEL, CAN and DC2 characters
16	:	ETX and EOT characters
32	:	HT, LF, VT, and FF characters
64	:	All other control characters (i.e., with ASCII values between 0 and 31) not included above

The various numbers can be added together to provide combinations of forwarding conditions. For example, a value of 50 will cause forwarding on CR, ETX, EOT, HT, LF, VT and FF characters.

Parameter 4 - Forwarding timer value

This parameter controls one of the other conditions for forwarding buffered data, on expiry of an idle timer. If there are buffered characters and then no character is received by the PAD port for a certain amount of time, the buffered characters are forwarded automatically. This is very important for character-based interaction. A typical use of this is when using a screen editor from a PAD port. It is essential for characters to reach the editor from the terminal as soon as possible so that the network is as invisible as possible. Network-induced delays are very noticeable when using screen editors.

If the value of this parameter is 0, forwarding will not occur because of the idle timer. If the value is between 1 and 255, then buffered characters may be forwarded on expiry of the timer. The value is in units of 50 milli-seconds, so a value of 20 means that characters will be forwarded if no character is received within 1 second.

Parameter 5 - Flow control by PAD

This parameter, opaquely described as 'Ancillary device control' in the CCITT recommendation, controls whether or not the PAD port will try to flow control the terminal. This becomes relevant when the terminal is sending characters to the PAD port, but the PAD port is running out of capacity to handle the data. If enabled by this parameter, the PAD port will try to stop the characters coming from the terminal. If using software flow control, it will send an XOFF character to the terminal. If using hardware flow control, it will drop the CTS line to the terminal.

Possible values of this parameter are:

> 0 : No flow control will be used
> 1 : Flow control will be used when
>   in data transfer state only
> 2 : Flow control will be used in
>   both data transfer state and
>   command state

It is *definitely* a good idea to have flow control enabled at all times. Although not so important for terminals connected to PADs, if a computer is connected to a PAD port, it is almost certainly essential. If the computer is transferring data at high speed into the PAD port and the port cannot handle the data rate, the only way to avoid loss of data is to use flow control.

Parameter 6 - Suppression of PAD service signals

This parameter controls whether or not PAD service signals will be sent to the terminal. These service signals are the message that tell the user what is happening to the PAD port. This includes things like whether a call set up attempt has been successful, etc.

If the value of this parameter is 0, service signals are suppressed. If the value is 1, service signals will be sent to the terminal. This parameter is normally set to 1.

Parameter 7 - Action on break

A break is what you get when you press the key marked 'break' on the keyboard of a terminal. Essentially, a break is a badly formed character that can be interpreted as a special condition. This parameter determines what happens when a break is received at the PAD port when in the data transfer state.

Possible values for this parameter are:

> 0 : Nothing happens at all
> 1 : An X.25 level 3 Interrupt packet
>   is sent on the call
> 2 : A X.25 level 3 Reset packet
>   is sent on the call
> 5 : Send an Interrupt packet
>   followed by an X.29 Indication
>   of Break message (more on this later)
> 8 : Escape from data transfer state
> 21 : Same as 5 but also discard characters
>   received from the call (i.e., those that
>   would normally be sent to the terminal)

This parameter often has the value 5. If the terminal is calling a Triple X host computer, typing break on the terminal will often result in the host computer aborting what it is doing at the time. In this case, the break key is acting as an abort key. To get a more rapid response, if a lot of data is being sent to the terminal, a value of 21 can be used. This is faster, because the data en-route to the terminal is discarded very rapidly.

Parameter 8 - Discard output

This parameter controls whether data received from an active call is sent to the terminal when in data transfer state. If the parameter is set to 1, the data is discarded. This is actually how parameter 7 value 21 works: when a break is received from the terminal, parameter 8 is set to 1 to discard the data received from the call. If parameter 8 is set to 0, data is sent to the terminal normally.

Normally, parameter 8 is only set to 1 as an action after receipt of a break from the terminal. It is set back to 0 when the host sends an X.29 set or set and read message (all will be revealed later) indicating that parameter 8 should be set to 0. If a Reset is sent or received, then that will also set parameter 8 to 0.

Parameter 9 - Padding after carriage return

This parameter controls how many padding characters will be added when a carriage return is sent to the terminal. The value of this parameter can be from 0 to 255. This parameter will normally be 0 as most modern devices do not need any padding characters. Only some of the slow, old printing terminals may need this. The padding character is a NUL.

Parameter 10 - Line folding

This parameter controls whether data received from the call and sent to the terminal will be formed into lines of a specified maximum length. If the parameter is set to 0, no line folding will take place. If the value is non-zero, line folding will take place at the appropriate column.

As an example, suppose that parameter 10 is set to 80 and a line of characters is received that is 130 characters in length. The first 80 characters will be displayed normally. Then a carriage return and line feed will be sent to the terminal (plus padding if required) followed by the remainder of the characters.

Parameter 11 - Port speed

This is somewhat ingeniously described as 'binary speed' in the CCITT recommendation. It actually refers to the speed in bits per second at which the port is operating.

The parameter can have the following values:

0	:	110 bits per second
1	:	134.5 bits per second
2	:	300 bits per second
3	:	1200 bits per second
4	:	600 bits per second
5	:	75 bits per second
6	:	150 bits per second
7	:	1800 bits per second
8	:	200 bits per second
9	:	100 bits per second
10	:	50 bits per second
11	:	75/1200 bits per second
12	:	2400 bits per second
13	:	4800 bits per second
14	:	9600 bits per second
15	:	19200 bits per second
16	:	48000 bits per second
17	:	56000 bits per second
18	:	64000 bits per second

As you can see, the numbering of the various speeds is stunningly illogical. The '75/1200' entry means that the port transmits data at 1200 bits per second and receives it at 75 bits per second (Prestel modem style).

Incidentally, the CCITT recommendation happily notes that the 'higher' speeds were only included to avoid revision of the standard in the future. This is rather incredible, since they have left out 38400 bits per second, which will become more and more common as PADs get faster. (Oh well!)

Parameter 12 - Flow control of the PAD

The setting of this parameter determines whether or not the PAD port will allow the terminal to flow control characters being transmitted by the PAD port.

If this parameter has the value 0, the terminal cannot flow control the data from the PAD port. If the value is 1, it can. This parameter should normally be set to 1 to avoid loss of data from the PAD. This is even true for ordinary terminals connected to PAD ports running at speeds of 9600 bits per second or above. Although almost all terminals can be set to run at these speeds, they cannot all display at this rate and will start losing data after a little while unless flow control is enabled on the PAD port and the terminal.

Parameter 13 - Line feed insertion after carriage return

There are various options available for what to do when a carriage return is sent to the

terminal in data transfer state and when a carriage return is received from the terminal in data transfer state.
Possible values are:

0	:	No line feed insertion
1	:	Insert line feed after carriage return sent to terminal
2	:	Insert line feed after carriage return received from the terminal and sent on the call
4	:	Insert a line feed when a carriage return is echoed to the terminal

Combinations of these values may be used. Usual combination values are 5, 6 and 7.

Parameter 14 - Line feed padding

This is somewhat analogous to parameter 9 except that the padding in this case is added after a line feed is sent to the terminal. The value may be between 0 and 255. The padding character is a NUL.

As with parameter 9, this is only normally required for old, slow, printing terminals.

Parameter 15 - Editing

The value of this parameter determines whether buffered characters may be edited while still in the PAD. Obviously, this cannot be used if parameter 4 is non-zero, because you cannot guarantee that the characters being edited are still in the PAD!

If this parameter has the value 0, editing is off and characters are processed normally. If the value is 1, the characters defined by parameters 16, 17 and 18 perform the appropriate editing functions.

It is usual for editing to be on if forwarding on idle timer expiry is not required, as it is easy for typing errors to be corrected before a line is sent on the call. Since the editing is performed in the PAD itself, no network delays are introduced.

Parameter 16 - Character delete character

The value of this parameter determines which character will cause the last character in the buffered data to be deleted. This is normally DEL (sometimes called RUBOUT). The value of this parameter can take values from 0 to 127.

Parameter 17 - Buffer delete character

The value of this parameter determines which character will cause all of the buffered characters to be deleted. This is normally 24 - CAN (generated by <CTRL+X>). The parameter may take values from 0 to 127.

Parameter 18 - Buffer redisplay character

The value of this parameter determines which character will cause the buffered characters to be redisplayed. This is normally 18 - DC2 (generated by <CTRL+R>). The parameter may take values from 0 to 127.

Parameter 19 - Editing PAD service signals

This parameter defines what happens when buffered characters are edited using the character delete and buffer delete functions. The different types are provided to cope with both VDU type terminals and printing terminals.

Possible values are:

0	:	No editing PAD service signals
1	:	Printing terminal
2	:	VDU type terminals
8	:	Send a backspace
32-126	:	Send character defined by value

This is fairly meaningless without further explanation. The further explanation is to be found buried in the X.28 recommendation. Put simply, if value 0 is set for this parameter, nothing is sent to the terminal when the editing functions are used.

If the value is 1, printing terminal style responses will be sent to the terminal. When a character is deleted, a '\' character is sent to the terminal. When the buffered line of characters is deleted, the string 'XXX' is sent to the terminal followed by a carriage return and line feed.

If the value is 2, VDU type terminal responses will be sent to the terminal. When a buffered character is deleted, a 'backspace space backspace' sequence will be sent. This effectively rubs out the deleted character from the screen. When a buffered line of characters is deleted, enough 'backspace space backspace' sequences are sent to rub out the entire line.

If the value is 8 or between 32 and 126, the response to deleting a buffered character is to send the character defined by the value of the parameter. For example, if the value is 8, a backspace is sent. If the buffered line is deleted, the response is as for value 1.

Note that, if parameter 6 is set to 0, then no responses are made to the editing functions.

Parameter 20 - Echo mask

This parameter allows some control over which characters are echoed if parameter 2 is set to 1 (i.e., echoing on). This can be useful to avoid intelligent terminals being too intelligent and trapping echoed characters from the user as commands to the terminal.

Possible values are:

0	:	No mask (all characters echoed)
1	:	No echo of carriage returns
2	:	No echo of line feeds
4	:	No echo of characters VT, HT, FF
8	:	No echo of characters BEL, BS
16	:	No echo of characters ESC, ENQ
32	:	No echo of characters ACK, NAK, STX, SOH, EOT, ETB, ETX
64	:	No echo of editing characters as designated by parameters 16, 17 and 18
128	:	No echo of all other characters with values between 0 and 31 not mentioned above plus the character DEL

As usual with these sort of parameters, various values can be added together to give a combined function. For example, a value of 24 means that ESC, ENQ, BEL and BS are not echoed.

Parameter 21 - Parity treatment

This parameter defines whether or not parity checking or generation is to be used.

Possible values are as follows:

0	:	No parity checking or generation
1	:	Parity checking on
2	:	Parity generation on
3	:	Parity checking and generation on

In practice, having parity checking on is a bit of a nuisance as the PAD cannot do anything useful except to send a BEL to the user or something like that. Parity generation may be useful if the terminal demands a particular type of parity. If possible, it is best to leave parity turned off wherever possible as it will only cause trouble.

Parameter 22 - Page wait

This parameter defines how many line feeds will be sent to the terminal before stopping on a page wait condition (i.e., it defines the depth of a page). Paging by the

PAD can be useful when continuous data is being sent to the terminal and the user actually wishes to read it! The condition is cleared when a character is sent by the terminal to the PAD. X.28 suggests that this is an XON character! Since XON is the character most likely to be trapped elsewhere in the communications path, it is also probably the worst character to choose.

If the page wait feature is not required, this parameter is set to 0. If paging is required, the parameter can have values between 1 and 255.

7.2.2 The X.28 Recommendation

The X.28 recommendation describes precisely how these 22 parameters translate into the user interface.

Unfortunately, the interface defined by X.28 belongs in the steam age - very few users of personal computers would find a strict X.28 PAD even vaguely acceptable. If you don't believe it, try using a PSS dial-up PAD port; it is very educational. What most PAD designers do instead is to incorporate the ideas expressed in X.28 into a more acceptable form of user interface. For this reason, there is no point going into detail about X.28.

7.2.3 The X.29 Recommendation

X.29 is the last of the 'XXX' recommendations. It defines how the X.25 is to be used for Triple X calls, mainly defining how the remote host can modify the X.3 parameters of a PAD port. To give a classic example of why this is useful, take the case of a call from a PAD port to a Triple X host computer. In most cases, once the user has called the host computer and the call is accepted, the user must log in to the computer system. To do this, a password will have to be entered. As passwords are supposed to be secret, it would be a bad move if the PAD decided to echo the password back to the terminal. To prevent this happening, the host can send an X.29 'set parameter' message to the PAD port to indicate that parameter 2 should be set to 0. This prevents echoing. Once the password has been sent to the computer, it sends another X.29 set parameter message to set parameter 2 back to 1.

The X.29 Protocol Identifier Field

X.29 says that the first 4 bytes of the Call User Data (CUD) field of a Triple X call packet should contain the X.29 Protocol Identifier Field (PIF). The first byte contains the bit pattern 00000001 indicating that the call is a standard CCITT Triple X call. The other three bytes are defined to contain all zeros. Sometimes, however, these last three bytes are used to contain extra information about the configuration of the PAD port. This is the case with PSS. This is non-standard and generally the last three bytes are not interpreted in any way.

As the PIF takes out 4 bytes of the CUD field, there are only 12 bytes left on a normal call packet and 124 bytes on a fast select call packet for extra addressing information.

X.29 PAD Messages

PAD messages are special data packets that can be transferred between the two ends of a Triple X call, which perform functions like parameter setting on a remote PAD port. Normal end to end data packets have the Q bit in the GFI field of the X.25 level 3 data packet clear. PAD messages, on the other hand, have the Q bit set to 1. This allows the PAD to distinguish one from another very easily.

The first byte of a PAD message is the message type code. Possible values for these are given below:

Message code	Type
00000000	Parameter indication
00000001	Invitation to clear
00000010	Set parameters
00000011	Indication of break
00000100	Read parameters
00000101	Error message
00000110	Set and read parameters
00000111	Reselection

The functions of these messages will now be described.

Parameter Indication

This message is sent in response to a read parameters or set and read parameters message. After the first byte of the packet (the Parameter Indication message code), there can be a sequence of 'parameter fields'. The first byte of each parameter field is the parameter reference. This determines to which of the X.3 parameters the parameter field refers. The second byte of the parameter field contains the current value of the parameter for the specific PAD port. If the Parameter Indication message is in response to a Set and Read message, then bit 8 of the parameter reference will be set if the PAD could not accept the attempt to set the parameter for some reason.

If bit 8 of the parameter reference is set, the parameter value field is used to encode the reason for the problem. Possible values are:

Parameter value field	Error Type
00000000	No additional information
00000001	The parameter reference does not exist or has not been implemented in the PAD
00000010	The parameter value is invalid or has not been implemented in the PAD
00000011	The parameter value cannot be altered from the current setting
00000100	The parameter is read only
00000101	The parameter follows an invalid parameter separator

In the last case, the 'parameter separator' is a parameter field with the parameter reference set to 0 and the parameter value set to 0. This is used to allow non-standard parameter references to be included.

Invitation to Clear

The Invitation to Clear message is used to request that the PAD port clear the call. This is most often used when a user calling a remote host computer from a PAD port logs off from the host computer. If the host computer just cleared the call straight away, any information in transit (log off information in this case) may well be 'overtaken' by the clear and lost. To ensure that this does not happen, the host computer can send out an Invitation to Clear PAD message after the log off information. The PAD port will see the Invitation to Clear only after all of the data has been received. The PAD port responds to the Invitation to Clear by clearing the call.

Another possible use for this PAD message is for information services. Usually, an information service, when called, may give a page of information and then terminate the call. Again, the computer providing the information service should use the Invitation to Clear PAD message instead of just clearing the call.

Set Parameters

This message can be sent to PAD port to set some or all of its X.3 parameters to specified values. The coding of the parameter fields is identical to the Parameter Indication message.

If no parameter fields are present, the X.3 parameters for the port should be restored to their 'initial configuration' (i.e., their values before the call was started).

Indication of Break

The Indication of Break message may be sent following an Interrupt packet depending on the value of X.3 parameter 7. If the value of parameter 7 is 5, the Indication of Break message is sent without a parameter field.

If the value of parameter 7 is 21, the Indication of Break message sent has one parameter field. The parameter reference is 8 and the parameter value is 1. This indicates that the PAD port has set parameter 8 to 1 to discard data received on the call. The host computer, upon receiving this message, should issue either a Reset or a Set Parameter message, to restore the value of parameter 8 to 0.

Read Parameters

This message is issued by a host computer to a PAD port in order to read the current values of the X.3 parameters.

If the Read Parameters message has no parameter fields, the PAD port treats this as a request to send the values of the entire X.3 parameter set. It does this by sending a Parameter Indication message with 22 parameter fields.

If the Read Parameters message does contain parameter fields, then only those X.3 parameter values requested are returned in the Parameter Indication message.

Error PAD Message

The Error PAD message is sent if a PAD message is received that is in error for some reason. The Error PAD message has two bytes following the message code. The first byte is the error type. The second is the invalid message code.

Possible values for the error type field are given below:

Error Type Value	Meaning
00000000	Received PAD message contained less than 8 bits
00000001	Unrecognised message code in received PAD message
00000010	Parameter field format of received PAD message was incorrect or incompatible with message code
00000011	Received PAD message did not contain an integral number of bytes
00000100	Received Parameter Indication message was unsolicited
00000101	Received PAD message was too long

Set and Read Parameters

This message is a combination of the Set message and the Read message. The values of the X.3 parameters are first set according to the Set message and the value are then returned in the Read message.

Reselection PAD message

This PAD message can be sent to a PAD port to request that it calls a different address. On receipt of this PAD message, the PAD port transmits to the terminal all data received from the call. It then clears the call and sets up another call to the address specified in the Reselection PAD message.

The format of the Reselection PAD message is shown in Figure 7.2. The format of the message is very similar to that of the X.25 level 3 Incoming call/Call request packet. It is worth noting that this is an optional feature and may not be implemented in all that many PADs.

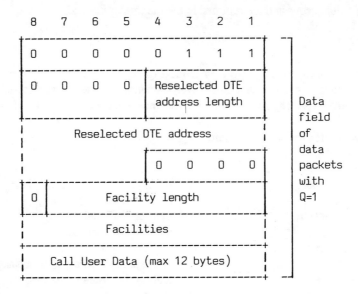

```
        8   7   6   5   4   3   2   1
      +-------------------------------+ --
      | 0   0   0   0   0   1   1   1 |   |
      +-------------------------------+   |
      | 0   0   0   0 | Reselected DTE|   |
      |               | address length|  Data
      +---------------+---------------+   field
      |  Reselected DTE address       |   of
      |               +---------------+   data
      |               | 0   0   0   0 |   packets
      +-----+---------+---------------+   with
      |  0  |    Facility length      |   Q=1
      +-----+-------------------------+   |
      |        Facilities             |   |
      +-------------------------------+   |
      |  Call User Data (max 12 bytes)|   |
      +-------------------------------+ --
```

Figure 7.2 Reselection PAD message format

7.2.4 Triple X 1980 and 1984

The version of Triple X described above are the 1984 versions of the CCITT recommendations. There are some differences between the 1984 versions and the 1980 versions that are important.

Possibly the most significant difference is that in 1980 there were only 18 X.3 parameters instead of 22. This has an implication for interworking between a 1980 version and a 1984 version. In particular, if a 1980 host sends a Read Parameters message with no parameter fields to a 1984 PAD port, the PAD will send back all of the 1984 parameters. What the host will do with the values for parameters 19-22 will depend on the host implementation. In one real example, the host software actually crashed in this situation. This is something to watch out for.

7.3 The Yellow Book Protocol

As mentioned in the introduction to this section, the Yellow Book (YB) protocol is a Transport Service (TS) layer protocol. This corresponds to level 4 of the OSI 7 layer model.

The idea of the protocol is to provide a uniform interface to the higher level protocols independent of the underlying network layer protocols and capabilities. In addition, the TS layer may add some functions that do not exist in the lower level protocols.

162

There are two main phases of the YB protocol - the connection creation and termination phase and the information transfer phase.

7.3.1 Connection Creation and Termination Phase

In order to establish a YB connection, the YB CONNECT message is used. The CONNECT contains the TS address of the destination and information about the facilities required there. If the CONNECT is acceptable to the destination device, it returns the YB ACCEPT message to the caller. If the call is not acceptable, a YB DISCONNECT message is sent to the caller.

Active connections are terminated by the exchange of DISCONNECT messages.

7.3.2 Information Transfer Phase

In this phase, YB DATA messages are transferred between the two endpoints of the YB connection. These messages are of arbitrary length. The end of a message is signalled by a PUSH message. This basically says that the end of the message has been reached.

YB EXPEDITED messages may also be sent between the two endpoints of a YB connection. These are not subject to the normal flow control processes for DATA messages and may overtake DATA messages in transit.

An active YB connection may be re-synchronised by the use of a YB RESET message.

There is one final YB message that may be used in the information transfer phase. This is the ADDRESS message and was defined to be used to pass TS level addresses of third parties between the two endpoints of a YB connection. As there are severe logical difficulties in this (as described in the next section) the ADDRESS message is almost never used.

7.3.3 TS Level Addressing

One of the most important features that are added by the use of a Transport Service like the YB protocol is the extended addressing capability that it offers. This is particularly important when X.25(80) is used to provide the network layer as it does not support the extended addressing facility present in X.25(84). The 12 or 14 digit DTE address is good enough to get to a particular device on the network, but often that is not good enough. The device might well be a host computer system that supports multiple facilities like file transfer, electronic mail and interactive access. The TS address provides the extra information required to select the particular facility required.

Figure 7.3 shows another situation where extra addressing information is required. In this case, two different networks are connected together via a gateway. The technologies may differ: one might be an X.25 network while the other might be an Ethernet network. The addressing is different and incompatible. The use of a Transport Service like the YB protocol provides the flexibility required to solve this problem.

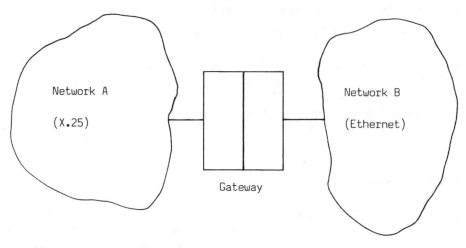

Figure 7.3 Networks connected by a gateway

Figure 7.4 is an example of how the TS level addresses work in the YB protocol. First of all, look at the left hand column showing the CONNECT. The called address is the TS address of the destination device. As can be seen, the TS address is actually a specification of the route between the two devices. The elements of the TS address do not need to be explicit DTE addresses, or their equivalent in the appropriate network technology. Instead, they can be mnemonic versions of the address that are 'mapped' at the appropriate gateway into an absolute DTE address. As the CONNECT passes through each gateway, the first element of the called address is stripped off. This provides the route information to the next gateway or the destination device. The calling address, however, gets new elements added to its front each time it goes through a gateway. By the time it gets to its final destination, the calling address forms a complete representation of the path back to the caller.

The ACCEPT message has one address parameter, the 'Recall address'. This is used to identify to the caller to which of possibly several destinations the CONNECT was routed. As an example of where this may be useful, suppose a host computer has several connection into an X.25 network called HOST1 and HOST2 at the TS level. The recall address would then indicate which of the two connections was used. When the ACCEPT reaches the caller, the recall address contains a complete address that can be used to recall the specific host connection.

So there are two basic types of address modifications that can occur: the called address style where elements are stripped off from the front and the calling address style where new elements are added to the front of the address. The recall address uses the calling address style of address modification.

164

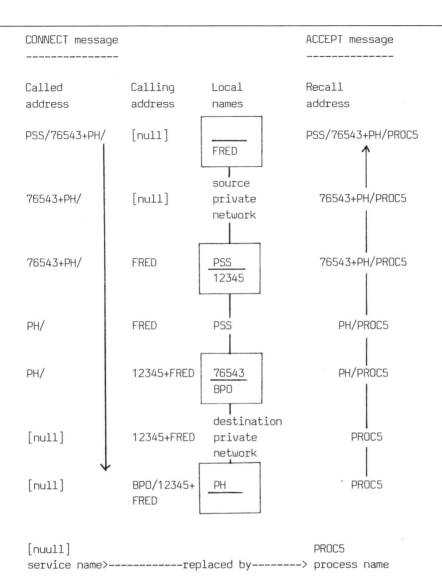

```
CONNECT message                            ACCEPT message
---------------                            --------------


Called        Calling       Local          Recall
address       address       names          address

PSS/76543+PH/ [null]         _____         PSS/76543+PH/PROC5
                            FRED
                                            ↑
                             |              |
                            source          |
76543+PH/     [null]        private        76543+PH/PROC5
                            network         |
                                            |
76543+PH/     FRED           PSS_          76543+PH/PROC5
                            12345           |
                                            |
PH/           FRED          PSS            PH/PROC5
                             |              |
                                            |
PH/           12345+FRED    76543          PH/PROC5
                            BPO             |
                                            |
                            destination     |
[null]        12345+FRED    private        PROC5
                            network         |
                                            |
[null]        BPO/12345+     PH_           · PROC5
              FRED


[nuull]                                    PROC5
service name>------------replaced by-------> process name
```

Address transformations in a sequence of networks and nodes.
The boxes represent nodes.   The strings within a box denote the
addresses of that node in the corresponding networks.

Figure 7.4 Yellow Book addressing

The ADDRESS message was intended to carry these TS level addresses between the
two endpoints of an active YB connection in the information transfer phase. However,
because the TS address is actually a route specification between two endpoints, the TS

address of a particular endpoint depends on where you are. So when an address of a third party is sent from one endpoint to another, the address of the third party must be modified each time it goes through a gateway. This would ensure that by the time it reached the receiver of the ADDRESS message the TS address would correctly specify the route to the third party from the receiver.

The question is which address modification style should be used by the gateways, called address style or calling address style? The answer depends on whether the ADDRESS message is moving towards or away from the third party. The trouble is that the gateways do not necessarily have access to this information and the whole thing goes wrong.

So, in practice, it is almost impossible to pass this type of address from endpoint to endpoint. The OSI concept of the NSAP address which is global in relevance solves this problem as the NSAP is always valid.

7.3.4 Using Yellow Book Over X.25

Although the YB primitives, CONNECT, ACCEPT, DISCONNECT, DATA, PUSH, EXPEDITED, RESET and ADDRESS have been introduced, nothing has been said about how they are actually realised in practice. This can vary between network technologies as long as the gateways between them carry out the correct conversions.

The CONNECT Message

The CONNECT message has up to four parameters. The first parameter is the Called Address. The second is the Calling Address. The third parameter is the 'Quality of Service' parameter. The idea of this was that a specified quality of service could be requested by the caller. In practice, this is not really used and is almost always null. The final parameter is the 'Explanatory text' field that can be used for providing some extra information; this is often null.

The CONNECT message is encoded into an X.25 level 3 Incoming call/Call request packet. The four parameters are conveyed in the Call User Data field of the packet. If a standard format Incoming call/Call request packet is used, only 12 bytes are available (four out of the 16 are used for the protocol identifier field). If the fast select facility is used, up to 124 bytes will be available.

The parameters themselves are encoded into fragments. Each fragment has a header byte that gives information about the fragment. The contents of the header byte are given below:

Bit in header byte	Meaning
8	If this bit is set to 1, this fragment is the last one for this parameter
7	Normally set to 0 exceptin CONNECT (see below)
1-6	This is the length of the fragment in bytes.

166

As a 6 bit field is available for the fragment length, the maximum length of a fragment is 63 bytes. If the parameter is actually more than 63 bytes long, more than one fragment must be used. All but the last fragment should then have bit 8 of the fragment header byte set to 0 to indicate that they are no the final fragments of the parameter.

What happens if the CONNECT parameters will not fit into the Call User Data field of the Incoming call/Call request packet? If this does happen, the caller sets bit 7 of the first header fragment. When the called device receives this CONNECT, it must accept the level 3 call with a Call connected/Call accepted packet. The caller can then send the remaining parts of the CONNECT in one or more qualified level 3 data packets (i.e., data packets with the Q bit set in the GFI field of the packet header). The first byte of the first of these qualified data packets is the CONNECT message code - 16 (decimal). All of the qualified data packets forming the CONNECT message have the More bit set in the packet header except for the last in the sequence. The X.25 More bit is therefore used to indicate the end of messages.

In practice, the fast select facility is almost always used with the YB protocol so that, in most cases, the parameters will fit in the Call User Data field and avoid the rather messy process described above.

The ACCEPT Message

The ACCEPT message is used in response to a CONNECT message if the connection is acceptable. The first parameter of the message is the Recall address that was described earlier. The second parameter is the quality of service. The idea here was that the parameter would indicate the actual quality of service provided for the call. As with this parameter in the CONNECT, it is normally null. The last parameter is the explanatory text.

The ACCEPT message is preceded by an X.25 level 3 Call connect/Call accepted packet. The ACCEPT itself is carried in a sequence of qualified data packets. The first byte of the first packet in the sequence contains the message type code - for the ACCEPT this is 17 (decimal). The remaining bytes in the message contain the three parameters encoded into fragments as for the CONNECT parameters.

The DISCONNECT Message

The DISCONNECT message is used to either reject an attempt to set up a connection or else to terminate an active connection. The DISCONNECT message has three parameters. The first parameter is a machine orientated error code. That means that it is an incomprehensible number. The second parameter is the 'address of error'. This actually means that the parameter contains the address of the device that generated the DISCONNECT. It is built up in the way as for the recall address in the ACCEPT message. This parameter can be quite useful as it is not always obvious where a DISCONNECT has come from; it may have come from the remote end of the connection or from a gateway somewhere on the route.

The third and final parameter is the explanatory text field. This may contain further information about the reason for the DISCONNECT.

The actual encoding of the DISCONNECT message onto X.25 level 3 depends on what the DISCONNECT message is doing. If the DISCONNECT message is in response to a connection attempt that consists of just an Incoming call/Call request packet, the DISCONNECT message becomes a Clear indication/Clear request packet.

If the DISCONNECT is being used to clear an active connection, it is sent in a qualified data packet as for the CONNECT and ACCEPT messages. The first byte of the first packet of the sequence contains the DISCONNECT message code - 18 (decimal). The remainder consists of the three parameters encoded as fragments as before.

In some cases, it is adequate to use the Clear indication/Clear request packet to convey the DISCONNECT message.

The DATA Message

The DATA messages are very simply carried in X.25 level 3 data packets that have the Q bit in the GFI field of the packet header clear (i.e., non-qualified data packets).

The PUSH Message

The PUSH message is used to indicate that the previous DATA messages formed a complete message. The PUSH message is not in actually encoded in a packet as such. The last packet of the preceding DATA message is sent with the More bit in the packet header set to 0. Therefore, as with the qualified data packets, the More bit is used as an end of message marker.

The EXPEDITED Message

The EXPEDITED message is encoded into an X.25 level 3 Interrupt packet. The expedited data is carried in the data field of the Interrupt packet.

The RESET Message

The RESET message has three parameters that are very similar to the DISCONNECT message. The RESET message is actually encoded into a Reset indication/Reset request packet followed by a sequence of qualified data packets containing the three parameters. The message code for the RESET message is 19 (decimal). In many cases, just the Reset indication/Reset request packet will be issued indicating that the three parameters were all null.

The ADDRESS Message

To be complete, the ADDRESS message has two parameters. The first parameter is the address itself; the second the 'qualifier' field, used to say whether or not the address is moving towards or away from the addressed object. The ADDRESS message is encoded into a sequence of qualified data packets. The message code for the ADDRESS message is 20 (decimal).

7.3.5 Yellow Book in Practice

The Yellow Book protocol definition contains some detailed state diagrams that helped ensure that implementations were compatible. In the Academic Community there are a very large number of Yellow Book implementations on a wide range of computers of all sizes. Interworking between these systems over the JANET network has been very successful and has made moving files around the network pretty simple.

Perhaps the biggest problem with it is that the Yellow Book never went much beyond the academic community and has now been overtaken by the OSI transport service.

7.3.6 The TS29 Protocol

The TS29 protocol is definitely in the odd-ball league. This is a version of the Triple X protocol but run over the Yellow Book transport service instead of just X.25 level 3.

Why try to run an interactive call over a transport service? The advantage is the extended addressing and the network transparency that the transport service provides. The problem is that X.29 uses qualified data packets to implement its PAD messages. Yellow Book uses them also for its control messages. Unfortunately, there is only one level of qualification available, so something has to be done. The only thing that could be done was to 'bodge' in a second level of qualification. The X.25 level 3 Q bit is used by Yellow Book as normal. The first of the data field of non-qualified sequences of data packets is used to provide an extra qualification level. If the first byte of such a sequence is 0, the rest of the sequence contains end to end call data. If the first byte is 128 (decimal), the rest of the sequence contains a PAD message.

TS29 has gained only a very restricted number of applications within the academic community and will die a death in the near future. There is no real need for an OSI version of TS29 as the Incoming call/Call request packet allows sufficient addressing information without the intervention of the transport service.

7.4 The Blue Book File Transfer Protocol
7.4.1 General Concepts

The 'Blue Book' Network Independent File Transfer Protocol (NIFTP) was developed within the United Kingdom to fill a significant gap in the International Standard protocols in the early 1980s.

The purpose of a file transfer protocol is to provide a mechanism for transferring files between host computers over a network. The point about having a standard file transfer protocol is that it allows the transfer of files between computers from different manufacturers. This was very important for the academic community, which had its national network (JANET) connecting together a wide range of host computers in colleges and universities throughout the country.

One of the general concepts of file transfer protocols is that of the 'Virtual Filestore'. The virtual filestore is a single standardised representation of how a set of files can be organised. The virtual filestore concept is required because different host computers with different operating systems may vary widely in the way in which they organise their files. For example, some operating systems have a 'flat' structure which do not allow the filestore to be structured in any way. Others have 'hierarchical' structures, which allow files to be grouped into subdirectories within the main filestore. Somehow, the file transfer protocol has be able to cope with these differences when transferring files between different types of filestore.

It is the task of the protocol implementation to take care of the real to virtual filestore mapping. Where the host computer has a sophisticated filestore structure, it may not be possible to map all of the capabilities onto the virtual filestore supported by the file transfer protocol. At the other extreme, the real filestore may be very simple, so that not all of the virtual filestore capabilities will have any equivalent in the real filestore. In either case, the file transfer protocol implementation must make intelligent decisions about the real to virtual filestore mapping.

When using a file transfer protocol, one host computer wishes to send or receive a file from another host computer. The host computer requesting the action is known as the 'initiator'. Blue Book also calls the initiator the 'P end'. The other host computer is known as the 'responder'. Blue Book also calls the responder the 'Q end'.

Figure 7.5 shows the relationship between the P and Q ends of the file transfer. An important part of the file transfer protocol is that which allows the P end to obtain information about the filestore at the Q end of the transfer. The P end is in charge of the transfer and determines whether or not it should proceed.

There are three important phases within a complete file transfer:
The Initialisation phase establishes the precise details about how the file is to be transferred. The P end and Q end 'negotiate' values for the transfer attributes in this phase. It is also possible at this point to specify that the transfer is to restart a previously aborted one. This can be very useful when transferring large files which may take a long time to transfer. If the connection fails for some reason near the end of the transfer, it would be necessary to restart the file from the beginning again. If the restart facility is used, then only the remainder of the file needs to be transferred.
The Data Transfer phase follows and is the actual transfer of data. This phase includes mechanisms to manage and control the flow of data between the two ends of the transfer.
The Termination phase completes the transfer of the file and indicates the final state of the transfer.

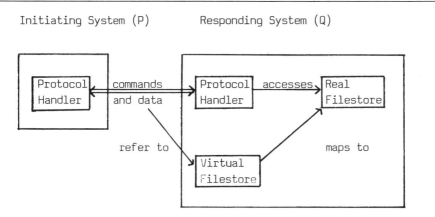

Initiating System (P)   Responding System (Q)

Figure 7.5 Relationship between P and Q

7.4.2 Encoding of Blue Book Commands and Data

Commands used within the Initialisation and Termination phases along with data in the Data Transfer phase are transmitted as 'FTP records'. The FTP records consist of a number of subrecords, each with a header byte and up to 63 data bytes making up the body of the subrecord. This structure is shown in Figure 7.6.

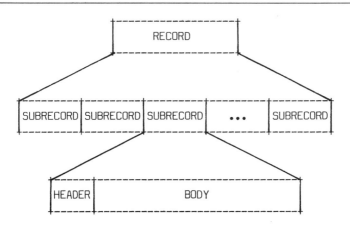

Figure 7.6 FTP record structure

Bit 7 of the header byte is used to indicate whether or not the subrecord is the last in the record. Bit 6 of the header byte is used to indicate whether compression is being used. If bit 6 is 0, compression is not in use and the byte count in bits 5-0 gives the number of bytes in the subrecord. If bit 6 is 1, compression is being used. In this case, the byte count in bits 5-0 gives the number of times that the single byte of data following the header must be repeated when decompressing the record. This feature can save a fair amount of transfer time depending on the contents of the file being transferred.

The commands used in the Initialisation and Termination phases are encoded into FTP records as described above. The structure of the commands is shown in Figure 7.7. The command identifier contains a code indentifying the specific command. The parameter count is the number of parameters that are contained within the command.

```
+---------------+---------------+---------------+- - - - - -+
|Command        |Parameter      |First          |Further    |
|Identifier     |Count          |Parameter      |Parameters |
+---------------+---------------+---------------+- - - - - -+
```

Figure 7.7 FTP command structure

The parameters used within the commands are made up of three parts as shown in Figure 7.8. The parameter qualifier is itself structured and this structure is also shown in Figure 7.8. The monitor flag can be used by the P end to demand that an explicit value for that attribute be included in the response from the Q end.

Bits 5 and 4 determine the type of the value field if there is one. Strings are encoded as a length count byte followed by that number of characters. Bits 2-0 specify an operator that is to be used with the value. This operator is used within the attribute value negotiation process.

The commands used within the Data Transfer phase are encoded as subrecords with a header containing all zeros. (This header cannot normally occur in a data record as the protocol defines that zero length data subrecords not delimiting the end of a record do not occur.) The structure is shown in Figure 7.9. The zero header is always followed by two bytes. The first identifies the Data Transfer phase command, while the second is an argument that depends on the particular command.

7.4.3 The Initialisation and Termination Phases

The first command used within this phase is the SFT - Start File Transfer. This is sent from the P end to the Q end and specifies the attributes that the P end is requesting for the transfer. The command identifier for the SFT is 04. The P end may specify a particular value for an attribute (using the EQ operator), an upper bound for a value (using the LE operator) or a lower bound for a value (using the GE operator). If the P end just wishes to check a value for an attribute at the Q end, it can use the ANY operator with the monitor flag set. This forces the Q end to send back the value that it has for that attribute.

```
+-----------+-----------+-------+
|Attribute  | Qualifier | Value |
|Identifier |           |       |
+-----------+-----------+-------+
```

Parameter structure

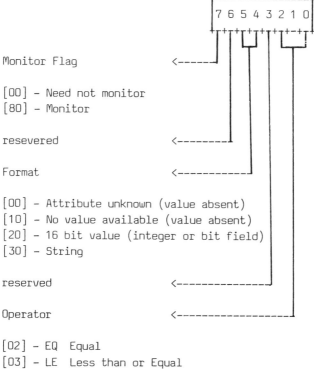

```
                              +----------------+
                              | 7 6 5 4 3 2 1 0|
                              +-+-+-+-+-+-+-+-+-+
Monitor Flag              <------┘   |   |   |
                                     |   |   |
[00] - Need not monitor              |   |   |
[80] - Monitor                       |   |   |

resevered                 <----------┘   |   |

Format                    <--------------┘   |

[00] - Attribute unknown (value absent)
[10] - No value available (value absent)
[20] - 16 bit value (integer or bit field)
[30] - String

reserved                  <------------------┘

Operator                  <------------------┘

[02] - EQ  Equal
[03] - LE  Less than or Equal
[05] - NE  Not Equal
[06] - GE  Greater than or Equal
[07] - ANY Any value acceptable
           Other values are reserved.
```

Figure 7.8 Qualifier structure

```
+-------------+-------------+-----------+
| Zero Header | Command     | Argument  |
| byte        | identifier  | byte      |
+-------------+-------------+-----------+
```

Figure 7.9 Transfer control command structure

There are a large number of different attributes that may be specified within the SFT command. Here, we describe a few of the more important attributes in some detail. Note that attribute identifiers are given as two hex characters.

The Mode of Access attribute (attribute identifier 01) must always be present within the SFT, as it specifies the direction of transfer of the file and the mode of access to the filestore. The value is a 16 bit value. Bit 15 is used to indicate the direction of the transfer. If bit 15 is 0, the transfer is from the P end to the Q end. If Bit 15 is 1, the transfer is from the Q end to the P end. The other bits are used to encode the mode of access. If the transfer is from the P end to the Q end, this can specify that the file is to replace an existing one, be appended to an existing file or just be created. If the transfer is from the Q end to the P end, this can specify whether or not the file is to be deleted after being read.

The Initial Restart Mark attribute (attribute indentifier 0B) is used to specify the point in the file at which a previously aborted file transfer is to restart. The value indicates the mark at which the transfer is to resume. These marked points can be inserted in the Data Transfer phase and are described later.

The State of Transfer attribute (attribute identifier 0F) is used to indicate the current state of the file transfer and whether or not a failed transfer can be restarted or not.

There are four categories of states: the Viable state means that the transfer is acceptable; the Rejected state that the transfer was not acceptable (an example would be an unacceptable attribute setting requested by the P end in the SFT); the Terminated state that the transfer has completed (there are two forms, one for satisfactory termination and one where there has been a problem with the transfer); the final state is Aborted. There are two forms indicating whether or not a retry of the transfer is possible.

The Filename attribute (attribute identifier 40) is used to identify the file at the Q end of the transfer. The filename is encoded as a string. In fact, Blue Book does not constrain the format of the filename string and so the precise form of the filename may vary between implementations.

The Username attribute (attribute identifier 42) is used to specify under which username the filename specified is to be found. This attribute is often used to provide authorisation for access to the filestore at the Q end of the transfer.

The Username Password attribute (attribute indentifier 44) is normally used in conjunction with the username attribute to authorise access to the filestore.

The File Password attribute (attribute identifier 45) can be used if the Filename requires a password in order to access the file in the filestore.

The Information Message attribute (attribute identifier 71) is used to convey text messages, usually to explain why a transfer was not accepted or why it was aborted. The value of this attribute is a string containing the information message text.

If the attribute values in the SFT command from the P end of the transfer are acceptable to the Q end, it will respond to the SFT with an RPOS command, a positive reply. The command identifier for the RPOS command is 02. For each attribute specified in the P end's SFT, the Q end will respond appropriately. If an attribute referred to is unknown to the Q end, it will respond with a parameter indicating that it was unknown with the operator set to ANY and no value.

If the P end specified an upper or lower bound on the values of attributes (using the LE or GE operators) the Q end can respond by selecting a value and using the EQ operator in the parameter. If the Q end cannot support any of the values in the range specified, the Q end should not respond with an RPOS; an RNEG should be sent instead. The Q end can also include attributes that were not specified on the original SFT.

If the transfer is not acceptable to the Q end, it will respond with an RNEG command, a negative reply. The command identifier for the RNEG command is 03. The RNEG should contain a State of Transfer attribute value indicating why the transfer was rejected. In addition, it may include an Information Message attribute to provide further explanation for the rejection if required. If there were problem with any of the attribute values requested by the P end in the SFT, response parameters for these attributes should be included in the RNEG to assist the P end in identifying the specific problem with the requested transfer.

Assuming that the P end receives an RPOS in response to its SFT and that it is happy to proceed with the transfer, it will send a GO command to indicate to the Q end that it is entering the Data Transfer phase. The command identifier for the GO command is 01. The GO command takes no parameters, so that the parameter count is always zero.

The STOP command is used by the P end to request that the transfer be terminated. The command identifier for the STOP command is 00. There are four circumstances in which the STOP command may be used. If the attribute values specified in the RPOS from the Q end are unacceptable, then the P end will send a STOP command to indicate this to the Q end. The STOP command will have the same parameters as those in the RNEG command described earlier. If the P end receives an RNEG in response to its SFT, it will respond with the STOP command. It will respond to an RPOS if it indicates that it is restarting a file transfer at the end of the file (there is no need to go into the Data Phase in this case). Lastly, it is sent by the P end to request termination of the transfer after the Data Transfer phase has completed.

The STOPACK command is send by the Q end of the transfer in response to a STOP command from the P end. The command identifier for the STOPACK command is 05. The only parameters conveyed by the STOPACK are the State of Transfer and Information Messages.

7.4.4 The Data Transfer Phase

In addition to the contents of the file transferred in this phase, there are eight 'transfer control commands'. Four can be used by the sender of the data while the other four can be used by the receiver of the data.

The SS command is used to indicate that the data transfer is to begin. The command identifier for the SS command is 40. The sender of the data sends this command at the start of the transfer. The argument for this command is the first restart mark point (i.e., where in the file the transfer is to begin). This is always zero unless the transfer is the resumption of a previously aborted attempt.

The MS command, Mark Point, can be inserted by the sender into the data to specify the position of a restart mark. The command identifier for the MS command is 41. The argument for this command is the mark number. The mark points are numbered consecutively. Therefore the argument of an MS command is that on the preceding MS or SS incremented modulo 256.

The CS command, Code Select, is used by the sender to specify whether subsequent data is text or binary. The command identifier for the CS command is 42. The argument byte specifies what parity the data will have and whether it is IA5 (ASCII), binary, EBCDIC or a private code.

The ES command, End of Data, is transmitted at the end of the data to indicate that all of the data has been sent. The command identifier for the ES command is 43. There are four forms of this command distinguished by the value of the argument. ES(OK) is used to indicate that the data transfer has completed without error. In this case, the argument is 00. ES(H) is used to indicate that the sender is entering the hold state (see later). The argument value for this form is 10. ES(E) is used to indicate that there has been an error detected by the sender. Various values for the argument from 20-22 and 28-2A encode the reason. ES(A) is used to cause immediate termination of the Data Transfer phase. Various values for the argument between 30 and 34 encode the reason for the abort.

The RR command, Restart Request, is used by the receiver to request retransmission from the restart mark number quoted in the argument to this command. The command identifier for the RR command is 44. When the sender receives the RR command, it will respond with an SS command indicating that the transfer is starting again.

The MR command, Mark Acknowledge, is sent by the receiver to indicate that it has correctly received all the data up to the restart mark number quoted in the argument. The command identifier for the MR command is 45. When the sender receives an MR command, it knows that if it needs to restart the transfer, then it only needs to transfer the data after the last restart mark point that was acknowledged.

The QR command, Quit, can be used by the receiver to indicate to the sender that it wishes to terminate the transfer or request a temporary hold. The command identifier for the QR command is 46. As for the ES command, there are four forms of the QR command distinguished by the value of the argument. The QR(OK) is used to request that the sender transmit an ES(OK) to terminate the transfer normally. In this case the argument is 00. The QR(H) is send by the receiver to request a temporary hold. The sender will respond with an ES(H). The receiver clears the condition with an ER(H). In this case, the argument is 10. The QR(E) is used to request termination of the transfer when an error has been detected by the receiver. The argument takes values from 20-22 depending on the nature of the error. The QR(A) requests that the transfer be aborted immediately without response from the sender. The argument takes values from 30-36 depending on the reason for the abort.

The ER command, End Acknowledge, is used by the receiver either to acknowledge the reception of an ES command or else to clear a hold condition. The command identifier for the ER command is 47. There are three forms of the ER command. The ER(OK) is used to indicate that the Data Transfer phase has been completed without error. The argument in this case is 00. The ER(H) is used to clear a hold condition. The argument in this case is 10. The ER(E) is used to indicate that the transfer has been terminated because of an error. The argument in this case is from 20-22 or 28-2A depending on the error.

7.4.5 Appendix III Blue Book

The file transfer protocol described above outlines the complete Blue Book NIFTP protocol. If everything is implemented fully, things can get a little top heavy and probably support a large number of capabilities that are never required in practice. This is what is required on a large mainframe implementation that has to cope with a wide range of demands, but implementations on small machines may only require a subset of the full implementation. The Blue Book NIFTP specification takes note of this and includes a 'functional specification' for a small implementation of Blue Book NIFTP. This is known as 'Appendix III' NIFTP.

7.4.6 Example Blue Book Transfers

In Figure 7.10, the Q end is not able to accept the attribute values indicated in the P end's SFT command. The Q end sends back an RNEG giving the reasons why the transfer is not acceptable. The transfer is finished by the STOP - STOPACK sequence.

Figure 7.11 shows a complete data transfer from the P end to the Q end. After the RPOS is received from the Q end, the P end sends a GO command to move into the Data Transfer phase. The P end (the sender in this case) then sends an SS with a restart mark number of 00 to indicate that this is not a restarted transfer. Data records follow terminated by an ES(OK) indicating that everything has been transferred correctly. After the Q end has responded with an ER(OK), the STOP - STOPACK sequence finishes off the transfer.

Finally, Figure 7.12 shows a rather complex example involving a restart request. The transfer goes ok until the receiver loses data and then requests the restart at the appropriate restart mark number.

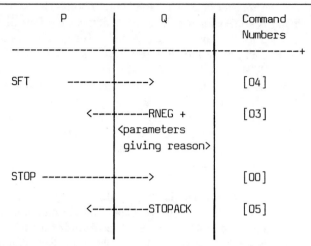

```
                  P              Q           Command
                                             Numbers
          ----------+-----------------+-------------+
    SFT        ------+------>                  [04]

               <---+------RNEG +               [03]
                   <parameters
                    giving reason>

    STOP --------------+------>                [00]

               <---+------STOPACK              [05]
```

Figure 7.10 Transfer unacceptable to Q

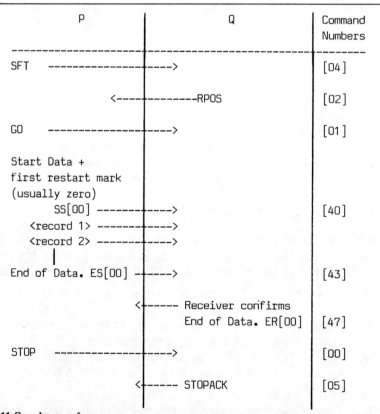

```
                   P                      Q             Command
                                                        Numbers
          ---------------------+-------------------------------
    SFT        --------------------+------>                [04]

                  <---+----------RPOS                      [02]

    GO         --------------------+------>                [01]

    Start Data +
    first restart mark
    (usually zero)
            SS[00] -------+------>                         [40]
       <record 1> -------+------>
       <record 2> -------+------>
           |
    End of Data. ES[00] --+------>                         [43]

                    <+------ Receiver confirms
                            End of Data. ER[00]   [47]

    STOP       -------------------+------>                 [00]

                    <+------ STOPACK                       [05]
```

Figure 7.11 Complete transfer

```
        Sender        | Receiver        | Comments
        --------------+-----------------+------------------------
        
        SS [00]  -----+---->            | Start of Data command
        
        (data)
        
        MS [01]  -----+---->            | Mark
        
        MS [02]  -----+---->            | Sender halts awaiting
                      |                 | mark ack from receiver.
                 <----+----MR [02]      | Receiver acknowledges
                      |                 | first two marks.
        MS [03]  -----+---->            |
                      |                 | Sender continues transfer
        MS [04]  -----+---->            |
                      |                 |
                 <----+----MR [04]      | Receiver acknowledges
                      |                 | previous marks
        MS [05]  -----+---->            |
                      |                 |
        MS [06]  -----+---->            |
                      |                 |
                 <----+----QR [10]      | Receiver loses data,
                      |                 | requests hold.
        ES [10]  -----+---->            | Sender pauses in
                      |                 | response to QR [10].
                 <----+----RR [05]      | Receiver requests restart
                 <----+----ER [10]      | Mark [05] and releases
                      |                 | hold.
        SS [05]  -----+---->            | Sender resumes transfer
                      |                 | from mark number [05].
                 <----+----MR [05]      | Receiver acknowledges
                      |                 | mark [05].
        MS [06]  -----+---->            | etc.
                      |                 |
                 <----+----MR [06]      |
```

Figure 7.12 Use of restart facilities

7.5 FTAM

FTAM stands for File Transfer, Access and Management. It is the OSI file transfer protocol and is therefore similar in concept to the Blue Book NIFTP described earlier. FTAM will become the dominant file transfer protocol in the future as OSI networks become the norm.

Figure 7.13 shows the basic concepts involved in FTAM. Entity A is the file service user initiating the activity. It is known as the Initiator. Entity B is the target of the activity initiated by entity A and is known as the Responder. Depending on the direction of transfer of data, one of the entities is the sender while the other is the receiver.

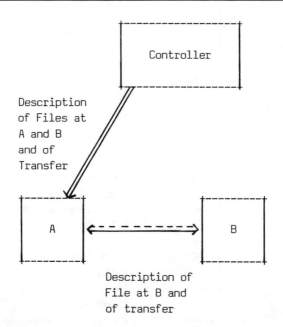

Figure 7.13 FTAM concepts

The FTAM protocol covers a very large variety of situations and implementations are therefore potentially enormous. To cope with this, the protocol specification includes a set of 'functional units'. The idea is that an implementation either implements them completely or not at all. Also, there are defined five classes of service each of which provide different styles of service.

The 'transfer class' allows for straightforward transfer of files with minimal protocol overhead. The 'management class' allows manipulation of the remote filestore by a series of independent confirmed exchanges but does not include the file transfer capability. The third class , the 'transfer and management class' combines the first two to give file transfer and management capabilities. The fourth class is the 'access class' which allows manipulation of data within the file at the remote filestore.

The fifth and final service class is the 'unconstrained class'. This leaves the selection of the functional units to the designer of the application using the FTAM service. This gives a very flexible protocol but no guarantee of compatibility with other implementations.

The particular class to be used are negotiated when the FTAM protocol is initialised.

FTAM provides a number of functions associated with the file service which may be useful in some environments.

The first of these is access control (i.e., controlling access to files). FTAM supports the concept of a list of conditions that must be satisfied in order to gain access to a file.

Mechanisms are also provided supporting charging and accounting for file access.

FTAM also supports concurrency control. This basically means that access to shared files may be locked when information is being updated.

Finally, FTAM includes in its error recovery protocol methods for ensuring that file transfers and modifications are performed successfully even after a wide variety of communications failures have occurred. This may well be essential for distributed applications updating a common database as it guarantees that changes have been made correctly. This facility is known as the CCR - Commitment, Concurrency and Recovery protocol.

As with the Blue Book NIFTP, FTAM uses the concept of the virtual filestore to unify access to real filestores. The FTAM implementation has to map the virtual filestore into the real filestore supported by the host computer.

7.5.1. The File Service

Figure 7.14 shows how an FTAM session proceeds. An FTAM regime is the period of time for which both the initiator and responder are in a particular state.

The FTAM regime initialisation phase establishes the basic connection between the applications using the service.

The File Selection phase uniquely identifies the file to which subsequent operations will refer. This may include creation of the specified file.

The File Management phase allows the file service user to perform management functions of the specified file. This may include operations such as changing the attributes of the file.

The File Open phase establishes the capabilities required for the actual transfer of the file.

The Data Access phase is where all of the action occurs. Is is in this phase that data transfers and manipulations take place.

The File Close phase terminates the Data Access phase and confirms that all of the previous operations have completed.

The File De-selection phase releases the file that had been selected previously.

The FTAM regime termination phase closes down the FTAM connection and is the final step in the process.

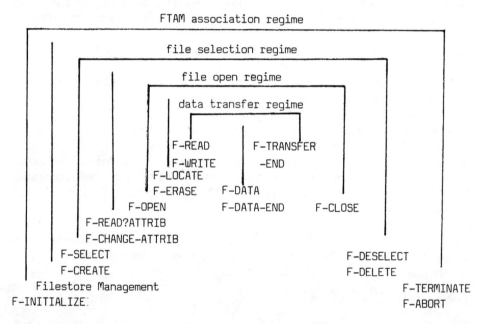

Figure 7.14 FTAM Session

7.6 X.400

X.400 describes the basic structure of an electronic mail system. In fact, X.400 is just one of a set of CCITT recommendations defining the system. The other recommendations are X.401, X.408, X.409, X.410, X.411, X.420 and X.430. Each one defines different aspects of the complete system.

In X.400 terminology, the recommendation describes the system model and service elements of the 'Message Handling System' or MHS for short. X.400 also defines the 'Message Handling' (MH) services that MHS providers offer to users to allow them to exchange messages on a store and forward basis. There are two MH services provided. The first is the 'interpersonal messaging' (IPM) service. This is used for communicating with Telex services for example. The second service, the 'message transfer' (MT) service, supports general purpose message transfer.

Figure 7.15 shows the basic MHS model. A user is either a person or an application running on some computer system. The *user agent* (UA) assists the user in the preparation of messages. The UA then interacts with the *message transfer system* (MTS) in order to transfer the messages.

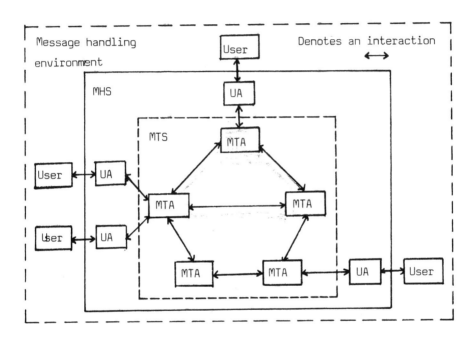

Figure 7.15 Functional view of the MHS model

Inside the MTS are a number of *message transfer agents* (MTAs). These are like packet switches in that they route a message from an originating UA to an intended recipient UA.

An X.400 message consists of an *envelope* and the *content*. The envelope carries the information that is to be used when transferring the message (addressing, for example). The content is the actual information that is being transferred.

There are three different types of envelope: submission, delivery and relaying. The submission envelope contains the information that the MTS requires to provide the required service. The delivery envelope contains the information related to delivery of the message. The relaying envelope contains the information required when transferring the message between MTAs.

There are various ways in which the MHS elements can be implemented. The simplest situation is where the originating and recipient UAs along with the MTA is physically in the same host computer system. The users communicate with the UAs using some sort of I/O device (this could be a terminal or fax machine). Another possibility is that the I/O device is intelligent enough to contain a UA itself. The intelligent I/O device is then connected, possibly via a network, directly into an MTA to allow message transfers with other UAs.

One of the major features of the X.400 MHS is its ability to convert the contents of messages from one type of message to another. There are nine different types of encoded information support by X.400. These are Telex, ASCII text, Teletex, G3 fax, Text Interchange Format 0 (TIF0), Videotex, voice, Simple Formattable Document (SFD) and Text Interchange Format 1 (TIF1). The conversion rules between the various types are defined in X.408. Unfortunately, the most common phrase found is 'This requires further study', although some of the conversions have been defined. Some of the conversions are obviously impractical. For example, converting from G3 fax to voice would indeed be a considerable intellectual challenge!

8

Security in Packet Switched Networks

8.1 Introduction

What do we mean by security when it comes to packet switched networks? One aspect of security in this context is the control of access to secure data. Secure data is basically that which should not be generally available. Personnel information and financial records fall into this category.

Usually, secure data is held in databases on computer systems which may be connected to a communications network. In many cases, it is difficult to control access to the network and therefore the host computer systems on the network must protect themselves against attack from intruders. This is what is meant by 'access control'. Only those people who need to access the data should actually be able to access the data. Unauthorised attempts to access the data should not only be detected and prevented, but also signalled to the operators of the system so that they are aware of these attempts.

Access controls usually use some form of password protection to provide security. This means that somebody wishing to access secure data must provide the correct password (or passwords) before access is granted. Passwords are effectively the keys to the safe.

A second aspect of security in packet switched networks is relevant when secure data has to be transferred across the network. In many cases, it may be impossible to guarantee that it is not possible for someone to gain access to one of the communications links and monitor the data flowing on the link. In such cases, it may well be up to applications using the network to take measures to ensure that no such attempts will result in useful information being obtained and that any attempts to alter the data in transit can be detected and rejected.

Data in transit in a packet switched network may be made secure by using 'data encryption'. This means that the data is first specially encoded in such a way that only the intended receiver is able to reconstruct the information. Any unauthorised intruder would not be able to deduce anything from the encrypted data.

After having identified some simple scenarios where security measures are required, the section will go on to describe some techniques that can be used to make a network secure.

8.2 When is Security Required?

Perhaps an easier question to answer would be, when is security not required? Even in the most straightforward of networks, some form of security has to be employed.

For example, most devices in the packet switched network (PADs, switches, etc.) will have network management facilities which can be accessed across the network. These remote management facilities may well have very powerful capabilities including the total shutdown of the network. Although these facilities are essential to the authorised managers of the packet switched network, it is also essential that no one else is able to gain access.

Another case may be where a network service needs to be accessed by some users of the network but not by others. This may be because of scarce resources or perhaps because use of the network service has to paid for by the user.

The previous examples have been of situations where access controls are needed. Often, it is necessary for packet switched networks to be used to carry data which should not be readable by unauthorised users of the network. An example of this is where a general purpose packet switched network is also used to carry accounting information. The information will almost certainly be confidential and certainly it should not be possible for the information to be altered by a network intruder.

8.3 Controlling Access

What are the main threats to the security of data in host computer systems that require access controls?

One threat is 'browsing'. This is when an intruder searches through the memory of a computer or its filestore looking for useful information. Often in multi-user computer systems, the computer's memory may not be cleared between running tasks for different users. If the intruder is lucky, the previous task that used the memory now occupied by his task left some important information lying around in memory. This is a classic way of locating other user's passwords and, in extremely unfortunate cases, large chunks of the file containing all of the valid passwords for the host computer system. If any one of these should have special system privileges, the intruder then may be able to access all of the data stored within the computer.

Another threat to access control is 'leakage'. In this case, a task with valid access to secure data may be able to pass the information to other tasks (and users) who should not have access to the data. This may either be accidental or intentional on the part of the software writers and maintainers.

The most basic form of access control that the host computer system can have is the 'user number/password' system. A user calling into the host computer is first asked for a user number and then the password associated with user number. The user number may be public knowledge (i.e., it does not need to kept secret). The password, on the other hand, must not be public knowledge. The host computer checks the user number/password combination against a file of valid user number/password pairs. If the combination is found within the 'validation file', the user is granted access to the system. The host computer may still restrict the privileges that the user has within the system. The validation file may also contain a list of privileges associated with the user number that the user cannot change.

Although this type of system is fine for preventing unauthorised access where the consequences of a security breach are not particularly serious, there are a number of problems with this system. Firstly, the validation file of user number/password combinations is liable to attack by intruders. In many cases it is not acceptable for even the system managers to be able to access this file in order to read its contents.

The validation file can be protected against attack by use of a 'one-way cipher'. This means that when the validation file is created, the entries are not stored as the user number/password combinations themselves but as an 'encrypted' version. The fact that the cipher used to produce the encrypted form is one-way means that it is impossible (or very difficult) to reproduce the original text from the encrypted form in the file.

When a user supplies a user number and password, the combination is first encrypted using the same one-way cipher that was used to generate the validation file originally. If the encrypted form is found within the file, the user is granted access to the system.

This method of encrypting the validation file avoids the problem of unauthorised access to its contents as the contents are meaningless. One unfortunate side effect of this is that, if a user forgets a password, there is no way of finding out what the password was. The only thing to do is to create an entry for a new user number/password combination.

Although the encrypted validation file solves many of the problems, it does not provide a total solution. The user must still type in a user number and password. There are three well known techniques for obtaining user number and passwords.

One technique is to monitor the packet switched network links or other parts of the communications network. Eventually, user numbers and passwords will be seen and can be recorded for future use by an intruder. Actually, Ethernet networks are particularly vulnerable to this sort of attack because any node on the network can monitor every data packet on the Ethernet cable. Although this makes network management relatively straightforward, it is also a major security hole. Since most PCs and workstations can easily be fitted with an Ethernet interface and run software that monitors the data on the network, a program could be written to check for user numbers and passwords and store them in a file for later collection by the intruder.

The second method of obtaining user numbers and passwords is to write a program that masquerades as the genuine log-in sequence. All that the program actually does is to collect user numbers and passwords for later collection by the intruder. When the user logs in, the fake log-in program says something like 'system down until further notice'.

The third method is to search through dustbins in areas where there are hard copy terminals. Very often, users enter their user number/password combination in such a way that it can easily be read. There is no easy way to prevent this except to make sure that users understand this danger.

One simple way of limiting the possible use of a user number and password obtained in these ways by an intruder is to check the origin of a call into the system. This is sometimes known as 'dial back' security. The caller supplies the user number and password. The system, after having validated the combination, then extracts the known correct source address and calls back to that address. Alternatively, in most packet switched networks, the host can check the address that the incoming call from the user was made from. In this case, the user number/password/source address combination is checked against the validation file. Any attempts to call in from the wrong source address will result in failure.

Where the source is itself a computer system (intelligent workstation, for example), it is possible to avoid ever sending user numbers and passwords in a readable form across the network. In this case, the host computer system challenges the caller with an encrypted form of the current date and time. The caller decodes the date and time and checks that it is correct. If so, the caller responds with an encrypted form of the current date and time along with its password. The host system decodes the password and can then perform the normal validation on the result. The date and time is included to insure that nobody can just monitor the encrypted password and then 'play it back' to the host computer system later. If this was attempted, the date and time would be wrong and the attempt would fail.

8.4 Data Security

In many cases, the weakest link in the system is the communications network itself. The network may cover a large geographic area and use public communications services. This generally means that physical security (i.e., preventing access to the network devices and communications links) may well be impossible. There are many situations, however, where data must be transferred with high security. Cryptography is often used to protect data in situations where physical security cannot be guaranteed.

There are two separate requirements for data security. The first is secrecy where the actual information itself must be kept secret. Even if an intruder is able to gain access to the information on the network, it must not be in a form that is useful. The second is for data authenticity. Here the object is to ensure that only those authorised can send specific data across a network, usually with the aim of modifying data base information.

One technique that an intruder can use is 'passive wiretapping'. In this case, the intruder monitors the information flowing on a communications link. The aim is to extract useful information from either the information itself or statistics about the information (the packet rate to a particular destination or perhaps some specific structure to the information). This technique, also known as 'eavesdropping' can be protected against by encrypting the information before transferring it across the network. An introduction to encryption techniques follows later.

The second technique that may be used is 'active wiretapping'. This means that the information itself is actually modified by the intruder. One possibility is that information messages are altered by the intruder. Another is that previous information messages, obtained by passive wiretapping, are 'replayed' into the information message stream with the aim of appearing to be valid messages. As with passive wiretapping, encryption techniques can be used to effectively protect against active wiretapping.

A good example to illustrate a situation where some of these techniques might be used are the Automatic Teller Machines (ATMs) that tend to sprout out of the walls of banks and building societies. These have to be connected over public communications links to the central computers. The information flowing between the ATM and the central computer must be protected against passive wiretapping as an intruder could obtain useful knowledge just by monitoring the transactions.

Even more important is that the information be protected against active wiretapping. It is clearly very important that unauthorised intruders cannot modify bank accounts just when they feel like it.

8.5 Cryptographic Techniques
8.5.1 Introduction

Cryptography has its own set of jargon words. A cipher is the method used to encode the data in a 'secret' form. The process of encoding the data with the particular cipher is known as 'encryption'. The reverse process, that of extracting the original information from the encrypted data is known as 'decryption'. The original information is known as 'plaintext' while the encrypted form of the plaintext is known as 'ciphertext'

Figure 8.1 shows how the information flows in a communications system protected by cryptographic techniques. The plaintext information from the transmitter flows first into the encryption device. This may either be a separate hardware system, or else part of the software system within the computer system that is the transmitter of the information. In either case, it is very important that no access is possible to the plaintext information between the transmitter and the encryption device as this is a potential security hole.

The encryption device employs some encryption algorithm to the plaintext to generate the ciphertext. The E_k symbol indicates that E is the encryption algorithm while K specifies the particular 'key' that is used to encrypt the information (more about this later). The ciphertext is then transmitted across the communications network to the information receiver. Before the information is presented to the receiver, it is first passed through the decryption device. The symbol D_k indicates that D is the decryption algorithm while K specifies the key.

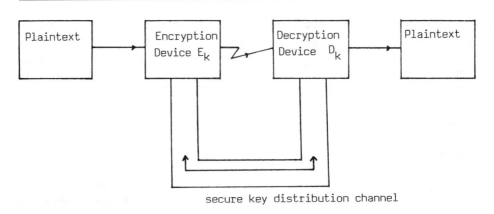

Figure 8.1 Information flow

As plaintext is being passed between the decryption device and the receiver, it is very important that no access is possible to the information. If a separate hardware device is used to perform the decryption, then very often it may be physically mounted within the receiver's computer system to ensure that physical access to it is difficult or impossible. If the decryption device is actually a program running on the receiver's computer system, then it is up to the access controls within it to ensure that unauthorised access to the plaintext is not possible.

Two things characterise the cryptographic system described above: the encryption/decryption algorithms (E and D) and the key K. Depending on which algorithms are used and the reason for using cryptography, either E or D or both may be public knowledge. The key K is always secret. In many ways, it is analogous to the use of the password in access control. It is therefore very important that the key to be used can be communicated to the transmitter and the receiver in total security (this is known as the secure distribution channel).

8.5.2 Basic Cryptographic Concepts

As we have mentioned earlier, cryptographic techniques can be used to provide two types of protection against intruders, secrecy and authenticity.

In order to provide secrecy, it should be 'computationally infeasible' to systematically determine the decryption algorithm D_k from knowledge of the ciphertext even if the corresponding plaintext is known. This is very important as otherwise success in deciphering one message transmitted using a particular key may lead to all messages sent using that key to be deciphered. 'Computationally infeasible' means that it is not possible within a reasonable time scale to compute the desired result.

An example of the problem is where all of the encrypted messages have the date at a certain place within the messages. Since the actual date is known by the intruder, the intruder would then know the ciphertext corresponding to the plaintext. If it were possible to obtain D_k from this information, the cryptographic system would be extremely vulnerable to attack.

A second, and perhaps more obvious, requirement for secrecy is that is should be computationally infeasible to determine the plaintext from the ciphertext.

In order to provide secrecy, it is essential that D_k is secret. It is not necessary that the decryption algorithm be kept secret, but it is essential the combination of D and the key K be secret. E_k may be revealed provided knowledge of E_k does not permit knowledge of D_k to be computed from it. If E_k is public knowledge, it means that anybody can send secret information which can only be deciphered by the intended receiver possessing the decryption algorithm D_k. Figure 8.2 shows the concepts involved in secrecy.

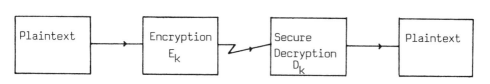

Figure 8.2 Secrecy

Authenticity has somewhat different requirements. Firstly, it should be computationally infeasible to systematically determine E_k given the ciphertext, even if the corresponding plaintext is known. If this were possible, an intruder could compute E_kK and then generate ciphertext, using the intruder's plaintext. The receiver would not necessarily be able to determine that the information came from an unauthorised source.

The second requirement is that it should be computationally infeasible to systematically find ciphertext which produces valid plaintext when deciphered by the receiver. This prevents an intruder from randomly generating ciphertext which produces the desired plaintext without knowing E_k.

To provide authenticity, E_k must be secret. The algorithm E may not necessarily be secret, but the combination of E and the key K must be. The decryption algorithm D_k may be revealed if it is not possible to compute E_k from it.

If D_k is public knowledge, then anybody receiving the information will be able to recover the plaintext and be sure that it came from the authorised transmitter. Figure 8.3 shows the concepts involved in authenticity.

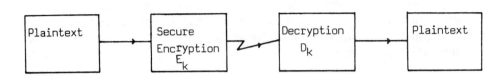

Figure 8.3 Authenticity

There are two basic classes of cryptographic systems. In the 'one-key' or 'symmetric' system, only one key is used for both encryption and decryption algorithms. In general, this means that both E_k and D_k must be kept secret. If this is done, the system provides both secrecy and authenticity.

The 'two-key' or 'asymmetric' system uses two keys, one for the encryption algorithm and a different one for the decryption algorithm. It must be computationally infeasible to determine one key from the other.

8.5.2 Public Key Encryption

Public key systems are an example of two-key systems. In this case, one of the two keys is made public while the other is kept secret. The public key may be published in something analogous to a telephone directory if required.

If the intended receiver's public key is used to encrypt information, then only the intended receiver can recreate the plaintext information (using the receiver's secret key). This mode of use provides secrecy.

If the transmitter uses its secret key to encrypt the information before transmission, then any receiver can recreate the original plaintext information using the original transmitter's public key. This mode of use provides authenticity.

Public key encryption can be used to provide both authenticity and secrecy simultaneously. First, the plaintext information to be transmitted is encrypted using the transmitter's secret key. The resulting information is then re-encrypted using the intended receiver's public key and then transmitted to the intended receiver.

The receiver first deciphers the received information using its own secret key. This is the secrecy part of the process. The resulting information is then deciphered back to plaintext using the transmitter's public key. This is the authenticity part of the process.

8.6 Encryption Algorithms

The purpose here is to provide a very brief overview of some of the common algorithms used within cryptographic systems.

8.6.1 Transposition Ciphers

The concept in transposition ciphers is to rearrange the letters in an information message in such a way as to hide the information content of the message. Basically an anagram is made of the message. All of the characters in the message remain the same, it is just the ordering of the characters that is different.

It is possible to identify that a transposition cipher has been used by checking the relative frequencies of occurrence of the letters in the ciphertext. This will be similar to the frequency in the original plaintext. The code can be broken using the frequencies of occurrence of digrams (two letter combinations) and trigrams (three letter combinations) to assist with the reordering of the letters.

8.6.2 Simple Substitution Ciphers

The idea here is to replace each character in the set of characters used in the plaintext with another in the set of characters used in the ciphertext.

As a simple example, take the case shown below:

```
Plaintext:       ABCDEFGHIJKLMNOPQRSTUVWXYZ
Ciphertext:      ZYXWVUTSRQPONMLKJIHGFEDCBA
```

Using this simple substitution cipher, the message:

```
SENDREINFORCEMENTSWEAREGOINGTOADVANCE
```

becomes:

```
HVMWIVRMULIXVNVMGHDVZIVTLRMTGLZWEZMXV
```

which, at first sight at least, hides the information content pretty well.

Another form of this type of cipher is where a 'shifted alphabet' is used to encrypt the information letters. This type of cipher is also called a 'Caesar cipher' because Julius Caesar used such a cipher where letters of the alphabet are shifted by three positions to the right:

```
Plaintext:       ABCDEFGHIJKLMNOPQRSTUVWXYZ
Ciphertext:      DEFGHIJKLMNOPQRSTUVWXYZABC
```

Here, the key is the number of characters that the alphabet is shifted.

This sort of cipher can generally be broken by analysing the frequency of occurrence of the letters in the ciphertext. If the frequencies can be obtained for the appropriate type of plaintext, it may be possible to find a relationship between the letters of the plaintext and the ciphertext.

8.6.3 Polyalphabetic Substitution Ciphers

To solve the problem with simple substitution ciphers (the fact that the frequency distribution of letters remains constant) polyalphabetic ciphers can be used.

An example of a polyalphabetic cipher is the Vigenere Cipher. Here the key is specified by a sequence of letters:

$K = k_1 k_2 ... k_d$
where each k gives the amount of shift in the corresponding letter.

Suppose that the plaintext is 'FREEDOM' and that the key is 'RANDOM'. The ciphertext will be:

```
Plaintext:        FREEDOM
Key:              RANDOMR
Ciphertext:       WRRHRAD
```

8.6.4 The Data Encryption Standard

The Data Encryption Standard (DES) is the nearest thing there is to a useful standard encryption technique that can be implemented in integrated circuits in order to provide high speed, safe, encryption of information. The DES was announced in 1977 by the National Bureau of Standards in the USA.

The DES encrypts 64 bit blocks of information with a 56 bit key. Then, using a combination of substitutions and transpositions, the algorithm generates the ciphertext. The same algorithm is used to decipher the information (the DES is a one key system).

There have been many criticisms of the DES, ranging from the most fundamental one (should there be a standard at all) to concerns about how secure the cipher is. The latter concentrates on the length of the key - many argue that the key should be 112 bits long to make the DES secure.

8.6.5 Rivest Shamir Adleman Scheme

The Rivest Shamir Adleman scheme (RSA) is based on the difficulty of finding the prime factors of large numbers.

The RSA is an example of an 'exponentiation cipher'. The RSA scheme encrypts a plaintext message block M into a ciphertext block C. The bits in M are treated as a number in the range 0 to n-1 (n depends on the number of bits in the message block).

The ciphertext is then computed by:

$$C = M_e \bmod n$$

e and n are the key to the encryption. In order to recover the plaintext message block M from the encrypted message block C, the following is performed:

$$M = C_d \bmod n$$

Here, d is the decryption key.

In practice, the encryption key e and n can be made public so that the RSA scheme can be used as a public key encryption system. The important thing is that it is computationally infeasible to compute d from the knowledge of e and n.

This is done when e, n and d are originally computed. First of all, two large secret prime numbers are required. N is then calculated from:

$$n = pq$$

e and d are then chosen, so that:

$$e.d = 1 \bmod [(p-1)(q-1)]$$

Having chosen one of the two numbers, d, for example, it is straightforward to calculate the other provided that p and q are known.

It is therefore the two prime numbers p and q that provide the security of the RSA scheme. In order to break the scheme, it is necessary to factor n into p and q.

If 100 digit numbers are used for p and q then n will be 200 digits. At the rate of one step per microsecond, it has been estimated that it would take several billion years to factor n.

Practical Aspects

Part 3 goes into the practical aspects of packet switched networks.

When to Use Packet Switching

This chapter deals with when it is appropriate to use packet switching and how to get the most out of packet switched networks. It covers remote sites and multiple vendor environments amongst others.

Packet Switched Network Physical Interfaces

A variety of different physical interfaces are used within packet switched networks. This chapter covers the most important interface types in detail and describes under which conditions the different interface types should be used.

Equipment for Packet Switched Networks

This chapter covers the practical aspects of equipment for packet switched networks. The emphasis of the section is on what to look for and where the dangers areas are. Each element of a packet switched network is covered in turn.

9

When to Use Packet Switching

9.1 Introduction

In this chapter we are going to look at the situations where packet switching can be used to greatest effect. Although packet switched networks could, in principle, be used in any situation, there are many cases where other types of networks are more suitable.

As an example of where a packet switched network would not directly provide the best solution is where a number of effectively identical PCs need to be connected together. The idea is that each PC can get access to files either on the other PCs or perhaps on a shared file server. There are many true LAN technologies (Ethernet, for example), which can do a very good job here.

Generally, packet switched networks are used when things are not as simple as a group of identical PCs confined to a small physical space. Coverage of large distances and connection of a large number of end-point devices is the forte of packet switched networks.

9.2 Linking Remote Sites

Take the case of a large company that has offices spread out over a very large area, possibly a nationwide distribution of offices. In each office, there may be a number of terminals, printers, PCs, minicomputers and mainframes. It is necessary to connect all of these devices onto one big network, so that total interconnection is possible.

Packet switching provides the solution to this problem. Figure 9.1 shows how such a network could be implemented. In this case, it is assumed that only a few of the offices have a significant number of end-point devices (PADs and host interfaces). These offices become the 'regional switching centres' for the network. The packet switches are located at the regional switching centres. If the end-point devices are more widely distributed, it may be necessary to place a small packet switch at each of the offices in order to keep the number of communications links down to a manageable level.

The links between the small offices and the regional switching centres will almost certainly be leased from the local PTT (British Telecom or Mercury in the UK). The most common communications link in use currently is probably British Telecom's KiloStream system. These are point to point links, usually running at either 9.6k bits per second or 64k bits per second (2.4k bits per second is also available). The choice of speed will depend on the anticipated usage of the link. There is a significant cost difference over the whole range of speeds.

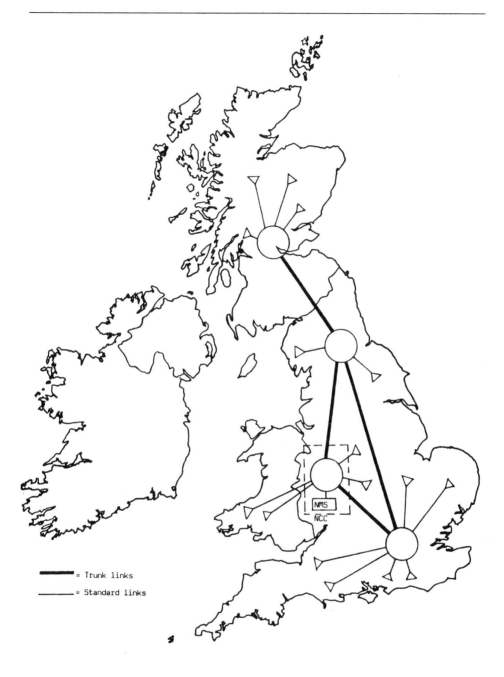

= Trunk links

= Standard links

Figure 9.1 Network linking remote sites

While KiloStream provides a digital link, it is also possible to use 'analogue' leased lines. These are basically specially conditioned, point to point telephone circuits. Modems are used at each end to provide the required digital interface. Leased line circuits are limited to about 19.2k bits per second and require quite fancy modems to operate at this sort of speed.

The regional switching centres themselves are connected together, providing the total interconnection required. The links between the regional switching centres are often known as 'trunk links'. These will have the heaviest loading of any links in the network as all packets moving between the regional switching centres must flow through them. This is where the 64k bits per second links are likely to be used with, 9.6k bits per second link between the regional switching centres and the outlying offices.

One of the regional switching centres is defined to be the 'network control centre' or NCC. The network control centre houses the network management system used to manage the network. Although the regional switching centres may have their own NMS for their region, there is usually an NCC in overall control. In a network of this size and covering this sort of area, full-time network managers will certainly be required. It is very important that the NMS provides information about problems very quickly to the network managers and in such a way that they can act on the information rapidly. Otherwise, problems with the network may build up into a backlog, resulting in unpredictable availability of the network as a whole.

Where very heavy use will made of the network, it may be necessary to use higher speed links to the outlying offices and for the trunk links. The next step up is to use 64k bits per second links to the outlying offices and MegaStream links, running at 2.048M bits per second for the trunk links between the regional switching centres. Where MegaStream links are being used, it may not be desirable to plug them straight in to a packet switch. In fact, very few packet switches can cope with MegaStream speeds at the moment. A more useful thing to do might be to use a 'MegaStream multiplexer'.

These multiplexers sit on the ends of MegaStream links and split the available capacity into a number of slower channels, possibly eight separate channels. These channels could then be taken to different packet switches in the regional switching centre allowing some routing redundancy. Some channels could also be used to connect directly to another regional switching centre via another MegaStream multiplexer, by-passing the packet switches at the local regional switching centre completely. Traffic not destined for an intermediate regional switching centre could then bypass it completely, reducing the loading on that regional switching centre.

It may also be of advantage if dynamic routing can be used between the regional switching centres. A trunk failure could be very disruptive unless rapid action is taken. Dynamic routing would allow the network to take action immediately. If a datagram protocol is used between the packet switches, then no information in transit need be lost even if a packet switch fails completely. In the case of X.25, the virtual call protocol could be run over a datagram protocol used between the packet switches in the regional computer centres. The datagrams would be transferred over the trunk links. The packet switches connected to the trunk links would then act as gateways between the X.25 protocol running to the outlying offices and the datagram protocol running over the trunk links. The use of datagram protocols over the trunk links usually means that all of the packet switches connected to the trunk links must be obtained from the same manufacturer. This removes one of the advantages in using X.25 in the first place, to get 'vendor independence', but the benefit may be worth it.

9.3 Multiple Vendor Environments

Mostly, companies try to have a consistent computer equipment purchasing policy. Compatibility and the ability to interwork is very important. However, things are rarely as simple as the extreme policy, that of buying equipment from only one manufacturer. Even this does not guarantee compatibility as over a period of time, old equipment may not be totally compatible with new equipment even from the same manufacturer.

Typically, some computer systems are good for some applications, others are good for other applications. Operating systems may vary according to the applications running on the computers. Sooner or later, there will be a requirement to allow file transfer, job transfer and general communications access to all of these different computers. It is in this situation that international standard protocols become really important. Most host computer systems worthy of the name will support X.25 at the very least. Even those that don't can generally be connected into an X.25 network using 'reverse PADs'. These allow access to the host computer system's asynchronous interfaces from the X.25 network.

Ethernet can also provide a solution to the multiple vendor situation. However, because Ethernet protocols are currently somewhat less standardised, different host computer systems may still not be able to communicate directly with each other. This situation will improve if OSI protocols are implemented. Ethernet (or other bus networks) do not really provide an effective solution to wide area networking (i.e., communications over large areas). Where Ethernet networks are used, these are generally connected to X.25 wide area networks via X.25 to Ethernet gateways. Although this does provide the required interconnectivity, things would be much simpler if X.25 was used throughout.

9.4 Difficult Environments

By a 'difficult' environment, we mean one that is difficult in the physical sense. A typical difficult environment is where the devices to be connected to the network are spread around several buildings, possibly separated by a public road or else by a significantly larger distance. In these cases, there is no choice but to resort to relatively slow leased lines or faster KiloStream connections.

Mass connection of a large number of terminals, possibly numbered in the thousands, also represents a difficult environment. This is especially true if the terminal users have to use character-based interaction with host computer systems. Screen editing is a classic example of the kind of use that large numbers of terminal users wish to make of a network. Screen editing operations can easily generate 20 packets per second per user. A large number of such sessions can generate very high loadings on any network.

Packet switched networks can provide very good solutions to networking in difficult environments. As each link in a packet switched network is separate from any other, the capacities provided and technologies used for each link can vary depending on the situation without any great cost or problems. For example, leased analogue lines can easily be included in a packet switched network to allow connection of remote devices. High speed links can be run over short distances using standard twisted pair cables. If there are areas with particularly high electrical noise, fibre optic cables can be used to provide high speed links without being affected by the electrical noise.

In the case of a network subject to very high loadings from screen editing sessions, packet switched networks can again provide, a very effective solution. Although networks like Ethernet have a basic cable capacity of 10M bits per second, each link in a packet switched network could run, with current equipment, at 250k bits per second. A medium size network might have 100 of these links, giving a total capacity of 25M bits per second. As 50 per cent utilisation of packet switched network links is quite easy to achieve, 12.5M bits per second could be carried on this packet switched network. This is far more than could ever be achieved with any Ethernet, or similar network, as it is very difficult to get more than a relatively small percentage of total cable capacity used productively.

Another useful aspect of packet switched networks where loadings are very high is that, if there is particularly large amount of traffic between two end-point devices, extra links can be added to ensure that packets are moved very efficiently between the two end-point devices. If it is possible, the two end-point devices could be connected to the same packet switch. This avoids heavy loading of the trunk links between packet switches.

9.5 Connection to Public Networks

Although a private network may satisfy a requirement for interconnection within a single company, there is very often a requirement to get access to other networks and to Value Added Network Services (VANS). Generally, the best way of getting to these external systems is to use a public network. Since these are almost exclusively X.25 networks, such as PSS, there is hardly any choice to be made. The only consideration is whether to go for a total X.25 solution, or whether to use a gateway between the private network protocol and the public network's X.25 protocol.

Very often, particularly in local government and central government communications systems, X.25 is being chosen throughout, so as to avoid gateways. Public organisations very often state that all equipment that they purchase must conform to international standards. Approval to connect to PSS is almost always a requirement for two reasons. Firstly, they may well want to connect their private network to PSS. Secondly, PSS connection approval is taken as a test of conformance and gives confidence that the implementation of X.25 is adequate for the job.

As most of these networks tend to cover large areas and include difficult environments, X.25 is very often the protocol chosen. This helps to prevent getting locked into a 'single vendor' situation and allows the network purchaser to shop around for the best equipment at the best price. The fact that X.25 is an international standard protocol and there are many manufacturers producing X.25 equipment means that equipment is constantly improving and prices falling.

10

Packet Switched Network Physical Interfaces

10.1 Introduction

The purpose of this section is to describe the various physical interfaces that are found on packet switched networking equipment. Even though the protocols run at higher layers may vary, there is only a fairly small range of interface types actually in general use.

10.2 X.21bis and V.24

The first of the layer 1 interfaces to be dealt with is the X.21bis interface, often also known as V.24. This type of interface is by far the most common at the present time and almost all X.25 equipment supports it. It is interesting to note that the CCITT recommendation states that X.21bis is just an interim recommendation until X.21 is used universally. This virtually guarantees that X.21bis will be around until the end of the universe.

Why are X.21bis and V.24 often used interchangeably? V.24 is basically a specification of how the 'interchange circuits' in the interface to between a DTE and a modem (the DCE) should operate. It specifies the 'interchange circuits' that may be present and how they can be used to control the operation of the modem and signal to the remote DTE. X.21bis uses those elements of V.24 that are required to provide level 1 support for X.25.

10.2.1 V.28

CCITT recommendation V.28 is one of the actual electrical specification of the interface that may be used with V.24 (i.e., it describes the characteristics of the drivers and receivers that are to be used in V.24 interfaces). In fact, X.21bis can be used with a variety of V series interfaces (V.10, V.11, V.28 and V.35) but is usually encountered in the form that uses V.28 electrical signalling.

Starting with the lowest level (ie that of the electrical signalling), V.28 will be described.

Figure 10.1 shows the general idea behind V.28 drivers and receivers. Note that there are two wires between the driver and receiver, with only one of them carrying the signal and the other the ground. This type of signalling is known as 'unbalanced'. The recommendation goes on to tie down the electrical characteristics of the interface pretty closely.

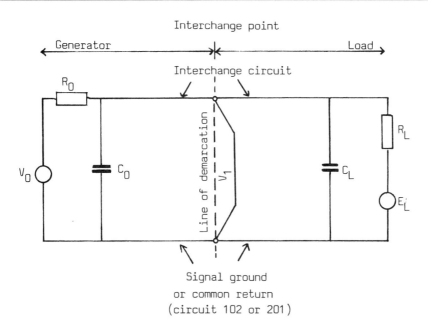

Figure 10.1 V.28 interface

The d.c. resistance (R_L) in the receiver must be between 3000 and 7000 ohms, with the open circuit receiver voltage not exceeding 2 volts. The shunt capacitance of the receiver measured at the interchange point must not exceed 2500 picofarads.

The driver should be able to withstand an open circuit and a short circuit between itself and any of the other drivers and receivers within the interface without damaging itself or anything else. Its open circuit voltage should not exceed 25 volts. The driver should generate a voltage at the interchange point between 5 and 15 volts in magnitude for load resistances (R_L) in the range 3000 to 7000 ohms.

The recommendation then goes on to specify how signals to be transmitted across a V.28 interface are handled. For the data interchange circuits, a binary 1 signal is sent by the driver as a voltage more negative than -3 volts. As a binary 1 is usually represented by a positive voltage, this means that data signals are effectively inverted for transmission. A binary 0 is sent as a voltage more positive than +3 volts.

The control and timing signals are handled in terms of their ON and OFF states. The ON state is indicated by a signal on the interchange circuit more positive than +3 volts.

The OFF state is indicated by a signal on the interchange circuit more negative than -3 volts.

Incidentally, the recommendation includes a happy note to the effect that, in some specific situations, the polarities stated above may be reversed!

The region between +3 volts and -3 volts is known as the 'transition region'. While the signal is in this region, the signal state is not all that well defined. The recommendation states that the time spent in this region (while the signal is changing from +3 volts or -3 volts or vice versa) should be limited to a millisecond or less.

The recommendation states that V.28 signalling is only good to 20k bits per second. This is partially because the 'maximum instantaneous rate of change' of the interchange signals is limited to 30 volts per microsecond. This is the rate at which the voltage can change in any one microsecond. This limit is imposed to stop very fast transitions on the interchange circuits. 'Fast edges' can cause a problem known as 'crosstalk' to occur. This is where signals on wires in the same physical cable interfere with each other. This can cause mis-operation of the interface if there is sufficient crosstalk.

What happens if nothing is connected to the input of a V.28 receiver? The recommendation allows receivers not to notice and therefore produce an undefined output (i.e., it could be a binary 1 or a binary 0). In most cases, however, the receivers treat this condition intelligently. The data circuits assume a binary 1 state and the control and timing circuits assume the OFF condition.

Virtually all modern interfaces using V.28 signalling utilise integrated circuit drivers and receivers to satisfy all of the requirements of the recommendation. Commonly, the positive voltage is between +12 volts and +15 volts with the negative voltage between -12 volts and -15 volts.

In many real applications, interfaces using V.28 signalling are used in situations not entirely covered by the recommendation. In one case, V.28 signalling was being used at 76.8k bits per second over a cable 30 metres long. Believe it or not, although the link was noisy, it did actually work. This sort of thing is not really recommended though.

The problem is that as the signal travels down the cable, the magnitude of the signal voltage reduces. As the voltage gets near to the 3 volt point, the signal gets very susceptible to electrical noise. The noise can take the signal onto the wrong side of the 3 volt mark and may cause the receiver to get the state of the signal wrong (generate a binary 0 instead of a binary 1, for example). This is even more serious for clock signals as it is the transitions of the clock signal that are important. As noise can generate extra transitions, the effect on clock signals can be very severe indeed.

Another effect of long lines is that the shape of the signals change. The sharp edges gradually get less steep and the signal more 'rounded'. This can make it very difficult for the receiver to reproduce the original signal correctly and again result in mis-operation.

10.2.2 The X.21bis Interchange Circuits

Having described the electrical signalling, we can now move onto the actual functions of the various data, control and clock signals in the interface.

The interchange circuits in the interface are grouped into the '100 series' and the '200 series'. The 100 series series are for general application and, in most cases, are the only significant signals. The 200 series are used for 'automatic calling'. This facility can be used in situations where it is possible for the DTE to specify to which remote DTE the connection is to be made (i.e., where circuit switching is provided). It is essentially a primitive method for calling, transferring data and then clearing connections to remote DTEs.

Since we are interested here in the parts of V.24 that are relevant to X.21bis and thereby in packet switched networks, only a subset of the 100 series will be described.

Circuit 102 - Signal ground or common return

This is used to provide the signal common return for the unbalanced interchange circuits if V.28 signalling is being used, or a d.c. reference potential for the interchange circuits if V.10, V.11 or V.35 signalling is being used.

Circuit 103 - Transmitted data (TXD or TD)

Transmitted data refers to the data transmitted by the DTE and received by the DCE.

Circuit 104 - Received data (RXD or RD)

Received data refers to the data received at the DTE and transmitted by the DCE.

Circuit 105 - Request to send (RTS)

This is a control signal generated by the DTE and an input to the DCE. It is used to control the data transmit function of the DCE. If the signal is ON, the DCE is able to transmit data received from the DTE. If it is OFF, then the DCE will stop transmitting data from the DTE.

Circuit 106 - Ready for sending (CTS)

This signal is often known as 'clear to send', hence the CTS abbreviation. This is a control signal generated by the DCE and an input to the DTE. If the signal is ON, the DCE is prepared to accept data from the DTE. If the signal is OFF, the DCE is not prepared to accept data from the DTE.

Circuit 107 - Data set ready (DSR)

This control signal is generated by the DCE and an input to the DTE. If DSR is ON, the DCE is ready to exchange further control signals with the DTE to initiate data transfer.

Circuit 108/1 - Connect data set to line (DTR)

This control signal is generated by the DTE and an input to the DTE. The signal is also known as Data Terminal Ready, hence the DTR acronym. When in the ON state, this signal indicates that the communications equipment should be connected to the line (i.e., go to an active state). When in the OFF state, the communications equipment should go to an inactive state.

Circuit 109 - Data channel received line signal detector (DCD)

This control signal is generated by the DCE and an input to the DTE. This signal is also known as Data Carrier Detect, hence the DCD acronym. When in the ON state, this signal indicates that the received data signal on the communications link is acceptable. When in the OFF state, this signal indicates that the received data signal is not acceptable.

Circuit 114 - Transmitter signal timing element (DCE source)

This signal is a clock signal generated by the DCE and an input to the DTE. The signal is commonly known as TSET-DCE. The clock signal is used to time the data signal transmitted by the DTE on circuit 103. Transitions of the data signal should occur when the clock signal on circuit 114 goes from OFF to ON.

Circuit 115 - Receive signal element timing (DCE source)

This signal is a clock signal generated by the DCE and an input to the DTE. The signal is commonly known as RSET-DCE. The transitions of the data signal transmitted by the DCE on circuit 104 will occur when the signal on circuit 115 goes from OFF to ON. The data should be sampled at the centre of the data bit (i.e., on the ON to OFF transition of the clock signal).

Circuit 140 - Loopback/Maintenance test

This control signal is generated by the DTE and an input to the DCE. When in the ON state, this signal indicates that the DCE should go into a maintenance mode. When in the OFF state, this signal indicates that the DCE should not be in a maintenance mode.

Circuit 141 - Local loopback

This control signal is generated by the DTE and an input to the DCE. When in the ON state, this signal indicates that the DCE should go into a 'loopback' mode. These allow various parts of the DTE/DCE connection to be tested without involving the communications link or the remote equipment. When in the OFF state, this signal indicates that the DCE should not be in loopback mode.

Circuit 142 - Test indicator

This control signal is generated by the DCE and an input to the DTE. When in the ON condition, this indicates that the DCE is in a maintenance mode. When in the OFF state, this indicates that the DCE is not in a maintenance mode.

10.2.3 The X.21bis Connector

The various V.24 circuits in the V.28 form of X.21bis appear on a connector known as a 'D25'. The mapping of V.24 circuit numbers to the D25 connector pins is defined in a specification published by ISO as ISO DIS 2110 and in the UK by the BSI as BS 6623: Part 1. Table 10.1 gives the essential information from these specifications for X.21bis.

10.3 X.21

X.21 is the 'correct' interface for packet switched network equipment that will gradually replace X.21bis in the fullness of time. Like X.21bis, X.21 borrows other X and V series specifications to provide various aspects of the recommendation. The first of these are X.26 and X.27, the two electrical signalling recommendations that X.21 permits. Just to confuse everybody, X.26 is identical to recommendation V.10 and X.27 is identical to V.11. Even more confusing is the fact that V.10 is very similar to RS-423 and V.11 virtually identical to RS-422. We will use the V.10 and V.11 forms here and forget about the rest.

10.3.1 The V.10 Interface

This is another unbalanced interface that is fairly similar in some respects to V.28. The main difference is that the recommendation specifies 100k bits per second as the maximum rate at which the V.10 interface should be used. It also gives a number of circumstances where V.10 should not be used.

1) Where the interconnecting cable is too long.

2) Where electrical noise makes operation impossible.

3) Where interference with other signals is to be minimised.

One of the main differences between V.28 and V.10 is that, whereas in V.28 the thresholds are at +3 volts and -3 volts, in V.10 the threshold are at +0.3 volts and -0.3 volts. Another difference is that, whereas in V.28 the voltage swing may be from -15 volts to +15 volts, in V.10 the voltage swing can only be up to -10 volts to +10 volts.

Table 10.1 X.21bis connector assignment

Pin number	Circuit
1	-
2	103
3	104
4	105
5	106
6	107
7	102
8	109
9	-
10	-
11	-
12	-
13	-
14	-
15	114
16	-
17	115
18	141
19	-
20	108
21	140
22	125
23	-
24	-
25	142

Since in many cases the voltage supplies used in practical implementations of V.28 are only 12 volts in magnitude, it may be just about all right to connect together V.10 and V.28 equipment without taking any special precautions.

The recommendation also has some comments about the length of cable over which V.10 will probably work (depending on the cable quality etc). At the maximum data rate of 100k bits per second, the recommendation suggests that only cable up to 10 metres be used. The maximum cable length recommended is 1000 metres at which length data rates should be kept below 1000 bits per second.

10.3.2 The V.11 Interface

The V.11 interface is the more interesting as it is a 'balanced' interface. Each signal has two wires associated with it. One carries the 'true' form of the signal, while the other carries the 'inverted' or 'false' form of the signal. This type of interface is also known as 'differential' signalling, because the original signal can be reconstructed by taking the difference between the received true form of the signal and the received false form of the signal.

The cables used to carry balanced interfaces are normally 'twisted pairs'. In this type of cable, the individual wires are grouped into pairs. Each pair of wires is twisted together with a pair used to carry the A and B forms of a signal. This technique ensures that any electrical noise coupled into the wire is equally coupled into both wires. Because the two signals are subtracted from each other at the receiver, any noise cancels out, leaving a clean signal, a surprisingly effective technique . The signals at the receiver can individually look quite horrible and be barely recognisable, but as long as the signal level is not too low and the noise is equal in both wires, the receiver can successfully recreate the original signal.

The recommendation identifies the false form of the signal as being the 'A' signal and the true form as being the 'B' signal. The 'A' signal is analogous to the unbalanced signals in the way the original signals are mapped into the transmitted signals.

For data signals, a 0 condition is transmitted as a signal where signal A is more positive that signal B. A 1 condition is transmitted as a signal where signal A is more negative that signal B.

For control signals, the ON state is indicated by the signal A being more positive than the signal B while the OFF state is indicated by the signal A being more positive than signal B. The general idea is shown in Figure 10.2.

As for V.10, the receiver thresholds are at +0.3 volts and -0.3 volts. The difference is that, in V.11, the received voltage is the difference between the signal A and the signal B. If V_A represents the voltage on the signal A and V_B represents the voltage on the signal B, then the receiver voltage is V_A-V_B.

The normal voltage ranges for the signals A and B are between 0 volts and 5 volts. In fact, the receiver specifications for the V.10 receivers and V.11 receivers are identical. If V.11 receivers are to be used with V.10 drivers, then the B inputs of the V.11 receivers are connected to ground.

The V.11 recommendation also has some comments about the maximum data rate and length of cable over which the interface can be used. At the maximum data rate of 10M bits per second, the recommendation suggests that cable length should be less than 10 metres. At the maximum recommended cable length of 1000 metres, the data rate drops to 100k bits per second.

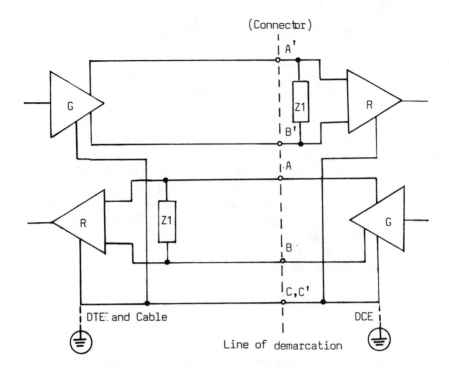

Figure 10.2 V11 interface

V.11 is the interface of choice when using X.21 and, in fact, most X.21 interfaces do use V.11 signalling as it gives excellent high speed performance over long cable runs without significant error rates. Certainly at rates of 64k bits per second and over, V.11 signalling is the most likely interface to be used.

10.3.3 The X.21 Interchange Circuits

The X.21 interchange circuits are very different from the V.24 interchange circuits used in X.21bis. In particular, every circuit has an A and a B component to carry the A and B signals.

The definitions of the X.21 interchange circuits can be found in recommendation X.24. X.24 is to X.21 what V.24 is to X.21bis. Only the parts of X.24 relevant to X.21 will be described here.

Circuit G - Signal ground or common return
This circuit interconnects the zero volt reference of the transmitter and receiver ends of the circuit.

Where V.10 signalling is being used, the G circuit is split into two - the Ga circuit and the Gb circuit. The Ga circuit is the DTE common return and is connected to ground at the DTE. The DCE can then use the signal as a reference for the receivers within the DCE. Gb is similar, except that the roles of the DTE and the DCE are reversed.

Circuit T - Transmit

The transmit circuit is used by the DTE to transmit data to the DCE.

Circuit R - Receive

The receive circuit is used by the DCE to transmit data to the DTE.

Circuit C - Control

The control circuit is used by the DTE to indicate to the DCE the state of the interface. During the data transfer phase, the control circuit should always be ON.

Circuit I - Indication

The DCE uses the indication circuit to indicate to the DTE the state of the interface. During the data transfer phase, this signal is always ON.

Circuit S - Signal element timing

This signal, generated by the DCE, is used to control the timing of the data on the transmit and receive circuits. Transitions on the transmit and receive circuits should occur at the OFF to ON transition of the signal on this circuit.

Circuit B - Byte timing

The signals on the byte timing circuit provide the DTE with byte timing information generated by the DCE. This circuit is not mandatory in X.21 and is rarely seen.

10.3.4 The X.21 Connector

The specification for the X.21 connector is contained in ISO 4903 and published in the UK by the BSI as BS6623:Part 3. Table 10.2 shows the essential information from this specification. The connector used is known as a 'D15' and is very widely available.

10.4 V.35

V.35 is an odd sort of interface that appears from time to time, usually on old fashioned mainframes. V.35 specifies that the data rate used should be 48,000 bits per second and so is not a general purpose interface. Another problem that V.35 suffers from is that the electrical signalling specified for V.35 is totally different to any other type in general use. Although V.35 in its role as an X.25 physical interface will hopefully die a very rapid death, it is described briefly here for completeness.

Table 10.2 X.21 connector assignment

Pin number	Circuit X.26	X.27
1	–	–
2	T	T(A)
3	C	C(A)
4	R(A)	R(A)
5	I(A)	I(A)
6	S(A)	S(A)
7	X/B(A)	X/B(A)
8	G	G
9	Ga	T(B)
10	Ga	C(B)
11	R(B)	R(B)
12	I(B)	I(B)
13	S(B)	S(B)
14	X/B(B)	X/B(B)
15	–	–

10.4.1 The V.35 Electrical Interface

The V.35 electrical interface consists of a diabolical mixture of V.28 and something completely unique. The V.35 control signals use standard V.28 drivers and receivers. The V.35 data and clock signals, however, uses differential signalling similar to V.11, but with a different specification.

10.4.2 The V.35 Interchange Circuits

The interchange circuits used in V.35 are given below.

Number	Interface	Function
102	-	Signal ground or common return
103	V.35	Transmitted data
104	V.35	Received data
105	V.28	Request to send
106	V.28	Ready for sending
107	V.28	Data set ready
109	V.28	Data channel receive line detector
114	V.35	Transmitter signal element timing
115	V.35	Receiver signal element timing

10.5 G.703

G.703 is a standard interface for operations at very high link speeds. For example, British Telecom's MegaStream presents a G.703 interface to the user's equipment. G.703 is specified at a number of different bit rates

10.5.1 Interface at 64k bits per second

The 64k bits per second interface involves three signals in each direction of transfer. The first is the 64k bits per second information signal. The second is a 64kHz timing signal (clock). The third is an 8kHz timing signal that is used to provide byte timing (i.e., it is used to mark the start and end of bytes being transferred across the interface).

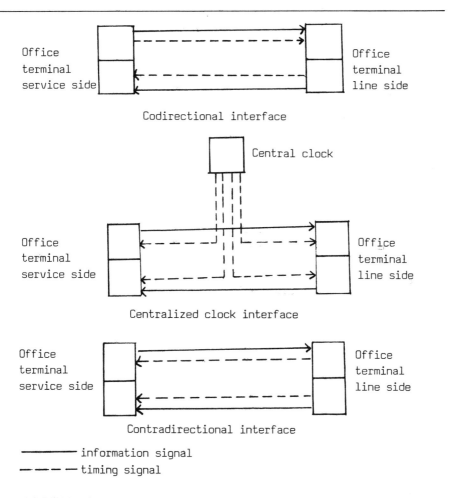

Figure 10.3 G.703 interface system

Three styles of interface are envisaged in the recommendation. These are shown in Figure 10.3. In the *co-directional interface*, timing signals are generated by the transmitter in each direction. In the *centralised clock interface*, a distinct clock is used to generate the required timing signals for both directions of transfer. In the *contra-directional interface*, the line side of the interface generates both clocks for the interface. This is analogous to the normal style of connection to modems.

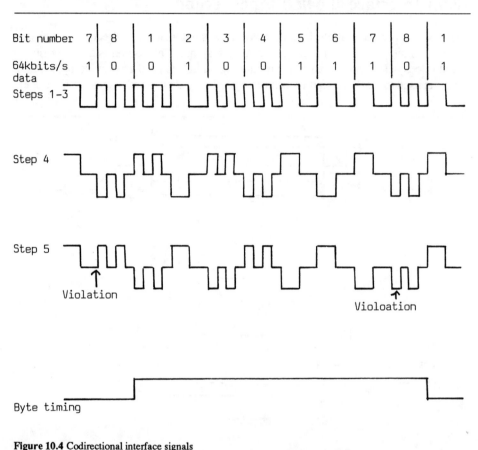

Figure 10.4 Codirectional interface signals

The 64k bits per second co-directional interface

The cabling for the co-directional interface consists of one balanced pair of wires for each direction of transfer. The two timing signals are encoded into the data stream. Figure 10.4 shows an example of how the system works. The encoding process consists of five steps:

Step 1 divides each 64k bits per second period into four unit intervals.
Step 2 encodes a binary 1 as the bit pattern 1100.

Step 3 encodes a binary 0 as the bit pattern 1010.

Step 4 encodes the signal as a three level signal by alternating the polarity of each consecutive 4 bit unit.

Step 5 encodes the byte timing signal into the data signal by violating the polarity alternation every eight units on the last bit of each byte.

The 64k bits per second centralised clock interface

The cabling for this interface consists of one symmetrical pair in each direction of transfer to carry the information signal. Two symmetrical pairs go from the centralised clock to each end of the link. Figure 10.5 is an example of the information and timing signals for the centralised clock interface. The information signals are encoded using the 'AMI' code. (AMI stands for Alternate Mark Inversion code and is a system that uses three level signalling to convey the information signal.) Successive binary 1s are represented by a sequence of alternating positive and negative polarity pulses with equal amplitude. Binary 0s are represented by a zero amplitude signal (i.e., no pulses).

The 64kHz timing signal is also transferred using the AMI code. The 8kHz timing signal is encoded into the 64kHz timing signal by introducing violations of the alternating polarity rule on the last bit of each byte on the information signal.

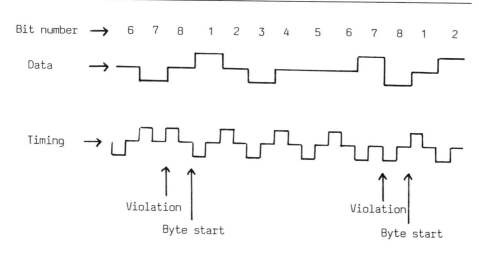

Figure 10.5 Centralised clock interface signals

The 64k bits per second contra-directional interface

This interface uses exactly the same information and timing encoding rules as the centralised clock interface. The only difference is that the two symmetrical pairs carrying the timing information start at the line side of the interface, instead of a centralised clock.

10.5.2 Interface at 2.048M bits per second

This version of the G.703 interface requires one coaxial or symmetrical pair in each direction of transfer. The signal is encoded using a system known as 'HDB3', which is short for High Density Bipolar 3.

HDB3 uses a three level signal to transfer information. The three states are denoted B_+, B_- and 0.

Spaces (binary 0s) in the signal are encoded as spaces in the HDB3 signal unless there are four spaces in a row (see later).

Marks (binary 1s) in the binary signal are encoded alternately as B_+ and B_- in the HDB3 signal in the same way as for the AMI code.

There are three rules for dealing with strings of four spaces. The first space of a string is coded as a space if the preceding mark of the HDB3 signal has a polarity opposite to the polarity of the previous violation and is not a violation itself. It is coded as a mark if the preceding mark of the HDB3 signal has the same polarity as that of the preceding violation or is by itself a violation.

The second and third spaces are always coded as spaces.

The last space of a string of four is always coded as a mark, the polarity of which is such that it violates the rule of alternate mark inversion.

The purpose of all of this is to ensure that adequate timing information is carried by the HDB3 signal and that the dc component of the signal is kept to an absolute minimum.

10.5.3 Other G.703 interfaces

The G.703 recommendation also carries specification for interfaces operating at 1.544M bits per second, 6.312M bits per second, 32.064M bits per second, 44.736M bits per second, 8.448M bits per second, 34.368M bits per second, 139.264M bits per second and 97.728M bits per second.

Equipment for Packet Switched Networks

11.1 Introduction

The purpose of this section is to give some idea of what to look out for when considering the purchase of packet switching equipment. Since most current packet switched networks are X.25, or at least, present X.25 interfaces to the outside world, the emphasis will be very much on the selection of X.25 equipment.

No specific, real, products will be mentioned in any detail. However, where it is possible, a rough price guide will be given to illustrate what can be bought for a certain amount of money. These prices should be viewed with some suspicion as, due to advancing technology and increasing competition, prices are falling all of the time.

Although manufacturers' specifications for products are generally correct, it is often important to look behind quoted figures to see their relevance and validity in real life operation. Often, the conditions in effect when a particular performance figure was obtained are not quoted. It is difficult for the potential customer to assess what these figures mean in practice. As a general rule, equipment should always be assessed operating in the role for which the equipment is being purchased.

In order to put the equipment into a realistic situation, it is usually necessary to try the equipment out at the customer's site. It is very common for potential customers to evaluate equipment at the customer's site before purchase. This allows the customer to establish performance figures relevant to the customer's application, something far more important than a manufacturer's rather abstract performance figures. If the manufacturer is confident of the equipment's performance, it will usually be possible to arrange such an evaluation. If the manufacturer (or supplier, if the equipment is being supplied via a third party) is unwilling to allow on-site evaluation, then the customer has to decide whether or not the equipment is up to standard.

Just before going on to discuss the individual devices in detail, it is worth defining what we mean in this book by a 'packet switch per second'. On any network connection, there will be a variety of packets flying about. For the purposes of measuring performance, the only packets counted are end to end packets containing data at the network layer. All other protocol and control packets at the network layer and below are excluded. In order to switch a packet, it must be received, routed and then transmitted. This whole process is considered to be one packet switch. Therefore, the number of packet switches per second is the number of end to end data packets that are received, routed and then transmitted in one second. In general, packet switching rates are averaged over a period of time to get a realistic figure.

11.2 Network Communications Links

There are many ways of providing a link between two devices. The choice in any particular situation depends upon three parameters: the distance between the devices, the speed at which the link has to operate and the cost.

11.2.1 Direct Connection

The simplest possible way of connecting devices together is simply to use a cable containing the appropriate number of wires between them. This is only possible within a single site. If it is necessary to cross a public road, a direct connection is usually impossible, as there are lots of rules preventing this sort of thing.

A factor when considering direct connection is the number of wires required to connect the devices together. This may vary from 4 wires up to 10 wires if control signals need to be sent. For example, an X.21 connection requires at least three pairs of wires (receive data, transmit data and clock). If the Control and Indication signals are to be sent, another two pairs are required. X.21bis connections require a minimum of four wires (receive data, transmit data, clock and ground) if a combined receive and transmit clock is used, going up to ten if separate clocks are used and all of the useful control signals are to be connected.

The distance between the devices is also a factor, as is the speed at which the link is to operate. For example, X.21bis can just about manage 100 metres or so at 9.6k bits per second. If the distance is increased, the speed has to be decreased. For example, at 500 metres (if the link works at all) it is unlikely that operation at more than 2.4k bits per second will be possible with a manageable error rate.

The only cost to be considered using direct connection is that of installing the cable in the first place. Even that may not be necessary if existing cable can be used for the network link. Often, the old 'star network' terminal wiring found at many sites can be pressed into use to provide packet switched network links. Even if new cable has to be installed, it only involves an initial capital cost with no recurrent element.

11.2.2 Line Drivers

Still on the subject of those situations where private cables can be used to connect together the two devices, line drivers provide a way of running fast links over long distances.

Generally speaking, line drivers only require two twisted pairs to provide a full communications link between two packet switched network devices. A simple synchronous line driver, powered from an X.21bis interface using V.28 signalling, can drive data at rates up to 19.2k bits per second over a distance of 6km. At low speed (1.2k bits per second), this rises to around 18km. The cost of a pair of these simple line drivers is around £300. Higher speed line drivers, capable of operating at 64k bits per second and using two twisted pairs between the two ends of the link, are also available. The cost for a pair of these line drivers is around £750.

There is usually a choice of internal or external clocking for the serial data on the link so that the line drivers can cope with all clocking requirements.

11.2.3 Analogue Modems

In situations where either there are not enough wires to allow a direct connection or use line drivers, or it is not possible to provide a private cable between the devices, modems can be very useful. Synchronous modems, the type suitable for packet switched network use, generally require either two or four wires between them. A modem is required at each end of the cable because they use clever signalling techniques to provide the connection. Two wire modems are almost always 'half duplex'. This means that, although transmission in each direction is possible, only transmission in one direction at a time is permitted. The modems periodically 'turn round' in order to allow transmission in the other direction. Rather more useful are four wire modems which allow 'full duplex' transmission. This means that each direction of transmission is independent of the other and can operate simultaneously.

If two wire modems are used, it is possible to use standard telephone circuits to provide the link between the two modems. This gives the system a 'dial-up' capability where the modem at one end of the link can dial up the other one across the telephone network. Once the link is established, the packet switched network protocols can be started. Four wire modems require 'leased lines'. These are special lines that have to be rented from the local PTT (British Telecom or Mercury in the UK). The precise type of signalling used between the modems depends on the speed at which they can run. 4 wire full duplex synchronous modems running at 2.4k bits per second use the CCITT V.26 recommendation. The recommendation also allows for a supervisory channel running at up to 75 baud in each direction. This could be used for remote monitoring of the state of the link.

Some modems use the V.26bis recommendation, which allows half duplex operation at 2.4k bits per second over the telephone network. Again, a 75 baud supervisory channel is allowed for within the recommendation. The recommendation allows for operation at the 'fall back' rate of 1.2k bits per second if it is found that the line cannot support the higher rate.

Modems capable of operating at 4.8k bits per second use the CCITT V.27 recommendation. This recommendation allows for either two or four wire circuits. There is also a V.27bis recommendation. The difference between the two is that V.27 specifies manual equalisation while V.27bis specifies automatic equalisation. Equalisation is the process of trying to undo the effects of the cable in-between the two modems. This consists of correcting for amplitude distortion (i.e., variations in the strength of the signal) and delay distortion (i.e., variations in the delay of the components of the signal) that could lead to corrupted data.

In the case of manually adjusted equalisation, the modems are equalised at installation time. Automatic equalisation is rather better as it can adapt to changes in the characteristics of the line over periods of time. This helps to keep the error rate minimised.

At 9.6k bits per second, modems use the V.29 recommendation which allows full duplex operation at this rate over four wire leased lines. Fall back rates of 7.2k bits per second and 4.8k bits per second are included if the line quality cannot cope with the higher speed operation. Recommendation V.32 provides the capability to run full duplex at 9.6k bits per second over the telephone network (quite an impressive feat).

Above 9.6k bits per second, there are no CCITT standards for modems in the 1984 recommendations. Some manufacturers do produce modems that run at 14.4k bits per second, but these use non-standard techniques so that the same manufacturer's modem has to be used at each end of the connection.

At rates much above 9.6k, it is necessary to use one of the digital circuits available from British Telecom or Mercury.

11.2.4 Digital Circuits

The ultimate way to connect packet switched network devices together over large distances is to use a digital circuit. The most commonly used digital circuit type is British Telecom's KiloStream service. KiloStream circuits can be obtained at rates from 2.4k bits per second up to 64k bits per second. At 48k bits per second and below, special bits are added to the transmitted information in each direction, invisible to the devices using the link. The purpose of these bits is to allow remote diagnosis of faults.

Figure 11.1 shows how the KiloStream system works. The Network Termination Units (NTUs) are modem-size blue boxes which provide the interface to the packet switched network devices at each end of the link. These are connected by a four wire circuit to a local KiloStream multiplexer. The local multiplexers are connected, via 2M bits per second lines, to demultiplexers at the 'Cross connect site'. Here the individual KiloStream circuits are joined to provide the required point to point connections.

If the two ends of the link are in the same area (i.e., they use the same Cross connect site), the installation charge for a 64k bits per second link is around £400 with an annual rental of around £2,000. If the KiloStream connections are to different Cross connect sites, then there is an extra charge depending on the distance between the two Cross connect sites. The installation charge is around £500 with an annual rental of around £3,500 if the distance is 10km.

A variety of interfaces to the packet switched network devices is available. X.21 is available at all speeds. X.21bis is available at 2.4k bits per second, 4.8k bits per second and 9.6k bits per second. There is also a V.35 version for 48k bits per second lines.

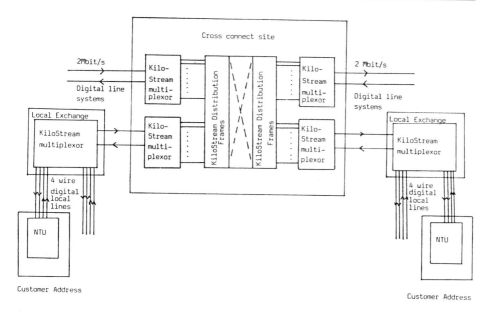

Figure 11.1 The KiloStream system

For those applications that require very high speed lines, British Telecom's MegaStream service provides a solution. There are four basic versions of MegaStream circuits: MegaStream 2 running at 2.048M bits per second; MegaStream 8 running at 8.448M bits per second; MegaStream 34 running at 34.368M bits per second; and finally MegaStream 140 running at 139.264M bits per second.

The interface to MegaStream circuits uses a the G.703 recommendation, described in Chapter 10.

The cost of a MegaStream circuit depends on the speed of the link and the distance over which the link runs. As a guide, a MegaStream 2 circuit from one device to the local MegaStream exchange, running over 1,000 metres, costs around £10,000 to install and around £700 per year in recurrent charges. A similar link is required to the device at the other end of the link. If the devices are connected to different MegaStream exchange, then a 'main link' is required between the two exchanges. The installation charge for a 15km main link is around £700 with an annual rental charge of around £5,000.

Mercury offer a number of services at 64k bits per second, 2M bits per second and above, mirroring British Telecom's services to some extent. The Mercury system is not as well-developed at the moment, although this situation will no doubt change in the future.

11.2.5 Public Networks

A slightly different method of connecting devices together is to make use of a public data network. The most important example of this in the UK is British Telecom's Packet SwitchStream, more commonly known as PSS. PSS is itself an X.25 packet switched network which offers three basic methods of connection. Two of them are ways of getting access to PSS while the third provides an interface for X.25 equipment.

Character devices (terminals, for example) can get access to PSS either using a dedicated, leased, circuit or else via the telephone network (dial-up access). If a private X.25 network is connected to PSS, it is possible to access the private network from a terminal by calling the private network across PSS.

PSS can also be used to connect together parts of an X.25 network that may be spread around the country. These are known as 'Packet Terminals' in PSS terminology. The difference between using a point to point link, such as those described earlier and using PSS to provide links between packet switched network devices is in cost and connectivity.

Fixed point to point links (KiloStream, leased lines, etc.) are not charged for usage. A fixed annual rental is charged, no matter how much use is made of the link. Public data networks not only charge an annual rental, but also make usage charges, based on the amount of time that calls are active and the amount of data transferred on each call.

If the link between the two devices is very heavily used, then a fixed point to point link will be cheaper than using a public data network. On the other hand, if the loading is likely to be light, use of the public data network might provide a more cost effective solution. This is particularly true if KiloStream links are to be used, as they can get quite expensive when the distance between the two ends of the link is large.

There are a variety of speed options available for PSS packet terminal connections. The slowest line, 2.4k bits per second, costs £850 to install and around £2,000 annual rental. The 9.6k bits per second lines cost £950 to install with an annual rental of around £3,700. To the annual rentals must be added some other smaller charges depending on the number of logical channels required, etc.

The charges for use are based on the amount of time that calls are active and the number of 'kilosegments' of data transferred. A segment is 64 bytes of data. The charge is around £0.30p per hour for the call connect time and £0.30p per kilosegment for data transferred.

One thing to watch for with PSS connections and most other things that have to be installed specially is the amount of time that it takes to get the lines installed. Delays of the order of months are the rule rather than the exception, so it is important to plan ahead.

11.3 Packet Switches

The choice of a packet switch is obviously very important in any packet switched network. This is because any unreliability or other problems have far more impact in a packet switch than in any network end-point device (with the possible exception of the Network Management System).

If the performance of the packet switch is inadequate, then no matter how fast the end-point devices are, they will only achieve the throughput that the packet switch allows. If the packet switch can only support a limited number of network connections, lower than that expected in operation, a condition known as 'network congestion' will occur. This is clearly undesirable as it limits the use of the packet switched network.

Packet switches can be grouped into three rough categories: low performance; medium performance; and high performance.

Low performance packet switches are suitable only for small packet switched networks or perhaps as small satellite packet switches connected to higher performance main packet switches. Typically, a low performance packet switch can handle network links running at up to 9.6k bits per second. The maximum number of network links may also be very limited, usually 16 or less. In the case of X.25 networks, the maximum packet size supported by this type of packet switch is likely to be 256 bytes.

This type of packet switch usually only has a single processor (often a Z80 microprocessor of some type) and there is frequently a limited amount of buffering space available. This means that just a relatively small number of virtual call channels can be supported at any one time. This may be as low as 50 virtual calls running through the packet switch at any one time. If the switch has 16 links, this is an average of just over three calls per link. This is clearly going to be adequate for only the smallest networks.

The packet switching rate will also be relatively low. This is because just a single processor has to run the link layer, network layer, switching and management functions. The rates obtained are usually below 50 packet switches per second. For comparison, a 9.6k bits per second link running at full speed can transfer about 8 128 byte packets per second. So a packet switch which runs at 50 packet switches per second can only run about six links at full utilisation.

Another figure to look at is how many network links the packet switch can run simultaneously at the quoted link speeds. A single microprocessor may have trouble running the link level protocol for a large number of links at full speed. The way that manufacturers quote this figure is as an 'aggregate link rate'. Basically, this is the maximum total rate that can be achieved. If the sum of the link rates in use on the various network links are added up, they should not exceed the maximum aggregate rate. If a packet switch is capable of running ten 9.6k bits per second links simultaneously, then it should have an aggregate link rate capability of at least 96k bits per second.

If a packet switch's aggregate link rate is exceeded, the effects may not be noticeable immediately. If the loading of the links is low enough, it may be possible to get away with an aggregate link rate higher than that supported by the packet switch. The problem will rear its ugly head when link loading goes up, however. Typical effects are that the link error rates go up rapidly. As this can result in an even greater load on the processor (re-transmitting link layer frames), the effect can be made worse. The net effect can be to reduce the useful throughput to almost zero; very many frame retransmissions go on with few useful frames being transferred. Often, by reducing link rates in this situation, total throughput can actually go up by avoiding this situation.

The best way of quoting prices for packet switches is to give a the price per link. Usually packet switches with a large number of links have a lower cost per link than smaller switches because the basic cost of the packet switch is shared between the links. £500 per link is about the maximum that should be paid for a low performance packet switch of the type described here. Therefore, a 10 link low performance packet switch should cost around £5,000 or less. These packet switches generally only have X.21bis interfaces, as they are perfectly adequate to cope with the low link speeds.

The next step up is a medium performance packet switch. Here we are looking at something that can switch up to about 500 packets per second and cope with a much higher aggregate link rate than low performance switches. 500 packet switches per second represents an aggregate link rate of 500k bits per second. This means that multiple processors, or at least fairly intelligent link layer interfaces, will almost certainly be used if the packet switch is not to be limited by its maximum aggregate link rate.

Medium performance switches also have a choice of interface types. X.21bis, X.21 and V.35 are usually available, possibly along with an X.27 interface. X.21 and X.27 allow the links to be run at high speeds over reasonable distances. In particular, the links can be run at 64k bits per second allowing connection to 64k bits per second KiloStream links. The number of simultaneous network connections through a medium performance packet switch is going to be in excess of 250 and may be as high as 1,000.

Typical prices per link for such a packet switch will be from around £500 per link up to £1,000 per link, depending upon the precise nature of the packet switch, the number of facilities supported, the number of processors used, etc. This particular type of packet switch is currently the most competitive segment of the packet switch market and so the price per link is likely to reduce rapidly.

Finally, there are the high performance packet switches. These have packet switching rates in excess of 500 packet switched per second and may achieve 2,000 or even more. There are usually many processors involved, linked together by shared memory or some other high speed method of inter-processor communications. This type of packet switch can handle, and make reasonable use of, network links running at 2M bits per second. This is a very significant number as, assuming that a G.703 interface can be fitted to the packet switch (and it is suitably approved for connection), a BT

MegaStream can be plugged straight into the packet switch.

Price per link of a high performance switch may well vary from link to link. This is because there may be both standard and high speed network link interfaces available. High speed interfaces may be from £1,000 per port upwards with possibly lower cost standard links.

The area of high speed packet switches is relatively new and is possibly the area most affected by technical developments. We may well see the low performance switches vanishing and being replaced by the medium performance switches taking their place as the 'bread and butter' packet switches. High performance packet switches would then be used as either the trunk switches in a network, or wherever high packet throughput, or high link speeds are required.

Incidentally, and just to conclude the subject of packet switches, the simple relationship between the packet switching rate and the maximum aggregate link rate quoted is often forgotten. It can provide a very useful insight into the nature of manufacturer's performance figures. The following conversation, based on one that one of the authors had with a real network equipment supplier, illustrates how this can be useful in practice (the author is 'customer', the supplier is 'supplier'):

Customer: Your packet switch looks very interesting. How many packet per second can it switch?

Supplier: It can switch 200 packets per second.

Customer: Are those 200 128 byte network layer data packets per second?

Supplier: Yes.

Customer: What is the maximum aggregate link rate that your packet switch can support?

Supplier: 100k bits per second.

Customer: That is very interesting. Since a 128 byte packet is at least 1,000 bits, 200 packet switches per second implies an aggregate link rate of 200k bits per second at least, double the maximum figure.

Supplier: Hmmm.

Almost certainly, the packets per second figure was obtained with smaller packets. If the customer was expecting to be able to switch 200 128 byte packets per second through this packet switch, the customer is going to be unlucky.

The packet switching rate itself is only part of the performance story. Another thing to check is the number of call set ups per second that the packet switch can handle. This, rather less often quoted figure, can be useful in large networks where there is generally a large amount of activity. It can also be relevant in small networks when things go wrong.

Suppose for example, that some end-point device tries to set up a number of calls to another end-point device on the network. The idea is that the calls should always be maintained so that data can be transferred whenever necessary. Suppose that 30 calls are to be maintained. What happens if the destination end-point device becomes unavailable? The originator of the calls will try to re-establish the failed calls again. This will, of course, fail. Suppose the calls are retried every 30 seconds, the result is that every 30 seconds a burst of 30 call set ups per second are received at a packet switch to be processed. All will fail.

What happens at this point depends on the ability of the packet switch to process call set up attempts that fail. This will often be very much worse than the number of successful call set ups per second that the packet switch can handle, especially if it has to try alternate routes that also fail. The result can be that the packet switch is brought to a complete standstill. It spends all of its time trying to process call set ups that are doomed to failure. No time is left for switching packets on existing calls.

This is particularly serious as it means that the failure of one end-point device can result in other end-point devices being very seriously affected, even though the packet switch is still operating correctly. It is often said in this sort of situation that the failed device 'back-fired' into the packet switch. So it is essential to consider failure modes of a packet switched network to ensure that the remaining network can operate as normally as possible. If a failure in one location in the network is allowed to spread throughout the network, the reliability of the network as a whole will be severely impaired.

As far as physical aspects of packet switches are concerned, there are two basic choices: desk mounted and rack mounted. Desk mounted packet switches are, fairly obviously, the kind that can be placed on a desk somewhere. This implies that the packet switch is fully enclosed. The other alternative is the rack mounting variety. These are designed to fit into '19 inch racks' of the type commonly found in computer rooms for communications equipment. This type of mounting is almost always used for all, but the smallest packet switches as larger packet switches tend to be located in computer rooms and therefore are conveniently mounted in 19 inch racks.

11.4 PADs

PADs are the interface between most users and a packet switched network. The PAD rapidly becomes identified as being the network. (The mysterious packet switches and gateways that lie beyond are not normally visible and so have only a low key image in the eyes of PAD users.) Any problems with the PAD are likely to annoy a large number of users, especially if some problem seriously limits the work that they can do.

As with packet switches, it is possible to group PADs on the basis of performance. Again, there are three groups: low performance; medium performance; and high performance PADs.

Starting with the low performance PADs, these are likely to use a single processor, almost always a Z80 microprocessor, to run all of the software in the PAD. It is obvious from previous discussions of the load that this imposes that the performance obtained from such a simple architecture is going to be very limited.

The network link speed of this type of PAD will not run at any speed greater than 9.6k bits per second. Also, the asynchronous PAD ports (the interfaces to the PAD users) are limited to 9.6k bits per second. Although some PADs of this type claim to run at faster network link speeds, they suffer from the same problem as packet switches in that there is a maximum aggregate rate that can be supported. For a PAD with a single processor, both the network (synchronous) links and asynchronous ports have to be considered as they both load the processor. Experience shows that trying to run this sort of PAD at greater link speeds with many asynchronous ports in use results in lost network link frames. This results in a lot of attempts to transmit each frame, wasting an awful lot of time doing nothing.

Another problem is likely to be 'input data capture'. This refers to the PAD's ability to process incoming characters from the asynchronous ports. It is very important that the PAD should not lose any characters because there is no way of checking that characters have been lost. This is in contrast to the network link where frames are checksummed and lost bytes would result in checksum errors. An important figure is the maximum rate at which the asynchronous ports can be run with the PAD still guaranteeing to capture received characters. In the case of low performance PADs, this may also be affected by the rate at which the network link is running.

Many low performance PADs were designed purely to connect dumb terminals to packet switched networks. Fantastic input data capture capability was not considered important because people just cannot type that fast. As soon as personal computers started being connected, the problems started appearing. This is because computers can transmit data at the line rate (usually 9.6k bits per second) which corresponds to a character rate of 960 characters per second. If the PAD has 16 asynchronous ports all operating at this speed, it must be able to process 15360 characters per second if it is not to lose characters.

If this last situation seems unrealistic, consider the situation where PADs are used as reverse PADs. This is usually done to connect a host computer to a packet switched network for which there is no suitable host interface. The asynchronous PAD ports call across the network to similar ports on the host computer. It is quite conceivable that, if there are 16 calls active, all ports could be receiving data from the host computer simultaneously. Although flow control will be used to control the characters from the host computer, there will be times when there is a burst of characters to all 16 ports at the same time. It is these peak loads that the PAD must be able to handle if characters are not to be lost.

Another consideration is the amount of buffer space available within the PAD. In low performance PADs, this is likely to be quite limited. This can give problems when the PAD is being heavily loaded with all ports in use. It is quite common for low performance PADs to run out of buffer space and give up the ghost entirely by restarting. The result is, probably, 16 very unhappy users.

Screen editing is the operation that generates the most load on a PAD. Low performance PADs are really totally unsuitable for this sort of operation. Although it is possible to get reasonable screen editing performance using a 9.6k bits per second network link, the problem is the network level packet rate that low performance PADs can achieve. This is unlikely to be much higher than 50 (single character) packets per second. As for packet switching rates, the only packets counted here are network layer data packets. Some manufacturers try to include all types of packets, including link layer control frames, in order to get better figures.

Since a single user screen editing via a PAD can generate 20 packets per second pretty easily, only about two to three screen editing sessions can be supported effectively on a low performance PAD. Also, because the network link rate is only 9.6k bits per second, it is impossible for the 128 byte packet throughput to be much more than eight packets per second. Clearly, since the network link is only 9.6k bits per second and there is some protocol overhead, this will be insufficient to drive even one of the asynchronous ports at full speed!

Another problem with low performance PADs is that they generally have very poor user interfaces, offering the minimum number of features required to set up calls, transfer data and then clear the calls again. The ultimate in user-unfriendly interfaces is that exhibited by the PSS PADs, the PADs you get through to if you dial up the PSS service, completely unmemorable and incomprehensible commands and responses that seem designed to stop them from being used. As for getting meaningful information about the state of a call and the PAD port, forget it!

The only really good thing about low performance PADs is that they are relatively cheap. The 'standard' X.25 PAD has a single network link and 16 asynchronous ports. The price of such a PAD should not be more than around £3,000. Options may include a second network link. Some PADs allow the customer to start with a small PAD, say four ports, and build up over time to a larger PAD. In the ultimate extreme, there are the 'monoPADs' which have only a single asynchronous port.

Often, if a complete network is being purchased from a single supplier, it will be possible to get a very good deal on the PADs. Low performance PADs can be obtained from a wide variety of manufacturers and suppliers and is a very competitive area. However, as customers become aware that they are really inadequate for most current requirements, the share of the market held by low performance PADs is bound to reduce as time goes on.

The next step up are medium performance PADs. These generally use a 16 bit microprocessor, like the Intel 80186, or a number of microprocessors to split up the processing load. Medium performance PADs are characterised by the fact that their network links can be run at 64k bits per second. These PADs are generally targeted at KiloStream connection, hence the link rate capability. Medium speed PADs also offer higher asynchronous port speeds. These can be up to 19.2k bits per second, or, in some cases, 38.4k bits per second.

Due to the improved hardware, the software is usually better and can offer more facilities to the user. More user-friendly information displays and help facilities are usually provided. Sophisticated mnemonic name to explicit address mapping functions are usually available, saving the user having to enter long, unmemorable, address strings.

In some cases, the PADs may be able to support a 'Name Server' interface. A Name Server is an end-point device that has an extensive database of name to explicit address mappings. When a user tries to call using one of these names, the PAD first passes the name to the Name Server. The Name Server responds by providing an explicit address for the PAD to try. If the attempt to set up a call using that address fails, it may be possible to ask the name server for alternative routes. This entire process is invisible to the user. To avoid loading the Name Server too much, the PAD may implement a local 'cache' of mappings so that frequently used names can be mapped locally.

Typical 128 byte packet throughput rates for medium performance PADs are in the 50 to 100 packets per second range. The figure of 60 packets per second is very important as 60 packets per second represents a fully utilised 64k bits per second communications link. Prices for high performance PADs are in the range £3,000 up to £5,000 depending on the facilities provided and the performance offered. This area is relatively new and has only recently begun to get off the ground. However, medium performance PADs at reasonable prices are going to kill off the low performance end of the market totally over the next few years, as medium speed PADs are found to offer the minimum acceptable performance for many practical network applications.

Finally, we get to the high performance PADs. This is a very new market and there are relatively few PADs available with suitable performance. Minimum requirement for this category is a throughput of at least 100 128 byte packets per second and at least 200 single byte packets per second. Network link speed is almost unlimited as it is almost a requirement that dedicated link controller integrated circuits are used to provide the link layer interface. As these can support link rates of up to 10M bits per second, the link rate capability is not likely to be a problem for some time to come!

One thing to look out for in PADs which boast very high network link speeds is how much the PAD can actually use of the link capacity. In the case of PADs with link speeds in excess of about 250k bits per second or so, it is very unlikely that the PAD could make full use of the link. A high link speed capability can still be useful, though, as it keeps the frame transit delay on the link very low. This is very important in situations where very low delays are necessary (screen editing is a classic example). As an example, many PADs quote a maximum network link speed in excess of 64k bits per second. When actually tested, however, some PADs were found to be unable even to drive data through the link at half this rate.

High performance PADs get their speed by using several processors to support the considerable capacity required of these PADs. A possible functional separation was described in Chapter Three that allows the maximum amount of parallel processing to take place.

Asynchronous port speeds offered by these PADs are much the same as for medium performance PADs. The main difference is that a high performance PAD will be able to get good throughput on all of its ports simultaneously. To illustrate this, suppose that the PAD has 16 asynchronous ports running at 9.6k bits per second. In order that the PAD can output characters received from network layer data packets on all ports simultaneously (representing about eight 128 byte network layer data packets each), the PAD must be able to support a throughput of at least 128 of these data packets per second. As each 128 byte network layer packet is roughly 1,000 bits, this requires a link rate of 128k bits per second at least.

As with packet switches, this simple calculation can be used to verify the consistency of manufacturer's performance figures. The conversation below is again (very loosely) based on a real conversation between one of the authors and a supplier.

Customer: What is the maximum link rate that your PAD can support?

Supplier: 64k bits per second.

Customer: How many of the asynchronous ports can be outputting network layer data simultaneously?

Supplier: The PAD can run all 16 ports at 9.6k bits per second simultaneously.

Customer: How many 128 byte network layer data packets per second can the PAD handle?

Supplier: 75.

You will no doubt be delighted to know that this time the author concerned kept his or her mouth shut and did not point out the inconsistencies between the three figures.

Prices for (real) high performance range from about £4,000 upwards. Technology in this area is moving fast so that these prices will probably fall in time to come. Also, as the market for high performance PADs develops, volume will go up bringing prices down as a result.

As with packet switches, PADs are often available in desk mounted and rack mounted forms. PADs are often placed at random locations and therefore the ability to just place one on a desk is quite useful. It is also common to want to locate PADs near to a packet switch in order to concentrate the equipment in one location for operational purposes. In this case, rack mounted PADs will be more useful.

Just before leaving the subject of PADs, it is worth mentioning the hybrid PAD and packet switch. This is where either a packet switch has a limited PAD capability or else a PAD has a limited switching capacity. These hybrids have the advantage of combining functions within one physical unit with an appropriate cost reduction over using separate hardware for each system.

This is a minor advantage compared to the disadvantages. The functions performed by packet switches and PADs are really quite different and any combination of the two functions is going to mean that compromises have been made. So, apart from the smallest packet switched networks where the requirement is too small to warrant separate devices for each function, it is wise to give the hybrids a miss.

11.5 Host Interfaces

As usual, we are going to group host interfaces into three groups on the basis of performance: low performance; medium performance; and high performance.

Low performance host interfaces are classed as those that cannot run their network links at rates greater than 9.6k bits per second. Even this is a scorchingly fast rate compared to some of the really poor host interfaces with speeds of 4.8k bits per second or less. Although such interfaces can be used for file transfers over slow leased lines and the like, time had better not be important. At 9.6k bits per second flat out, it takes around 20 minutes to transfer one megabyte of information, the contents of a single PC AT type floppy disk.

Low performance interfaces are also totally inadequate for supporting interactive access from PADs. Although a 9.6k bits per second host interface can support a single 9.6k terminal reasonably well, if there are 10 sessions active, performance is likely to be less than adequate.

Low performance interfaces are usually found on old minicomputers and mainframes that assumed that access to the computer was going to be via its asynchronous ports. The packet switched network interfaces were grafted on at a late stage and are usually not very well integrated with the computers operating system. One of the authors had an experience with one such computer where, if the link to the packet switched network went down, it would not come up again until the whole computer had been restarted. This is not very popular on a multi-user computer system.

The area of host interfaces also covers packet switched network interfaces for PCs. This is a rapidly growing area, particularly in the case of X.25 cards, as the cost per connection to the network reduces due to the use of improved technology and greater competition. Many of these PC interface cards come into the low performance category due to their low link speeds. These interface cards basically consist of a serial interface. The PC's own processor has to run the network and link layer software, imposing a very heavy load on the PC and reducing the usefulness of the interface.

Medium performance interfaces are those that can support network link speeds up to 64k bits per second. This usually means that the interface cards have on board processors running the link layer protocol and possibly even the network layer protocol. These interfaces are generally adequate to support a reasonable number of interactive sessions from PADs and some file transfers all at the same time. One thing to consider here is the maximum packet rate that the host interface can support in order to ensure that the link rate can be fully utilised.

Very often there is an interaction between the loading on the host computer and the performance obtained from the packet switched network interface. How much one affects the other depends on how much of the software is run on the interface card and how much the host computer has to involve itself in the operation of the packet switched network interface.

The last category contains the high performance host interfaces. These are interfaces that can support packet switched network connections at rates greater than 64k bits per second. There are relatively few of these about at the moment, although some very good host interfaces running at 72k bits per second are available. Increased use of dedicated integrated circuits to cope with high link rates in the future will very much improve the capabilities of host interfaces.

It is difficult to give much of a price guide for host interfaces as they vary so much, depending on the type of host computer under consideration. The only comment to be made is that the price varies from a few hundred pounds up to several thousand pounds, depending on the computer. Interface cards for PCs vary from a few hundred pounds up to about £1,000.

11.6 Gateways

Similar comments apply to gateways as for host interfaces. The particular characteristics of a gateway depends on the types of network on each side of the gateway and the protocols in use. Possibly the most common gateways in large scale use are Ethernet to X.25 gateways. X.25 network link speeds of typical gateways can vary between about 9.6k bits per second up to 64k bits per second. This type of gateway is often used to provide a means of accessing wide area networks from an Ethernet local area network.

Validation gateways and charging gateways are mostly custom-built for particular applications, as requirements can vary so much between application. The most important consideration here is the ease of writing the software to drive the network interfaces on each side of the gateway.

Wherever possible, it is best to avoid gateways as they are traditionally slow and unreliable. Inconsistencies in mapping the functionality of different networks on each side of the gateway may also present problems, particularly in the area of network addressing.

Prices for gateways will obviously depend on the level of performance offered and the types of network on each side of the gateway. As a rough guide, prices between around £3,000 and £8,000 are representative.

As well as the type of gateways mentioned above, there are also the smaller scale PC local area network gateways, typically connecting NETBIOS networks into X.25 networks. These utilise PC network interface cards of the type described earlier. Prices for this type of gateway are roughly the same as for the interface cards themselves.

11.7 Network Management

For almost any packet switched network other than the very smallest, a network management system (NMS) is virtually essential. The precise features required of the NMS will vary depending on the particular type of network in question, but most features are common to all networks.

Monitoring device availability is probably the most important function from the point of view of the network managers. Ideally, the NMS should respond very rapidly to the loss of any device on the network or a communications link. The network managers should be alerted both visually and audibly to ensure that serious network events do not go unnoticed.

Collecting information about the operational state of the network is also important. It should be possible to record link loadings, link errors, packet switch loadings, etc., on disk, so that the information can be processed at a later date. Serious problems should alert the network managers straight away as they may be able to take action that prevents a more serious situation developing.

Collecting billing information from the network is another function that is commonly required. Again, it should be possible to save the billing information on disk, so that invoices to users can be generated automatically.
Managing the network configuration is also a function of the NMS. This could include PAD configurations, routing tables for packet switches and validation tables for gateways. Ideally, the NMS should be able to give a graphical display of the topology of the network. Even better is if the NMS can annotate such a display with real-time information about link loadings, etc. This can provide the network managers with a very good insight into how the network is performing at any time.

In some networks, the NMS contains the operating software used in the various network devices. The devices contain enough software to enable them to start up and call the NMS. The NMS now downloads the appropriate software to them. They car then begin to run in their operational role. This strategy has the advantage that it is very easy to upgrade the software in the network devices. All that has to be done is to upgrade the copy on the NMS and then download this into the target devices, often known as 'booting over the network'. The disadvantage is that the devices may not be able to run normally at all if the NMS is unavailable for some reason.

Normally, there is a main NMS which performs all of the functions described above. It is sometimes useful, however, to be able to get access to the NMS remotely. Typically, the NMS will be located in a computer room, so that the state of the network can be monitored by normal operations personnel. It may be desirable to edit configurations and monitor network status from a more pleasant location, such as an office.

In order to do this, the NMS must be able to handle remote NMSs. These call into the main NMS in order to access the configuration and real-time status databases maintained there. It is obviously important that such access only be available to suitable validated callers.

In the case of very large networks, remote NMSs may be used to help collect real-time information at a faster rate than would be possible if just a single NMS was used.

NMSs usually consist of a PC of some kind or a small minicomputer with the appropriate packet switched network host interface fitted. The choice of PC or minicomputer will largely determine both the cost of the NMS and the facilities offered. NMS prices vary widely. Low cost NMSs start at around £5,000 all the way up to around £100,000 for very sophisticated systems designed for large networks.

11.8 Supporting the Network

Choosing the correct equipment for a packet switched network is only half of the story. The network has to be installed and then supported during its operational life. Often, the same equipment is supplied by a range of manufacturers and suppliers. They may look superficially different, but in the end they may be exactly the same. There is a packet switch on the market at the moment which is manufactured by at least three different companies and supplied by a much larger number of companies.

The difference between the various suppliers is likely to be support. Support consists of two parts: software support and hardware support.

Software support, as its name implies, deals with the operating software used in the devices forming the packet switched network. As communications software is generally very large and complicated, it is important that bugs detected in operation can be corrected. The customer reports these problems back to the supplier. What happens then varies widely. In some cases, the software developers are brought in to correct the problem. In other cases, particularly when the original development was done overseas, it may not be possible to get the problem corrected.

Something to establish before the equipment is purchased is whether any payment is required to get bugs fixed. In some cases, bugs are fixed at the next release of new software, which probably means that the customer will have to purchase the new release to get the bug (or bugs) fixed. As an alternative, some suppliers offer a software support service, which operates a bit like insurance. The customer pays a certain amount per year and receives in return any new release of the software that may occur.

It may be important to establish the software development path that is planned for the equipment. For example, most X.25 networks currently use the 1980 version of the protocol. Many networks, however, will be moving to the 1984 version in time. It may be very important to establish that 1984 will be available on an appropriate timescale.

The second aspect of support is hardware support. This deals with how hardware failures in operation are dealt with. The services offered are usually of the 'guaranteed response' type. This means that it is guaranteed that a service engineer will appear at the customer's site within a specified time. The basic service level is usually eight hours. If better response is required, response times of four hours and even two hours may be available. The ultimate is to have permanent on-site engineers. Although it may not be practical to pay for a service company's on-site engineers, it may make sense to train up some in-house people to look after the equipment. If this is planned, it is necessary to ensure that the supplier is prepared to hand over the required circuit diagrams etc to allow this to be done.

Of course, the fact that an engineer turns up does not mean that the problem will be fixed immediately. Usually, the engineer turns up with a range of spares to cope with the more common faults. If the problem is more serious, there may still be a considerable delay before the fault is corrected. If it is essential that hardware failures are corrected rapidly, the best solution may be to have some spare devices on-site that can be used to replace faulty equipment.

Part 4

The Future

In the last part of the book we are going to take a look into the future. This is almost always a dangerous activity.

The first area under consideration are packet switched network protocols. The second area is network equipment where there are likely to be some very great changes in the future. Lastly, we take a look at where Value Added Network Services (VANs) are likely to be going in the future. This is probably going to be the most interesting area of all.

Up until fairly recently, packet switched networks have been in the technology development stage. In the foreseeable future, high performance packet switched networks with high reliability are going to be generally available at reasonable costs. Packet switched networks will then begin to be used as a reliable tool that is an almost invisible link between the user and whatever facilities the network can offer.

Clearly, it is pointless to have a very efficient network without anything interesting to call. Networks are by their nature only means to ends. The ends in question are the VANs that can be accessed via the networks.

12

Protocol Developments

12.1 Introduction

In this section of the book we are going to look at where packet switched network protocols may be going in the future.

In general, the move towards standardisation is going to slow down innovation so far as protocols are concerned. Most attention is now going to focus on technology (how fast packet switched networks can be made to run). The main protocol developments are likely to be in the areas so far not covered by standardisation.

12.2 Datagram Protocols

Networks, particularly packet switched networks, tend to be large in area and contain a large number of network devices. Even if the failure rate of an individual piece of equipment is very low, if there are large numbers of devices, the failure rate when considering the network as a whole will be very much higher.

The use of the multilink procedures (MLP) rather than the single link procedures (SLP) version of X.25 level 2 will be a major step forward in providing fault tolerance within the network. Although MLP is an improvement, it only works at the frame level and so requires more than one link between each network device to be effective. What is really required is a network level fault tolerance capability.

Failures in the network are detected by Network Management Systems (NMSs). Some NMSs are able to re-configure the network around failures to allow normal operation to continue as much as possible, in spite of the failure. It is obviously rather better if the network itself is able to do this. After all, if the NMS is isolated by a failure, it no longer has access to the remainder of the network to re-configure it. Even if the NMS has multiple links into the network, there will be some failures that prevent the NMS from accessing parts of the network.

The first part of the solution is to use distributed adaptive routing. Although this is not a new concept, its use has not been widespread. An extra layer of protocol is required to allow packet switches to communicate information about network configuration. Since this has not been standardised to any extent, there has been no general move to provide such protocols. As the move is away from proprietary protocols and towards international standards, nothing much will happen until there is an international standard for distributive adaptive routing.

The second part of the solution is to use datagram protocols within the network itself. End-point devices attached to the network could either run the network datagram protocol itself or else connect to the network using a virtual call protocol such as X.25 level 3. In a pure virtual call network, the failure of a packet switch in the network results in the loss of any virtual calls through that packet switch. In a datagram network, this type of failure is easily coped with without the loss of calls or data. Coupled with distributed adaptive routing, the network can respond very quickly to faults, reconfigure, and then continue operation normally.

Until such protocols are standardised, distributive adaptive routing will remain a manufacturer-specific system, preventing its widespread use.

12.3 Network Management Protocols

At the time of writing, network management protocols are still highly manufacturer-specific and, in some cases, jealously guarded. Even if the network management protocol is available in the public domain, every manufacturer tends to use different protocols.

Network management of packet switched networks is still at the stage where it is seen as an advantage not to be compatible with other manufacturers. When a manufacturer sells a network to a customer, the customer is almost expected to take the manufacturer's NMS. Some networks will not even operate without the manufacturer's NMS. The result of this lack of real competition is that many of the network management systems on offer are not particularly exciting. Just about the only thing that they do have in common is that they are very expensive, up to £100,000 in one case.

The situation with Ethernet is a bit different. Most of the network management of Ethernets consists of watching packets fly by on the Ethernet cable and checking what they are up to. Retrieving information from the devices connected to the cable is a rather secondary requirement.

Packet switched networks, due to the fact that the packets are distributed around the network, are intrinsically much more difficult from the network management point of view. It is not much use to look at a single link as only a very limited view of the network is obtained. The only way to do it is to get the network devices to monitor traffic on behalf of the NMS. This is what makes standard network management protocols essential for packet switched networks.

There are moves towards standardising packet switched network management protocols. When they arrive, the NMS market will change dramatically. Enormously expensive NMSs will vanish as competition brings the prices down. At the same time, functionality within the NMS will increase.

Until the benefits of competition arrive, NMSs will continue to be rather mysterious, expensive and ineffective.

12.4 Name Server Protocols

Name Servers are almost essential in large networks and very helpful in small networks. What they do is to map a memorable name for a particular network destination into the explicit address that the network itself needs.

For example, suppose the convenient name for a particular host computer system is 'hosta'. The explicit address for that might well be something really horrible, in many cases exceeding 60 characters. Most people find 60 character strings difficult to remember, particularly if there are 40 digit numbers in there somewhere!

What a PAD user, trying to call hosta really wants to do is to type:

```
call hosta
```

This is much better than typing the explicit address. It is then up to network to sort out what the explicit address happens to be. Some PADs are able to keep a table of name to address mappings internally. If hosta is in the table, there is no problem. Suppose hosta is not there, the PAD then has to be able to access more information than can be stored in the PAD.

If the PAD has access to a Name Server, it can call it up and check if the Name Server knows the name 'hosta'. If it does, it returns the explicit address for the PAD to try. If that fails there may be more maps available and so on. If the PAD is really clever, it will 'cache' the maps locally so that they can be used again.

This is all very well, but how do the PAD and the Name Server do this? The answer is that they use a Name Server protocol over a call between the PAD and the Name Server. Via this protocol, the PAD and Name Server can process the name to address mapping function. If the Name Server has a large amount of disk storage, there is no reason why it cannot hold names for every device on the network.

For OSI networks, a Name Server is possibly even more important. This is because the OSI NSAP addresses to not themselves carry any routing information (they are global addresses). Somehow, the network has to determine where a particular device is on the network.

The route between devices depends on the location of the calling and the called endpoint devices. This implies that the Name Server has to know the complete architecture of the network in order to provide the mapping function. In fact, this is not required so long as domain structuring of the address is used. This adds an element of routing information to the OSI NSAP address. Name Servers then only need to know about the domain in which it logically resides. This allows smaller Name Servers to be distributed throughout the network.

Although Name Servers have been in use for many years, they have not been in widespread use for the usual reason, the protocols have not been standardised. In the UK, the Joint Network Team (JNT) has defined such a protocol called the NRS Lookup Protocol (NLP). The NRS part stands for Name Registration Scheme. This refers to the database of callable end-point devices on JANET, the Joint Academic Network used by academic institutions throughout the UK.

Name Servers have the effect of hiding the underlying network addressing from the user, even if route addressing is used rather than global addressing. For example, it is possible for the Name Server to avoid faulty parts of the network by mapping names into a different explicit network address if there is an alternate route. Name Servers can impose a weak form of access control by validating connection attempts on the basis of the caller's location on the network. This can be used to reserve resources on the network for specific applications. If a user that is not validated tries to call a protected end-point device, the Name Server does not return a map and therefore prevents access.

13

Future Network Equipment

13.1 Introduction

In this section we are going to look at the possible development path for packet switched network equipment. The emphasis is likely to be in the areas of higher reliability, higher performance and greater ease of use, both for the network managers and the network users. The actual provision of the network service itself will be less of a consideration as the interconnection of network devices and end-point devices will be taken for granted.

13.2 Network Communications Links
13.2.1 ISDN

An Integrated Services Digital Network (ISDN) may provide the ideal means to interconnect future packet switched networks together across large distances. There are some distinct advantages to using an ISDN connection rather than a pure packet switched network connection.

The first advantage is that ISDN provides circuit switching capability. One characteristic of circuit switching is that delays through a circuit switching network are minimal. This is in contrast to the packet delays introduced when going through packet switches in a packet switched network. Once a path through an ISDN has been selected, a channel is available with guaranteed throughput totally unaffected by other users of the ISDN.

Another advantage of running over ISDN is that, as the connection is transparent, any protocol can be carried. This is in contrast to public packet switched networks where it is necessary to conform to the specific protocol supported by the public network.

13.2.2 FDDI

FDDI stands for Fibre Distributed Data Interface. FDDI is in fact a fibre optic implementation of an IEEE 802.5 token ring that, in its standard form, runs at 100M bits per second. A second form of FDDI, known as FDDI-II, can support both packet switched and circuit switched traffic whereas FDDI only supports packet switched data. The distinction made here is that a fixed data rate is guaranteed for circuit switched data. An enhancement to FDDI allows the ring to operate at 1.2G bits per second (i.e., 1200M bits per second).

Although FDDI itself is not a packet switched network, it could be used to interconnect packet switched networks over quite reasonable distances with very high data throughputs. In this role, FDDI would be called the 'backbone' supporting the packet switched networks.

FDDI may well provide a very effective method of interconnecting packet switched networks over so called 'metropolitan' areas where individual links in the ring can be greater than ten kilometres in length. Networks over this sort of area are known as 'MANs' which is short for Metropolitan Area Networks. A 1.2G bits per second ring could support a large amount of inter-network traffic very effectively.

13.3 Packet Switches

The architecture of packet switches is going to move to large scale use of parallel processing and the use of dedicated integrated circuits for link layer and possible network layer protocol support and fault tolerance.

13.3.1 Parallel Processing

The old style concept of using a single processor driving a packet switch with a large number of links is already looking inadequate. No matter how fast a single processor is, it will never compete with a number of less powerful processors operating in parallel. In general purpose computing, this is not always so, as the advantages obtained by using multiple processors depends on the 'concurrency' of the application. This basically means that the advantage depends on how much of the application can be processed in parallel rather than sequentially. If a single application can be split up into ten smaller ones that can be processed in parallel, parallel processing will be very effective. If the application cannot be split up, there will be no gain in speed.

Fortunately, communications in general, and packet switching in particular, can be very easily split into a number of concurrent tasks. The ultimate step is to use a separate processor for each link on the packet switch. Given that there is a high speed channel to route packets between the link processors, a very high throughput packet switch will be the result. The only central task is network management and general tasks of that nature. A separate processor, not involved in the packet switching process, could be used to take care of these sorts of tasks.

13.3 2 Dedicated Protocol Support Integrated Circuits

The only way to obtain very high link speeds with high utilisation is to use dedicated protocol support integrated circuits. There are a number of integrated circuits offering X.25 level 2 support on the market currently. These offer link speeds up to 10M bits per second without loading their controlling processor. As techniques improve, this speed may well be exceeded.

The use of Gallium Arsenide integrated circuits for dedicated link layer protocol support holds out the possibility for even higher link speeds, possibly as high as 100M bits per second.

In packet switched networks, pure link speed itself is only part of the story. It is important that high link utilisations are obtained also. In other words, it is important that the throughput of the higher layers in general, and the network layer in particular, are matched to those of the link layer if capability is not to be wasted.

Currently, all network layer implementations are written to run on general purpose processors with some support peripherals (DMAs, etc.). It may be necessary to move to dedicated network layer support integrated circuits, in the same way as for the link layer, in order to achieve very high network layer throughput. At the time of writing, attempts at producing X.25 level 3 integrated circuits have been rumoured from time to time. So far, no real products have appeared. If there is sufficient market requirement and all of the technical problems can be solved, network layer protocol integrated circuits could be produced. The entire packet switching function could be combined into a small number of high speed integrated circuits. The result would be low cost, very high performance packet switches.

13.3.3 Fault Tolerance

Most packet switches currently available completely die if the main processor fails. A large number of users of a packet switched network may be affected. Even if datagram protocols and distributed adaptive routing techniques are used, devices connected to the failed packet switch will still be unavailable.

There are two possible solutions to this problem. The first solution is to ensure that all end-point devices have at least two network links, so that they can be connected to different packet switches. This is fine where possible, but may be expensive or impractical depending on the situation.

The second solution is to reduce the probability of the packet switch failing. Ideally, no single failure should affect performance of the packet switch as a whole. The best way of doing this is to duplicate the modules inside the packet switch in such a way that a failed module can be isolated and replaced by another identical module automatically and without interruption to network traffic.

In most cases, it is either very difficult or very expensive to provide a full fault tolerant capability. On the other hand, only a partial fault tolerance may be required. For example, it may be decided that a main processor failure must not cause a total packet switch failure but a failure of a particular link interface is tolerable. In this case, it would only be necessary to duplicate the functionality of the main processor rather than try to duplicate the functionality of the entire packet switch. This would result in a saving in cost and complexity.

13.3.4 PADs

The future for PADs as a whole is not particularly certain. PADs provide a less than ideal way of connecting devices to a network. While there are still many simple terminals and computers around that cannot support direct connection to packet switched networks there will be a large scale requirement for PADs. As it becomes cheaper to provide a direct connection for each terminal and computer and users require the extra functionality that results, the demand for PADs will decline.

PAD performance will continue to improve as the software and hardware used improves. The emphasis will then move to the facilities supported by the PAD. Currently, most PADs provide little more than that specified by the X.3 recommendation. This only deals with things like echo state and whether to add linefeeds to carriage returns, etc.

One common problem that could be solved in the PAD is mapping between terminal types. For example, suppose a host computer system only supports one range of terminal types and a user has a different type of terminal. Normally, this situation would severely restrict the use of the host computer system. Screen editing would be out of the question. If the PAD could map between the terminal types, this incompatibility would disappear.

Another problem occurs with network services that generate Prestel type graphics. Most terminals (and quite a lot of terminal emulation software for personal computers) cannot directly display this information. If the PAD could convert between the raw Prestel type graphics and something that looks reasonable on the terminal, this would open up the use of the network service to a larger number of users.

Another possibility is to provide intelligent support for screen editing within the PAD. The use of something like the SSMP protocol (described briefly in Chapter Five) within the PAD would considerable reduce the load placed on the network by screen editing. Most screen editing operations are performed locally and involve no network traffic. It is only when the intervention of the host computer system is absolutely required is any network traffic generated. Even the traffic that is generated consists of a number of large packets rather than the very large number of small packets that screen editing normally generates.

13.4 Host Interfaces

Since, in the future, every host computer system from the largest supercomputer to the smallest general purpose computer will have a direct connection to some sort of network, host interfaces will become even more important than they are now.

Current host interfaces are adequate for file transfer type applications over wide area networks which do not require exceptionally high performance. They are currently inadequate for local area network type applications which require high speed or for supporting large numbers of interactive sessions from PAD users.

It is to be hoped that manufacturers of host computer systems will provide much faster packet switched network interface support, which can cope with a large number of calls and a high link and packet rate.

13.5 Gateways

Roughly the same comments apply to gateways as for host interfaces. Since gateways represent a performance bottleneck in the link between two different networks, it is very important for gateways to support large numbers of connections and high packet rates.

13.6 Network Management Systems

Network management systems (NMSs) are rapidly becoming an essential part of any packet switched network. Development of useful NMSs is rather behind demand at the moment but this situation is changing very quickly.

There are perhaps two big problems facing designers of NMSs. The first is the non-standard nature of network management protocols. Even if a manufacturer can provide an NMS for its packet switched network products, the NMS will almost certainly not be able to cope with products from other manufacturers. Very few NMSs provide the network managers with the ability to customise the operation of the NMS to the extent that it can cope with different network management protocols. This limitation makes 'total management' of the network almost impossible.

The second big problem is that of how to present the collected information to the network managers. It is very unlikely that the network managers have a deep understanding of packet switched network protocols, so that information presented at that sort of level is not very useful. Ideally, the NMS should inform the network managers of problems at a higher level, preferably with a recommendation as to what action to take to correct problems.

The use of colour graphics displays, annotated with usage information collected in real time from the network can provide the network managers with a good feel for how the network is operating.

The network managers should also be able to specify the particular events that are important and should have available a number of alarm levels, depending on the seriousness of the event.

Ultimately, the NMS itself could take action to improve the performance of a network by altering routing tables without intervention by the network managers. This capability would allow it to route around failed links and failed packet switches. If public data networks are involved in the network, the NMS may also be able to re-configure the network usage from time to time in order to make use of differences in cost at different times of the day on different public data networks.

Value Added Network Services

14.1 Introduction

Value Added·Network Services, or VANs for short, are services provided for network users and are accessible over the network. Examples of VANS are electronic mail services, online database search services, general information services, etc. Although there are VANS available today, the whole area is still at an early stage. As more use is made of networks, so more demand will be created for useful VANs accessible from those networks. In this chapter we are going to take a look at some of the VANS that may be in widescale use in the future.

14.2 Image Libraries

High quality images involve a large amount of data. This can be of the order of megabytes depending on the resolution of the image and the number of colour and intensity levels used. It is virtually impossible to transfer high quality images over current packet switched networks due to the length of time it takes to transfer them.

As the performance of packet switched networks improves, it should be possible to transfer high quality images all over the country in minutes or seconds. This makes possible network accessible 'image libraries'. There are all kinds of possible applications for image libraries. Satellite images could be stored in an image library for access at any later date by users of satellite data. Books that include many complex colour diagrams and photographs could be stored in an image library. Assuming the the transfer time per page was not excessive (or that accessing of following pages is concurrent with the display of the current page), this would allow books to be read online.

14.3 Information Services

There are all kinds of possibilities for network accessible information services. Again, a high performance network is essential if 'browsing' through the information stored is to be possible. This is one of the big problems with Prestel. Unless you know exactly which page you require, it can take ages to move through the directory system to find the correct page.

If the information can includes graphics, online manuals are possible. For example, a

PAD user guide could be placed on an information server. If a PAD user needs to refer to the manual, the user calls the information server and looks through for the relevant section. Physical (i.e., paper) manuals can almost never be found when they are most needed and are often out of date. It is very much easier to update an electronic manual which is kept in one place than physical manuals which are kept all over the place.

Network address directories are also good candidates for information servers. Although Name Servers simplify network addressing as far as users are concerned, it is still necessary to know what the valid names are for particular destinations. The ability to call up a network address directory in order to find the correct name is very useful, particularly in large networks.

Library computer systems are now in widescale use. These keep track of the books in the library. This includes things like an inventory of all of the books owned by the library, whether they are in the library or out on loan and to whom the books have been loaned. If the library computer system is connected into a network, these facilities become accessible to users of the network. Without actually going to the library it is possible to check if a required book is owned by the library and whether or not any copies are available. If there are copies available, it is then possible to reserve a copy for later collection, or delivery.

Useful Addresses

British Standards Institute (BSI)

British standards and ISO standards can be obtained from:

> BSI
> Linford Wood
> Milton Keynes
> MK14 6LE

CCITT

CCITT recommendations can be obtained from:

> General Secretariat
> International Telecommunication Union
> Place des Nations
> 1211 Geneva 20
> Switzerland

International Standards Relevant to Packet Switching

Introduction

In this appendix the major standards and recommendations relevant to packet switching are very briefly described. The gaps in the numbers are where standards or recommendations are not really relevant to packet switching. The idea is that, if confronted with an unfamiliar X series recommendation, for example, it should be possible to look it up in this Appendix and at least get some idea of what it is all about.

The CCITT G Series

G.702

G.702 specifies a hierarchy of digital bit rates. It describes how lower speed signals are to be combined into the higher speed 'primary rate' interfaces.

G.703

G.703 specifies the physical and electrical characteristics of hierarchical digital interfaces. This recommendation defines the characteristics of the primary rate interfaces. G.703 is described in Chapter Ten.

G.704

G.704 specifies the functional characteristics of interfaces associated with network nodes. This recommendation specifies the frame formats to be used over G.703 interfaces.

G.705

G.705 specifies the characteristics required to terminate digital links on a digital exchange. This includes things like timing tolerances.

The CCITT I Series

I.120

I.120 contains a basic description of Integrated Service Digital Networks (ISDNs).

I.130

I.130 specifies attributes for the characterisation of telecommunication services supported by an ISDN and the network capabilities of an ISDN.

I.210

I.210 specifies the principles of telecommunications services supported by an ISDN.

I.211

I.211 specifies the bearer services supported by an ISDN. It describes the basic user connections to ISDN and the services supported by ISDN.

I.212

I.212 specifies the teleservices supported by an ISDN.

I.310

I.310 specifies the network functional principles of an ISDN.

I.320

I.320 specifies the ISDN protocol reference model. This is described in terms of the OSI reference model.

I.330

I.330 specifies the ISDN numbering and addressing principles.

I.340

I.340 specifies the ISDN connection types.

I.410

I.410 describes the general aspects and principles relating to the recommendations on ISDN user-network interfaces.

I.411

I.411 specifies reference configurations for ISDN user-network interfaces.

I.412

I.412 specifies the ISDN user-network interface structures and access capabilities.

I.430

I.430 specifies the layer 1 basic user-network interface. It defines the bit signalling to be used and the electrical and physical aspects of the layer 1 interface.

I.431

I.431 specifies the layer 1 primary rate user-network interface. This describes the layer 1 interface for 1.544M bits per second and 2.048M bits per second primary rate connections.

I.440

I.440 describes general aspects of the ISDN user-network interface at the data link layer. This recommendation describes the basic aspects of LAPD - the D channel link access procedure.

I.441

I.441 is the actual LAPD specification. The LAPD protocol is actually fairly similar to the X.25 level 2 LAPB protocol.

I.450

I.450 describes the general aspects of the layer 3 ISDN user-network interface.

I.451

I.451 contains the actual layer 3 protocol specification. This defines the messages transferred over the D channel.

I.460

I.460 specifies the multiplexing, rate adaption and support of existing interfaces.

I.461

I.461 specifies the support of X.21 and X.21bis based DTEs by an ISDN. This is identical to X.30.

I.462

I.462 specifies the support of packet mode DTEs by an ISDN. This is identical to X.31.

I.463

I.463 specifies the support of DTEs with V series type interfaces by an ISDN. This is identical to V.110.

The CCITT V Series

V.1

V.1 specifies the equivalence between binary notation symbols and the significant conditions of a two condition code. This describes how binary 1s and binary 0s are represented in different systems (frequency modulation for example).

V.10

V.10 specifies the electrical characteristics for unbalanced double-current interchange circuits for general use with integrated circuit equipment in the field of data communications. This is identical to X.26. It describes the characteristics of the drivers and receivers for this type of electrical signalling and gives some guidelines for compatibility with other interfaces.

V.11

V.11 specifies the electrical characteristics for balanced double-current interchange circuits for general use with integrated circuit equipment in the field of data communications. This is identical with X.27. V.11 is similar to V.10 except that it deals with differential signalling.

V.21

V.21 specifies a 300 bits per second full duplex modem standardised for use in the general switched telephone network.

V.22

V.22 specifies a 1200 bits per second full duplex modem standardised for use in the general switched telephone network and on point-to-point 2 wire leased telephone-type circuits.

V.22bis

V.22bis specifies a 2400 bits per second full duplex modem using the frequency division technique standardised for use on the general switched telephone network and on point-to-point two wire leased telephone-type circuits.

V.23

V.23 specifies a 600/1200 baud modem standardised for use in the general switched telephone network. V.23 modems, often described as 'Prestel style' modems, operate at

600 or 1200 bits per second in one direction and 75 bits per second in the reverse direction.

V.24

V.24 is a list of definitions for interchange circuits between DTEs and DCEs.

V.26

V.26 specifies a full duplex 2400 bits per second modem standardised for use on four wire leased telephone type circuits.

V.26bis

V.26bis specifies a 2400/1200 bits per second modem standardised for use in the general switched telephone network.

V.26ter

V.26ter specifies a 2400 bits per second full duplex modem using the echo cancelling technique standardised for use on the general switched telephone network and on point-to-point two wire leased telephone-type circuits.

V.27

V.27 specifies a 4800 bits per second modem with manual equaliser standardised for use on leased telephone-type circuits.

V.27bis

V.27bis specifies a 4800/2400 bits per second modem with automatic equaliser standardised for use on leased telephone-type circuits.

V.27ter

V.27ter specifies a 4800/2400 bits per second modem standardised for use in the general switched telephone network.

V.28

V.28 specifies the electrical characteristics for unbalanced double-current interchange circuits. The characteristics of V.28 are described in Chapter Ten.

V.29

V.29 specifies a 9600 bits per second modem standardised for use on point-to-point 4 wire leased telephone-type circuits.

V.32

V.32 specifies a family of 2-wire full duplex modems operating at data signalling rates of up to 9600 bits per second for use on the general switched telephone network and on leased telephone-type circuits.

V.35

V.35 specifies a system for data transmission at 48k bits per second using 60-108kHz group band circuits. Although this standard specifies a modulation technique for shifting the baseband 48k bits per second signal into the 60-108kHz band, V.35 is usually used as a specification of an electrical interface for operating at 48k bits per second and mostly the modulation technique is forgotten.

V.100

V.100 specifies the interconnection between public data networks and the public switched telephone network.

V.110

V.110 specifies support of DTEs with V series type interfaces by an Integrated Services Digital Network (ISDN). This is identical to I.463. The recommendation gives mechanisms for converting between V series interfaces and the ISDN S-interface.

The CCITT X Series

X.1

X.1 specifies the international user classes of service in public data networks and integrated services digital networks (ISDNs).

X.2

X.2 specifies international data transmission services and optional user facilities in public data services.

X.3

X.3 specifies the packet assembly/disassembly facility (PAD) in a public data network. This recommendation specifies the operating parameters for the PAD user interface. This is described in Chapter Seven.

X.10

X.10 specifies categories of access for DTEs to public data transmission services provided by public data networks and/or integrated services digital networks through terminal adapters.

X.21

X.21 specifies the interface between a DTE and a DCE for synchronous operation on public data networks. It defines the connector and operation of interchange circuits for X.21 interfaces. This is described in Chapter Ten.

X.21bis

The X.21bis recommendation covers the use on public data networks of DTE equipment which is designed to interface to synchronous V series modems. This recommendation is similar in scope to X.21, except that it defines the use of the V series interfaces (V.28, for example) for use with public data networks. This interface is described in Chapter Ten.

X.22

The X.22 recommendation defines the interface between a DTE and a DCE operating at 48k bits per second. The interface supports a number of X.21 connections multiplexed into a single line.

X.24

The X.24 recommendation specifies the interface interchange circuits between a DTE and a DCE on public data networks. X.24 is the digital circuit version of V.24 for the V series interfaces.

X.25

X.25 specifies the interface between a DTE and a DCE for packet mode DTEs connected to a public data network via a dedicated circuit. X.25 level 2 is the OSI layer 2 protocol for packet switched networks, while X.25 level 3 is the OSI layer 3 protocol for packet switched networks. X.25 specifies the use of X.21, X.21bis or V series interfaces at the physical level (OSI layer 1). X.25 is described in detail in Chapter Six.

X.26

The X.26 recommendation specifies the electrical characteristics for unbalanced double-current interchange circuits for general use with integrated circuit equipment in the field of data communications. This is identical with V.10.

X.27

The X.27 recommendation specifies the electrical characteristics for balanced double-current interchange circuits for general use with integrated circuit equipment in the field of data communications. This is identical with V.11.

X.28

X.28 specifies the DTE/DCE interface for a start-stop (i.e., asynchronous) mode DTE accessing the PAD in a public data network situated in the same country. In other words, it specifies the user interface presented by a PAD at its asynchronous ports.

X.29

X.29 specifies procedures for the exchange of control information and user data between a PAD and a packet mode DTE or another PAD. This recommendation specifies how the operation of a PAD port can be controlled from across a packet switched network. X.29 is described in Chapter Seven.

X.30

X.30 specifies the support of X.21 and X.21bis based DTEs by an Integrated Services Digital Network (ISDN). As X.21 and X.21bis are not directly supported by ISDN, this recommendation specifies the conversion process to the ISDN S-interface. This recommendation is identical to I.461.

X.31

X.31 specifies the support of packet mode DTEs by an ISDN. This recommendation is identical to I.462.

X.32

X.32 specifies the interface between DTEs and DCEs for packet mode DTEs accessing a public data network through a public switched telephone network or a circuit switched public data network. X.32 provides mechanisms to allow a DTE to identify itself for purposes like billing, authorisation, etc.

X.75

X.75 specifies terminal and transit call control procedures and data transit system on international circuits between packet switched data networks. This is a variation on X.25 for use on links between X.25 networks. It is described briefly in Chapter Six.

X.92

X.92 describes hypothetical reference connections for public synchronous data networks.

X.96

X.96 specifies call progress signals in public data networks.

X.110

X.110 specifies the international routing principles and routing plan for public data networks.

X.121

X.121 specifies the international numbering plan for public data networks.

X.135

X.135 specifies delay aspects of grade of service for public data networks when providing international packet switched data services.

X.136

X.136 specifies blocking aspects of grade of service for public data networks when providing international packet switched data services.

X.140

X.140 specifies general quality of service parameters for communication via public data networks.

X.141

X.141 specifies general principles for the detection and correction of errors in public data networks.

X.150

X.150 specifies the principles of maintenance testing for public data networks using DTE equipment and DCE equipment test loops.

X.180

X.180 specifies administrative arrangements for international closed user groups (CUGs).

X.181

X.181 specifies administrative arrangements for the provision of international permanent virtual circuits (PVCs).

X.400

X.400 specifies the system model and service elements of a message handling system (MHS). This is described in Chapter Seven.

X.408

X.408 specifies encoded information type conversion rules for MHS. This specifies procedures for conversion between the various types of message support by MHS. These include things like Telex, G3 fax, etc.

X.409

X.409 specifies the presentation transfer syntax and notation used in MHS.

X.410

X.410 specifies the remote operations and reliable transfer server for MHS.

X.411

X.411 specifies the protocols used in the message transfer layer of MHS. There are two protocols specified. 'P1' is the message transfer protocol. 'P3' is the submission and delivery protocol.

X.420

X.420 specifies the interpersonal messaging user agent layer for MHS. It defines the operation of UAs for the interpersonal messaging service.

X.430

X.430 specifies the access protocol for Teletex terminals when making use of MHS. It specifies how Teletex terminals can make use of the interpersonal messaging system.

The ISO Standards

ISO 2110

ISO 2110 specifies the DTE/DCE interface connectors and pin assignments for the 25 pin connector. This is published by BSI as BS 6623:Part 1.

ISO 2593

ISO 2593 specifies the DTE/DCE interface connectors and pin assignments for the 34 pin connector. This is published by BSI as BS 6623:Part 1.

ISO 3309

ISO 3309 specifies the HDLC frame structure. This is published by BSI as BS 5397:Part 1.

ISO 4335

ISO 4335 is a specification for consolidation of elements of HDLC procedures. This is published by BSI as BS 5397:Part 2.

ISO 4902

ISO 4902 specifies the DTE/DCE interface connectors and pin assignments for the 37 pin connector. This is published by BSI as BS 6623:Part 2.

ISO 4903

ISO 4903 specifies the DTE/DCE interface connectors and pin assignments for the 15 pin connector. This is published by BSI as BS 6623:Part 3.

ISO 7478

ISO 7478 is a specification for multilink HDLC procedures. This is published by BSI as BS 5397:Part 6.

ISO 7498

ISO 7498 is the basic OSI reference model description. This is published by BSI as BS 6568.

ISO 7776

ISO 7776 specifies the X.25 LAPB-compatible DTE data link procedures. This is published by BSI as BS 5397:Part 7.

ISO 7809

ISO 7809 is a specification for consolidation of classes of HDLC procedures. It is published by BSI as BS 5397:Part 5.

ISO 8072

ISO 8072 is the OSI transport service definition. This is published by BSI as DD115.

ISO 8073

ISO 8073 is the OSI transport protocol specification. This is published by BSI as DD116.

ISO 8208

ISO 8208 specifies the X.25 packet level protocol for DTEs. This is published by BSI as DD117.

ISO 8326

ISO 8326 is the basic connection-orientated session service definition. This is published by BSI as DD111.

ISO 8327

ISO 8327 is the basic connection-orientated session protocol specification. This is published by BSI as DD112.

ISO 8348

ISO 8348 is the connection mode network service definition. It is published by BSI as DD119.

ISO 8571

ISO 8571 is the standard for the OSI FTAM protocol. This is published as four separate parts. It is published by BSI as DD113.

ISO 8649

ISO 8649 is the standard for the OSI common application service elements: commitment; concurrency; and recovery. This is published by BSI as DD109.

ISO 8650

ISO 8650 specifies the protocols for the common application service elements: commitment; concurrency; and recovery. This is published by BSI as DD110.

ISO 8822

ISO 8822 is the connection-orientated presentation service definition. This is published by BSI as DD101.

ISO 8823

ISO 8823 is the connection-orientated presentation protocol specification. This is published by BSI as DD102.

ISO 8824.2

ISO 8824.2 is the standard for the Abstract Syntax Notation (ASN.1). This is published by BSI as DD103.

ISO 8825.2

ISO 8825.2 specifies the basic encoding rules for Abstract Syntax Notation 1 (ASN.1). This is published by BSI as DD104.

ISO 8831

ISO 8831 specifies the concepts and services in JTM. This is published by BSI as DD105.

ISO 8832

ISO 8832 specifies the basic class protocol for JTM. This is published by BSI as DD106.

ISO 8878

ISO 8878 specifies how X.25 is used to provide the connection-orientated network service. This is published by BSI as DD122.

ISO 9040

ISO 9040 is the standard for the OSI Virtual Terminal services. This is published by BSI as DD129.

ISO 9041

ISO 9041 is the standard for the OSI Virtual Terminal protocols. This is published by BSI as DD130.

Glossary of Terms

Address: An address is a string of numbers or characters used to identify a specific point within a network.

ALOHA: ALOHA was an experimental packet radio network developed by the University of Hawaii.

ANSI: American National Standards Institute.

Application Layer: The application layer is layer 7 of the OSI seven layer model. It provides the facilities required to support the end user application.

ARPANET: ARPANET was one of the first packet switched networks. It was developed by ARPA (the Advanced Research Projects Agency within the U.S. Department of Defence).

Asynchronous: This is a means of transmitting data where each element of the data (usually eight bits) is self-contained and can be transmitted at any time. No separate clock is required as in the case of synchronous transmission. The asynchronous characters contain their own timing information, so that no extra clock signal is required.

BABT: BABT stands for British Approvals Board for Telecommunications. BABT checks that equipment designed to connect to public communications networks conforms to the required standards.

Balanced Circuit: A balanced circuit is a layer 1 electrical interface that uses differential signalling to transmit information.

Bandwith: This is the range of frequencies that a transmission system is capable of handling with acceptable signal distortion and reduction in amplitude.

Baseband: A baseband network is a network where only one communications channel can be using a network link at any time.

Baud: A baud is a measure of the number of signal element changes per second. Since the information rate may well not be equal to the rate at which the signal changes, the baud rate may not equal the number of bits per second.

Bit: Bit stands for binary digit.

Blue Book FTP: Blue Book FTP is part of the Colour Book protocol set. It is a network independent file transfer protocol.

Bits Per Second: This is the number of binary digits that can be transferred across a communications link in one second. The prefixes K (for thousand) and M (for million) are often used for high bit rates.

Broadband: Broadband networks are networks in which many communications channels can be using a single communications link simultaneously.

BSI: BSI stands for British Standards Institution. BSI is a good source for ISO standards.

Bus: A bus network is a network where all of the devices on the network are connected to a single cable. Ethernet is an example of a bus network.

Byte: A byte consists of eight bits. This is sometimes called an octet.

Call: A network call is a full-duplex communications path between two network connected devices. There is usually a call set up phase, an information transfer phase (in which information is exchanged) and a call clear down phase.

Cambridge Ring: The Cambridge Ring is an example of a ring topology local area network. It is only in limited use and is not an international standard.

CCITT: CCITT stands for Consultative Committee for International Telephone and Telegraph. The CCITT publishes a range of recommendations covering most areas of data communications.

Channel: A channel is a full-duplex path between two ends of a network call.

Character Switching: Character switching is a network technique for interconnecting large numbers of asynchronous devices. Characters received from an asynchronous device are reassembled within the character switch before being transmitted out on the outgoing half of a connection. This gives a character switch the ability to cope with devices running at different speeds.

Circuit Switching: Circuit switching is a network technique for interconnecting large numbers of synchronous or asynchronous devices. Using a technique known as sampling, a circuit switch simulates direct connections between lines.

Clock: A clock signal is a regular timing signal that is used to reconstruct transmitted synchronous data at the receiver.

Collision: A collision can occur in bus networks when two devices start transmitting packets onto the cable simultaneously.

Colour Book: The Colour Books define a set of network protocols used within the Academic Community.

CSMA/CD: CSMA/CD stands for Carrier Sense Multiple Access/Collision Detection. This is the access control technique used by Ethernet.

CUD: CUD stands for Call User Data. This field is found in X.25 level 3 Incoming call/Call request packets.

DCE: Data Circuit-terminating Equipment. The device and connections placed at the interface to a network by the network provider.

Dial-up Line: A dial-up line is one which uses the public switched telephone network. Before it can be used, the link must be established by one end dialling up the other.

Differential Signalling: Differential signalling is a technique where a pair of wires is used to transfer information. One wire carries the true form, while the other carries the inverted form. The receiver re-inverts the inverted form and adds it to the true form. The result is that any noise in the signal is cancelled, just leaving the correct information.

DISC: DISC is an X.25 level 2 unnumbered frame. It is used to indicate that the link is in the down state.

DTE: DTE stands for Data Terminal Equipment. A DTE is the counterpart of a DCE.

DXE: The term DXE is used to mean either DTE or DCE.

ECMA: European Computer Manufacturers Association.

EIA: The Electronic Industries Association.

Electronic Mail: Electronic mail is a way of sending text and graphics messages over a network.

Encryption: Encryption is a method of protecting data being transferred across a network. Encryption alters the data so that an eavesdropper would not be able to reconstruct the original information that is being transferred.

Ethernet: Ethernet is a baseband bus network that uses the CSMA/CD technique to control access to the Ethernet cable. The transmission rate is 10 million bits per second.

Fast Select: Fast select refers to a mode of operation of the X.25 level 3 protocol where various packets contain a significant amount of user data.

Fawn Book: Fawn Book is one of the Colour Book protocols. It defines SSMP.

FCS: FCS stands for Frame Check Sequence. An FCS is usually calculated from the contents of a frame or packet before transmission, then sent with the frame or packet. The receiver uses the FCS to determine whether or not the frame or packet has been received correctly.

Fibre Optic Cable: Fibre optic cables carry information in the form of light signals between network devices. Fibre optic cables are capable of operating at very high data rates and are immune from electrical noise in the environment.

Flag: A flag character is the sequence '01111110'. This is used in X.25 level 2 to delimit the start and end of frames.

Flow Control: Flow control is a mechanism whereby a receiver of data can stop the transmitter when the receiver cannot process the data at the rate at which it is being received. The use of flow control prevents the loss of data in such a situation.

Four Wire: Four wire circuits are used by synchronous modems that are able to operate in full-duplex. One pair is used to carry data in one direction while the other pair is used to carry data in the other direction.

Frame: A frame is a single entity at the link layer. The link layer protocol transmits and receives frames.

FRMR: FRMR stands for FRaMe Reject. It is an X.25 level 2 frame that is transmitted in response to a received frame which contained a serious error requiring a link reset.

FTAM: FTAM stands for File Transfer, Access and Management. FTAM is the OSI file transfer protocol.

Full-Duplex: A full-duplex connection between two end-point devices is a connection that can support simultaneous transfer of data in both direction.

Gateway: A gateway is a device that allows connections between end-point devices in two different networks. The network technologies used on each side of the gateway may be different.

Green Book: Green Book is one of the Colour Book protocols. It specifies a way of using the Triple X protocol.

Half-Duplex: A half-duplex connection is one where it is only possible to transfer data in one direction at a time. Periodically, the direction of transfer changes in order to allow transmission in the other direction.

HDLC: HDLC stands for High level Data Link Control protocol. Elements of HDLC are used within the X.25 level 2 protocol.

IEEE: Institution of Electrical and Electronic Engineers.

IPSS: International Packet SwitchStream.

ISDN: ISDN stands for Integrated Services Data Network. This is a circuit switching network that is designed to carry both voice and data traffic simultaneously.

ISO: ISO stands for The International Organisation for Standards. ISO is responsible for the OSI seven-layer network model.

JANET: JANET stands for Joint Academic Network. This is a private X.25 network which connects together all of the UK universities.

JTMP: JTMP stands for Job Transfer and Management Protocol. JTMP is one of the Colour Book protocols. It allows the distribution of computing jobs around a network.

KiloStream: KiloStream is a digital link service supplied by British Telecom. KiloStream links can operate at 2.4k, 4.8k, 9.6k, 48k and 64k bits per second.

LAN: LAN stands for Local Area Network. A local area network is one which spans a limited geographical area. Generally, a LAN is confined to a single building.

LAP: LAP stands for Link Access Procedure. It is a version of the X.25 level 2 protocol. LAP has been largely replaced by LAPB.

LAPB: LAPB stands for Link Access Procedure Balanced. It is a version of the X.25 level 2 protocol.

Leased Line: A leased line is a point to point link provided by a PTT. Modems are usually used at each end of the leased line to provide a link suitable for packet switched networks.

Line Driver: A line driver is a device that allows relatively high data rates to be achieved over long distances on point to point links.

Link Layer: The link layer is layer 2 of the OSI seven layer model. It provides a flow controlled, error free link between the devices at each end of the link.

Logical Channel Number: This is the unique number assigned at a DCE to DTE interface to identify packets belonging to a particular call.

Logical Channel Group Number (LCGN): This identifies the type of channel to which the associated logical channel number belongs.

Mail Server: A mail server is a computer system that provides an electronic mail service. A mail server is able to transmit mail to other mail servers and store received mail messages for later collection by the recipients.

MegaStream: MegaStream is a high speed digital point to point communications link service provided by British Telecom. The most common MegaStream link speed is 2.048 million bits per second.

MLP: MLP stands for MultiLink Procedure. This is a version of X.25 level 2 that is able to use multiple communications links.

Modem (B): Modem is short for MODulator/DEModulator. Modems allow digital data to be transmitted over voice circuits such as those in the public switched telephone network.

Multiplexer: A multiplexer is a device that allows a number of communications channels to be combined into a single communications channel.

Name Server: A Name Server is a device that contains mnemonic names to explicit address maps.

Network: A network is a very general term for a collection of devices that can communicate with each other over some common communications system.

Network Architecture: Network architecture includes concepts such as the topology of the network (ring, bus, star, etc.), protocols, operational characteristics, etc.

Network Layer: The network layer is layer 3 of the OSI seven layer model. The network layer is responsible for establishing connections across a network.

Network Management: Network management covers all of the operational aspects of a network. This includes configuration of the network, monitoring status and performance of the network and recording significant information for later analysis.

Network Management System: A Network Management System (or NMS) is a network device used to provide the network management functions for a network.

Network Manager: The network managers are the users of the Network Management System. Their role is to ensure that the network is operating correctly and to re-configure the network devices as required.

NIFTP: NIFTP stands for Network Independent File Transfer Protocol. NIFTP is another name for Blue Book FTP.

Node: A network node is a point at which network links come together. In a packet switched network, a node is usually a packet switch.

NSAP: NSAP stands for Network Service Access Point. This is the point at which the transport layer gains access to the services provided by the network layer.

OSI: OSI stands for Open Systems Interconnection. OSI was developed by ISO to permit interworking between computers from different manufacturers.

Packet: The network layer protocols transfer packets across network connections.

Packet Radio Networks: Packet radio networks are packet switched networks where the network links are in the form of radio links.

Packet Switch: Packet switches are devices that route packets within a packet switched network.

PAD: PAD stands for Packet Assembler/Disassembler. A PAD allows asynchronous, character based, devices to be connected to a packet switched network.

Password: A password is used to gain access to a computer system or file that is protected from general access.

PIF: Protocol Identifier Field. This field takes up the first four bytes of X.25 level 3 Incoming call/Call request packets. It is used to identify the protocol being used with X.25.

Point to Point: A direct connection between two pieces of equipment or two sites.

PVC: PVC stands for Permanent Virtual Circuit. A PVC is a connection in X.25 networks that is permanently in existence.

Physical Layer: The physical layer is layer 1 of the OSI seven layer model. The physical layer deals with the electrical and mechanical aspects of network connection.

Presentation Layer: The presentation layer is layer 6 of the OSI seven layer model. The presentation layer deals with the encoding and transfer of information from the application layer.

Prestel: Dial-up information service run by British Telecom. Prestel uses a low resolution colour text and graphics format to allow access to a wide range of information services.

Protocol: Protocol is a general term for the set of procedures stating how to operate a particular level of communications.

PSE: PSE stands for Packet Switch Exchange. This is basically another name for a packet switch.

PSS: PSS stands for Packet SwitchStream. PSS is the most important public data network in the UK.

PSTN: PSTN stands for Public Switched Telephone Network. This is basically the telephone network.

PTT: PTT stands for Post, Telephone and Telegraph authority. This is the term used to describe the major provider of communications services in each country.

Public Data Network: A public data network is a network run by a PTT that provides useful data services. PSS is an example of a public data network.

Red Book: Red Book is one of the Colour Book protocols. It defines the JTMP.

Repeater: A repeater is an active network element that extends the range over which a network can operate.

Reverse Charging: Reverse charging in a packet switched network is analogous to a reverse charge call on the telephone system. The called end-point device pays for services used rather than the caller.

Ring: A ring network is a network that uses a single cable in the form of a complete ring. Data circulates around the ring in one direction.

RS-232: RS-232 is an electrical signalling standard. It is very similar to V.28.

SABM: SABM stands for Set Asynchronous Balanced Mode. It is the X.25 level 2 frame that is used to bring a link into the up state.

SABME: SABME stands for Set Asynchronous Balanced Mode Extended. This is similar to SABM except that it requests that extended frame numbering be used.

Security: Security refers to the process of protecting resources or data from unauthorised access. Security may be in the form of protecting a network resource from general use, so that only validated users can get access. Alternatively, it may refer to the process of ensuring that data being transferred on the network is protected from eavesdroppers.

Session Level: The session layer is layer 5 of the OSI seven layer model. The session layer is responsible for controlling the dialogue between two applications. It provides methods for restarting a dialogue at a known point if the connection between the applications should fail.

SLP: SLP stands for Single Link Procedure. It is the version of X.25 level 2 that supports a single communications link.

SSMP: SSMP stands for Simple Screen Management Protocol. It is one of the Colour Book protocols. It defines a protocol that permits efficient use of packet switched networks for screen editing operations.

SVC: SVC stands for Switched Virtual Call. An SVC is a network connection where the call has to be first set up before communications can take place. After the information has been transferred, the call is cleared.

Synchronous: Synchronous transmission is a very efficient way of transferring data as no extra bits have to be included in the bit stream to provide timing information. Synchronous connections require clock signals to provide timing information to allow the receiver to reconstruct the transmitted information.

Token Passing: Token passing is an access control technique that can be used in bus and ring networks. A device cannot transmit information unless it is in possession of a token.

Token Ring: A token ring network is a network that uses a ring architecture with token passing access control.

Topology: Topology refers to the shape of the network. Possible topologies are rings, buses, stars, etc.

Transceiver: A transceiver is a combined receiver and transmitter.

Transport Layer: The transport layer is layer 4 of the OSI model. It is responsible for hiding the characteristics of the underlying network and providing a standard interface to the session layer.

Triple X: Triple X refers to the X.3/X.28/X.29 set of CCITT recommendations. Triple X defines the operation of X.25 PADs.

TS29: TS29 is a version of X.29 that has been modified to run on top of the Yellow Book transport service.

Twisted Pair Cable: Twisted pair cable consists of a number of pairs of wire. Each pair of wire is twisted around itself along the cable's length. This is ideal cable for use with balanced circuits (i.e., differential signalling).

VANS: VANS stands for Value Added Network Services. VANS are useful services that can be accessed by calling across a network.

WAN: WAN stands for Wide Area Network. The term is used to describe networks that cover large geographical areas.

Window Size: Window size refers to the number of unacknowledged frames or packets that may be outstanding (i.e., unacknowledged) at the link or network layer.

Yellow Book: Yellow Book is one of the Colour Book protocols. It defines a transport service and is normally run over X.25 to provide support for higher level protocols.

INDEX